365 Days
of Angel Prayers

365 Days
of Angel Prayers

Elizabeth Harper

Cathleen O'Connor PhD

Printed in the United States of America.
ISBN-13: 978-1499215373
ISBN-10: 1499215371
Library of Congress Control Number: 2014914443
CreateSpace Independent Publishing Platform
North Charleston, South Carolina

Dedication

This labor of love is dedicated to all the amazing teachers, healers
and everyday people who share the love and work of the angels.

It is also dedicated to the angels and guides who brought forth the idea of
this book and inspired so many to write from the heart.

A special dedication to our own Book Angel, Lora Cossolotto,
who flew in just in time to help us finish.

May the love and light of the angels be with you always and in all ways.

TABLE OF CONTENTS

February

March

June

July

August

September

November

December

Foreword

In the process of my spiritual awakening in the mid 80's I came to realize that all of us have many helpers in spirit that have been assigned to assist us! As my consciousness began to elevate, I started to truly understand how spiritually well cared for we are while on earth. It was during this time of seeking and looking to enhance my spiritual life that I was given a dictated message in writing from my angels that was so loving and healing, I knew it was from them! From this first spiritual message, an "Angelic Epiphany" happened and my spiritual life has been filled with enormous love and wisdom ever since!

It came to me through this angelic exchange that we all have a purpose or a mission for the greater good, but thankfully; we are never alone in fulfilling our life Work. It was so clear to me that God was sending angelic messengers to be by our side and that their presence was ever constant. You see, an angel's job is not only to do God's work, but also to guide, support, teach, and encourage, and more importantly love each one of us while we are here fulfilling our life purpose. Each one of us is truly blessed. The best part of our awakening is learning that we can actually form a real and meaningful partnership with our angels for anything in our lives that we would like to know, have, or do. Our spiritual team of angels is here to help us on every level, physically, mentally, emotionally, and spiritually and in every way imaginable. Learning how to form such a partnership with my angels was an amazing process for me, as I began to talk with them or pray with them daily.

Before even getting out of bed in the morning, I love to spend time with God and the angels. I begin my day in prayer to give thanks for all the goodness that has come into my life. I also ask for help with any events that are going on in my life. Asking is key to working with our spiritual team of angels, because when we ask for their assistance it gives the angels permission to work with us while we are here on Earth. There are also days when I write their loving messages and words of wisdom that come to me in my quiet time of prayer and meditation. It is so easy to communicate with angels for they are always there ready to connect with us!

Here is a prayer that the angels gave to me many years ago that I still frequently use. You can use it anywhere at any time:

Dearest God and Angels

Please bring to me the right people,
circumstances and events
that I may better do thy will.

Amen

It is in knowing that the angels are ready and waiting to connect with you that I invite you to make an even closer connection with your own spiritual support team of angels, guides, and loved ones through *"365 Days of Angel Prayers"*. Use this wonderful book on a daily basis as its authors suggest, as a tool to help maintain your divine connection. Welcome each day as you experience their loving messages they have sent and you will receive the goodness and love that flows from each page and each author. Enjoy and take comfort in knowing the continuing presence of God's angels among us!

Trudy Griswold, Author
Angelspeake ~ How to Talk With Your Angels

Trudy Griswold is a Spiritual life coach, teacher, intuitive, and author of four bestselling books on spirituality including *Angelspeake: How to Talk With Your Angels* and *The Angelspeake Book of Prayer and Healing*. As a gifted clairvoyant and clairsentient, Trudy assists individuals in opening more fully to their highest and best spiritual potential. Guided by the angels, Trudy believes that everyone has a life purpose or special calling and it is her privilege to help others in realizing theirs. Connect with Trudy at www.angelspeake.com.

Introduction

Welcome to a celebration of communication with the angelic realm. It's a celebration because once you open your heart to the angels amazing things start to happen. From the moment you invite their love and light into your life you begin a journey that uplifts your body, mind and spirit. And your journey and love of the angels begins to spread love and light upon all with whom you come into contact and many others who you will never meet. Because you are choosing to turn your energy to the angels you are also choosing to share that energy of love and healing with the human family of which you are a part.

We seem to be at a time in our history when the angels are sorely needed. And with the busy lives we all live it can be easy to forget to take the time to spiritually connect each day. That is why we decided to put this book together – so you would have a daily resource of inspiration, love, healing and prayer that will help you make time for those precious moments of remembering your connection to source.

The book is a gathering of daily angel invocations, blessings, prayers and essays written by people who work with the angels to manifest joy, healing, deep peace and love. Each day's inspiration has been submitted by someone who has a divine life purpose of communicating with the angelic realm and a deep desire to share that purpose on a global scale. Each entry in the book is a gift to you – a reminder that, no matter what your struggles in life, you are never alone – not in a theoretical sense but in a very real, tangible sense.

You have angels ready to assist you at any moment and can connect with them each day using the unique prayers and inspirational messages you'll find here – each one a beautiful jewel of love crafted with joy and angelic guidance. Like you, they are part of a great illumination of love and light! Some of the prayers are to specific Archangels, others might be directly to Divine Source;

some are for our furry angels who embody unconditional love for us; some are for Mother Earth – our most precious of Earth Angels; some honor the traditions of indigenous peoples; some are poetic; some are lyrical and have been put to music and some are deeply personal channeled messages.

There is no one 'right' way to pray for divine blessing, healing and assistance. What you will find as you work with this book is that the best communication is one that is in your own words and that comes from the heart. So allow yourself to be inspired to write your own prayers. You can work with this book by reading the prayer for each calendar day or use your intuition and ask to be guided to exactly the best prayer for you for any given day and just open to a page and read that page's entry. And you can make the book your own by adding to it if you are inspired to do so.

As you read each day's entry do so without expectation or judgment. Allow the words to come into your mind and heart and ask that you receive whatever is most healing for you to receive from that day's entry. Trust and know that you will receive exactly what is needed at the moment. And read the personal stories that begin each chapter – each chapter has a sponsor – someone who came to know the angels through a moment of crisis, an intervention of healing or a spontaneous experience of an angelic presence. Each of the chapter sponsors is a person just like you whose life was changed and moved onto a different path because of the appearance of the angels in their lives. And it took courage for some of them to follow that path just as it might take courage for you to follow your heart's purpose in life.

We were especially blessed with our project in the added support and contribution of four angel experts who offered prayers and their perspectives on the energies associated with the angelic realm. Kimberly Marooney, Karen Paolino Correia, Sunny Dawn Johnston and Roland Comtois share their amazingly beautiful prayers and essays that will uplift you and reassure you that the angels and divine beings of love and light surround you even in the most mundane activities of your daily life. You have a resource in this book of contact information for some of the world's best angel communicators so use that resource. Visit their websites, learn more about them; and when you can, thank them for the gift of love they have so generously offered to us all.

From the glorious foreword by *Angelspeake* author Trudy Griswold to all the stories and prayers contained within, you and this book are part of a circle of light spreading around the earth – neighbor to neighbor, town to town, country to country, faith to faith and heart to heart.

We are in deepest gratitude for your purchase of this book and your commitment to 365 days of angel prayers. May you be blessed each day with grace, healing and joy.

With love,

Elizabeth Harper and Cathleen O'Connor

January–February–March
The Energy of New Beginnings

with **Karen Paolino Correia**

Manifest Your Best Year Yet with the Angels

By Karen Paolino Correia

I was thrilled to be the angel messenger guiding you as you ring in the New Year. Coincidentally, this was the exact time of year my journey began with the angels in 1996. After 3 years of neglecting to take care of myself because I was too busy taking care of everyone else, working two jobs and living the life of a type A personality, I finally went for a checkup and within minutes my doctor found a lump on my throat. I went for a biopsy and I began my new year with a diagnosis of cancer at the early age of 34. Needless to say I was in shock and filled with fear.

Even though I was not religious at the time nor was I on any type of spiritual path, I knew I needed to pray, ask for help and seek multiple channels of healing. I spent hours in the bookstore looking for answers and I joined a meditation class at my gym.

During my first experience in meditation the facilitator guided us on a journey to a sacred garden where we could rest and invite anyone who wanted to sit with us. As I surrendered my doubt and allowed myself to experience, I felt a presence sit next to me and hold my hand. This experience was all so new and even though I felt comforted, my first thought was, *I must be making this up!* Yet when I emerged from the meditation and I later got in my car, the fear that had been hovering over me was gone and I felt peace through my entire body. Intrigued and wanting more, I continued the weekly meditation class and this presence of love continued to sit with me and eventually when I asked, she said, *"I am your guardian angel. You are going to be OK and healed from this cancer but you need to go through this. I will always be there for you and you will never be alone."* From that moment forward, I felt her presence always especially when I spent two weeks in isolation for a high dose of radiation therapy.

By September of that same year, I had completed surgery, radiation treatment and I was cancer free. My energy level was coming back and I was back at the gym only to overhear someone at the desk saying, *"I am having this amazing psychic come to my house"* and before I could catch myself, I was inviting myself to her party! Shocked and regretting my actions, I thought, *what if she tells me something bad when I am just emerging from a challenging, dark, journey.* But something told me to go, a nudge or a push, and looking back, I am so grateful I stepped into the unknown.

This complete stranger proceeded to read me as if she knew me. She told me about my life, my journey with the cancer and then the clincher, the life changing moment…she described my guardian angel exactly how I saw her in meditation and she told me everything my guardian angel told me and I had never shared these messages with anyone.

That was it, the light at the end of a long tunnel was finally in sight and a new door swung open for me to enter. Another realm, my angel was real and I had an opportunity to believe and trust that everything I had gone through had a purpose and there was so much more to explore. I made the choice to walk through the "door" that day and say yes to a whole other world, of divine guidance, support and miracles.

Believe me, I am not anyone special. I was not born seeing spirit nor do I have a special gift to connect and communicate with the angels. My desire to know and experience more opened the channel and tuned me into the infinite oneness that is always there for all that choose to re-member.

Many have forgotten who they truly are in this human experience but when you journey within through meditation and prayer you remember your eternal essence, the divine light within you. You wake up and remember nothing is separate and it is your natural birthright to reconnect with your divine spiritual family, who has always been there for you, in all ways.

My journey with the angels over the past 20 years has created a life better than I could ever imagine. I have experienced and now passionately teach others that you can manifest miracles and healing in every aspect of your life when you choose to co-create with the angels and believe me when I say, anything is possible…..

- Physical, emotional, mental and spiritual healing
- Manifest healthy, loving relationships and a soulmate if you wish
- Create financial abundance and prosperity
- Discover and live your purpose with fulfillment and joy
- Experience peace, self-love, joy and fun in your life
- Enjoy everyday miracles and a knowing that you are never alone and loved unconditionally for just being you!

How do you begin? This is a perfect time as you close one year and welcome in a new year. It is a sacred opportunity to release and let go of all that no longer serves you and invite and allow a new beginning where divine potential awaits you and anything is possible. In order to ignite the flow, follow these powerful intentions to manifest a year better than you could ever imagine.

1. ASK the angels to support and guide you every step of the way and initiate asking with the prayers in this book i
2. LET GO- Write down all that you choose to release…fears, blocks, circumstances, old patterns and beliefs and most importantly, doubt
3. MAKE A WISH LIST- Include anything and everything. Proclaim how you want to feel in your new year.
4. INVITE THE ANGELS TO CO-CREATE all that is necessary for your highest and best
5. PAY ATTENTION- Follow the clues, synchronicities and especially follow your intuition
6. EXPECT MIRACLES better than you could ever imagine!

Are you ready to invite the angels into your life?
or….enhance your ability to co-create with the divine to a whole other level?
Then say yes and be open and willing to manifest your best year yet?

"Dearest angels, Infinite Spirit, I recognize this moment as sacred. I am asking for your help, guidance and intervention so I can own my power and choose to release and let go of any thoughts, beliefs, feelings and all that no longer serve me for my highest and greatest good.

I am choosing to be re-birthed into a new beginning. I welcome in this New Year with positive thoughts, faith and the knowing that miracles are possible. I choose to believe that I am never alone, I am so loved and I have infinite divine support all around me, always. Please show me undeniable signs, miracles and confirmation of your presence so I can increase my faith.

As I fall asleep tonight, I welcome the divine to enter. Heal me and clear my mind, body and spirit so I may awaken to feel myself re-birthed into a new beginning where I manifest a year better than I could ever imagine. May it be filled with joy, love, peace, harmony and prosperity (and anything else you choose to affirm). Thank you! And so it is."

Karen Paolino Correia has combined her certifications in personal training, hypnotherapy, mediumship, and as an Angel Therapy Practitioner® (trained by Doreen Virtue) with the development of her own training programs in Soul Entrainment and her 8-week Angel Messenger Certification. Karen's pure intention in all her work is to empower others to heal and discover their true magnificence. She established her spiritual center for the soul, *Heaven on Earth*, in 1999. Karen teaches classes and workshops in a variety of healing and spiritual modalities and hosts guest speakers and teachers from around the world. She also facilitates her private practice, which includes Soul Entrainment, angel and mediumship readings, hypnosis for weight loss, and past life regressions.

Karen is the author of four books: *101 Ways to Meet Your Angels* (Adams Media, October 2011), *How to Contact Your Angels* (David & Charles Ltd., June 2011), *The Everything Guide to Angels* (Adams Media, October 18, 2009), and What Would Love Do? A 40-Day Journey to Transform Your Fears into Miracles of Love (Self Published, October 2005). Karen just completed her fifth book, *A 40-Day Affair with Your Self, a Journey of Self-Love and Owning your Magnificence* which is currently an online program and awaiting publication.

Karen Paolino Correia has been called "the real deal" and is known for her authenticity and her passion for her work. For almost two decades she has helped thousands of people around the world through her books, workshops, certification programs, and private sessions. She can be reached for speaking engagements and readings at http://createheaven.com.

JANUARY
"Poked" By Angels
Rev. Jennifer Shackford, CHt, RM, HHP, Spirit Communicator

The Angels came into my life at a very busy time. I felt like I was living the life of a hamster on the wheel and every day was the same vicious cycle. Before heading to my hectic corporate job, I would drive my 3 year old and 6-month old boys to daycare, plus (with any spare time I had) manage a household with my husband Peter. I had nothing in my life that distinguished me or nourished who I was and I was under the impression that once you were a mom, "I" no longer existed. But the more I shut ME out, the more I concentrated on them, the more lost I became. The only goal I wanted to accomplish in my adult life was that of being a mother. And now that I was, I didn't know how being ME and being the best mother I could be for my sons might co-exist. In actuality, I stopped nourishing my relationship with my husband as well as the one with myself; everything was about the boys.

Becoming a mother, a working mother, doesn't come with a handbook. In my effort to be a good mother I let all relationships in my life fade away. I stopped having lunch dates with my friends. I stopped shopping or going out. Pete and I had less date nights. I was physically and emotionally exhausted. I was living a "successful" life but I was empty inside and every morning I woke up dreading the day instead of embracing it. I turned to my strong Catholic faith and prayed to "The Blessed Mother" to help me feel better, to bring joy and happiness into my life. That was when a friend, Noelle, invited me to a psychic party at her house. From a very young age I have seen spirit and had visions of spirit, Angels, The Blessed Mother and Jesus, but because I had been taught it was evil I pushed it all down and away. Even though I was afraid I accepted the invitation and it was the answer to my prayers.

Through the psychic I was referred to Julie, a psychotherapist and Reiki Master. I contacted Julie, we talked a few times and she performed Reiki energy healing on me. During the one session of Reiki, I had visions of angels healing me, had conversations with my deceased grandparents, and saw Moses writing the 10 commandments on a cliff near a rock. It made me cough when she removed a lump in my throat; it felt as if a mountain had been dislodged. I was very emotional as years of fear were removed. I was in awe at the results of the Reiki session. I felt alive, energized and uplifted!

My same friend told me about a woman, Karen Paolino, in Pembroke MA, teaching Angelic Communication. I was very interested, but felt that we needed to leave it to the angels if I was meant to take this class. I told the angels that if it was meant to be to put the money for the class in my bank account. On April 1st, ten days before the class was about to start, I came across two deposits made from State Treasury and Fed Tax. One deposit was for $444.12 and the other $222.12. I immediately called our accountant to ask why we were getting a refund. She said she had input the figures into the wrong box and when she fixed it we ended up not having to pay! The $444 I needed for the class was available!

That Angel class was an answer to the prayer I sent to The Blessed Mother months before. I had prayed for happiness. From that first class to the present I have been happy and fulfilled with love and abundance. Invoking Angelic Guidance in my life has opened my eyes to witnessing thousands of miracles and synchronicities. I continue every day to ASK for their assistance, guidance and love. I now am blessed and filled with Faith, Love, Trust and Joy and share it with as many people who step forward to seek it for themselves. I live my life according to love as a Reverend, Angel Messenger, Reiki Master, Psychic Medium and Hypnotherapist. I set the intention everyday with God and The Angels to be a channel of love and healing to all who seek it. I am blessed with a full time spiritual healing practice. Doing what I love to do and raising my three children with Peter is overwhelmingly fulfilling. Today, not only am I Mom, I am Rev. Jennifer Shackford.

Reverend Jennifer Shackford trained to be an Angel Messenger and Advanced Angel Practitioner with Karen Paolino Correia, LHT, Angel Messenger, Soul Coach and Author. She has also trained with Rita Berkowitz, Spirit Artist, Spirit Communicator, and Spiritual Counselor and presently attends the New England School of Metaphysics and trains under Elaine Kuzmeskus, M.S., Director and Author, for mediumship, Teresa Lally for Certification in Table Tipping and Roland Comtois for channeling. Elizabeth Harper has also been an asset spiritually and professionally.

Jennifer is enrolled at the Divine Blessings Academy for her Bachelors in Spiritual Healing and Holistic Practitioner Certification with Instructor, Rev. LaVonda Young, PhD.

Jennifer is a Certified Psychic Medium and member of the American Federation of Certified Psychics and Mediums and is in several of their books and listed in the 2013-2014 editions of Best Mediums in the United States, ranked at number 20. Her page on their website is: http://americanfederation-ofcertifiedpsychicsandmediums.org/jennifer_shackford.htm. Jennifer is also affiliated with Bellesprit Magazine as a Diamond Psychic Healer. Learn more about Jennifer and her work at her website http://www.faithandangels.com or email her at faithinangels222@gmail.com.

JANUARY 1
Archangel Manifestation Prayer

By Rev. Jennifer Shackford

I call upon the Archangels to pave the way for an abundant future,
filled with love, happiness, gratitude and faith.
I set the intention this will be the best year of my life.

I call upon Archangel Michael
for the strength I will need to meet challenges in the year ahead.

I call upon Archangel Gabriel
for the words and communication needed to pave the way of my truth
and desires for my present and future successes and relationships.

I call upon and release all to Archangel Raphael
to enable processes for healing of my ego and higher self;
to no longer allow my past fears to control my present or future.

I call upon Archangel Uriel
to activate and embrace my true inner power and love;
to direct me easily and effortlessly to my soul lessons in this lifetime.

I call upon Archangel Raguel
to balance all relationships in my life with peace and harmony.
Allow me to recognize, accept and release any relationship
that is not for my highest and best, to send them gratitude and peace.

Dear Archangels,
I am always open and willing and deserving of your love and guidance.
Blessings of Love.

JANUARY 2
The Angels Are There

By Inger Marie Moeller

I climb a mountain to reach my soul
and fly with a bird from its nest.
I follow what God has set as a goal
for my life on this Earth, and the next.

The Angels are there when I need them the most
and help me through sadness and pain.
They take all my prayers to fly with their host
for Peace to mankind to gain.

The love, the joy, the grace that I feel,
I know are presents of light.
And grateful my heart for God will kneel
while Mother embraces me tight.

JANUARY 3
Archangel Michael

By Trish Grain

Archangel Michael,

I invoke Archangel Michael
for inner strength,
to help me cut cords
from any negative beliefs and emotions
and any addictions that no longer serve me.

I ask that you help me to release any fears and stress
so that I can let go of this situation.

I ask for your help so that I can forgive others and myself
so that I can live in peace.

I ask you to help me live in my own truth and to shine my light.

JANUARY 4
Angel Prayer for the New Year

By Suzanne Gochenouer

Dear Angels,

Guide me to a deeper knowledge
of how I can best serve my own needs,
as well as those of this world,
as I step into this beautiful New Year.

Fill me with the strength necessary
to meet any challenges,
and the knowledge to discern my right path.

Help me hear my soul's whispers,
and bring me true understanding
of my higher purpose as I work to shape my life.

Help me make my way through the coming year
with love, peace, and harmony.

Share with me the ability to hear,
and the wisdom ability
to listen to the voices of my angels,
and the confidence to allow myself
to trust my intuition fully each day.

Amen, amen, amen.

Thank you, thank you, thank you.

January Chapter Sponsor – Rev. Jennifer Shackford

JANUARY 5
Prayer for Good Health

By Elizabeth Harper

Archangel Raphael,
I am open to receive your emerald ray of healing light,
ready to be healed on all levels of my being,
and willing to let go of anything that stands in the way of good health.
Help me to release all patterns within my consciousness
that create illness and dis-ease.

Guide me to find the right healing modalities
to draw on for optimum health.
Direct me to the foods that will best serve
my pursuit of good health and happiness.
Give me the courage to realize that I am worthy
of living a healthy and healed life.

I am healthy.

I am whole.

I am healed.

Thank you!

And so it is.

January Chapter Sponsor – Rev. Jennifer Shackford

JANUARY 6
Divine Love

By Lisa Clayton

We love you dearly and are with you always, Beloved Child of Source.
Trust and receive our blessings every hour of each day.

Go forth, precious heart, with the light and essence in your soul
to vibrate pure, unconditional love the world needs and desires the most.
Fuel your Source with nutritious prayers and meditations
from the buffet of life's offerings.
Watch its potential grow into enlightened relationships with others.

Now is the time to love yourself unconditionally,
with no judgment of the past or fear of the future.
Let Divine Love immerse your life like you have never experienced.
Embrace the responsibility to feed and exercise your soul wisely
by calling upon us daily for Divine Love meals.

Trust and receive. Vibrate joy and love.
Do your inner work by loving and appreciating yourself…always.
Surprise your soul by giving it meals of love and appreciation
in every conscious breath and watch what happens!!

Walk with us in faith, spirit and love.
Love is your soul food. God is your Guide.
Angels are your Manifestation Managers
creating miracles and magic daily in your life.

Watch your blessings unfold and be grateful for our assistance
as we are always with you.

January Chapter Sponsor – Rev. Jennifer Shackford

JANUARY 7
Divine Presence

By Katrina L. Wright

Have no fear, for the angels are here!

Michael, Gabriel, Uriel, Chamuel,
they're all here surrounding and protecting me.
Yes, they're everywhere!

They've come because I called them in.
I feel their Divine Light presence permeate my senses on every level.

These heavenly Beings are anxiously awaiting to assist,
love and guide me on the rest of my earthly mission.

With gratitude, I am open to receive.

January Chapter Sponsor – Rev. Jennifer Shackford

JANUARY 8
Spirit of Peace

By Ann Phillis

Spirit of Peace, wash over me with love,
Lift me in your wings of compassion and heart.

Reveal my path, my journey ahead,
Lift my gaze, to see hope not dread.

Awaken my heart, my soul's graceful presence,
Infuse me with life force, always present.

Stir up my strength, my power to be,
Loving and kind, a true human being!

January Chapter Sponsor – Rev. Jennifer Shackford

JANUARY 9
Angel Prayer for a Divine Assignment

By Michelle Mullady

Beloved Angels of the Holy Spirit,
thank you for the grace, guidance and gifts you bring to my life.
I aspire to be a vessel of your love, power and healing,
bringing tranquility to the world.

Release me from my doubts and fears,
so I may choose to carry the flame of divine love,
shining it around me and igniting the hearts
and minds of all those who I meet.

Help me align with my unique contribution to the whole,
and realize my full potential.
I ask that you give me a heavenly assignment
that totally utilizes my natural talents, skills and interests.

I desire to be of devoted service.
Please use my time in deeply meaningful ways.
Clearly guide me with ease, joy and pleasure
to where and how I can help.
Thank you. And so it is.

Amen.

As you read this prayer, sit in silence. Create a channel between your conscious mind and the Holy Spirit. Call its blessings to encompass you, feel its gentleness and devotion. Breathe in its kindness and strength.

January Chapter Sponsor — Rev. Jennifer Shackford

JANUARY 10
A Prayer for Healing the Child Within

By Gina Barbara

Dear Angels,

I pray to you for your love and support
in healing the parts of me that I have knowingly and unknowingly rejected.

I ask that I become lovingly aware to hear the call for my love and attention,
to be given to the neglected parts of my 'Little Child Self';
as it is through love and nurturing to the gentle, kind, loving spirit, that I am,
that I now bring light to my shadow through which
'My little Child Self' can be acknowledged and healed.

I give thanks to the Angels for what I have received today.

JANUARY 11
More

By Lisa K.

Dear Ones,

Your life is always new.

It is a place where you are free to explore,
to achieve more,
and be willing to allow more into your life.

You've been waiting for more to come to you,
but you must know that you have to be open
for allowing more to be available to you.

Take this new beginning, the New Year,
to grant yourself permission to be open, without judgment,
and release your preconceptions of what can be,
so you can experience what will be if you only allow.

– Your Angels

JANUARY 12
Seraphim Angels, Come

By Bobbe Bramson

Seraphim Angels, Come, Come; Seraphim Angels, Come
Sing God's praises down to us. Shower us with your love.
Seraphim Angels, Come, Come, Come

Seraphim Angels, Come, Come; Seraphim Angels, Come
Purify with your fire of Love. Sanctify the name of the One.

Sing Ye: Holy, holy, holy
Kadosh Kadosh
Holy, holy, holy
Kadosh Kadosh Kadosh
Gloria in Excelsis Deo

Open up forgotten places within my heart
Touch within me, soft and gentle, the aching part
Oh, please, surrender me to God's Love
To the home I've been dreaming of...

Oh, Seraphim Angels, Come, Come; Seraphim Angels, Come
Pierce the lies that drag me down. Lift me up to higher ground.
Seraphim Angels Come, Come, Come

Sing Ye: Holy, holy, holy
Kadosh Kadosh
Holy, holy, holy
Kadosh Kadosh Kadosh
Gloria in Excelsis Deo

January Chapter Sponsor – Rev. Jennifer Shackford

JANUARY 13

Archangel Jeremiel:
Prayer of Divine Purpose

By Cathelijne Filippo

Beloved Archangel Jeremiel,
Please guide me on my path and help me live my Divine Blueprint.
Send me signs to clarify my Higher Purpose in life,
and help me make any adjustments needed
to live in accordance with the truth of who I really am.
Help me let go of any fears or worries I may have about living my Divine Purpose.

Dear Archangel Jeremiel,
Give me the strength and clarity to review my life.
Help me to see what resonates with my Soul and what does not.
Give me the courage to let go of all that no longer serves me
as I embrace that which reflects my inner truth.
Help me to follow the guidance of my heart, as it is the compass of my Soul.

I am now ready to share my inner Light with others in any way my Soul sees fit.
Let it be a journey of discovery and magic.

So be it!

JANUARY 14
My Angel, Beamer

By Sarah Dennison

I think of you,
my sweet, gentle boy
and I hear the Angels singing.

The Angels are singing the sweetest song I have ever heard.

Resting on a fluffy cloud in the bluest sky above,
surrounded by the Angels singing.
I close my eyes, and we are walking side by side.
We listen to the Angels singing.

Sitting by the water's edge, under the moon-lit, starry sky,
the silvery waves breaking on a distant shore.
Together, we listen to the Angels singing.

I feel you brush against my cheek,
while holding you close to me.
We listen to the Angels singing.

I watch you gently fade away,
as memories roll down my cheeks.

The Angels are singing,
leaving their sweet song
tucked safely in my heart.

January Chapter Sponsor – Rev. Jennifer Shackford

JANUARY 15
Breaking Through Illusions that Keep You Small

By Julie Geigle

Archangel Metatron,
I call on you now to help me align with my inner truth.
Help me to call in the angels and follow my divine guidance.
I cast out all negative thoughts and break through the illusions
created by my ego to keep me small.

I step into this knowingness and allow the magnificence that I am
to flow into and through my veins,
replacing all illusions and negative thought projections
with the purity and love from my soul.

As I align with God's will in my life,
I am shown the way,
and where there is no way miracles unfold and the path is revealed.

Illusions that served me once
are now disintegrating and fading from my sight.
My essence is as pure and sacred as a newborn child
and as I tap into this truth,
there is nothing that I cannot be, do or have.

Only love exists now. Only love.
Thank you, Archangel Metatron,
for helping me to remember who I am and why I came here.
By the grace of God it is so.
Thank you. Thank you. Thank you.

January Chapter Sponsor – Rev. Jennifer Shackford

JANUARY 16
The Light of this Day

By Cher Slater-Barlevi

God Goddess, All That Is,
I call forth my High-Self Spiritual Council:
my Teachers, Guides, and Angels,
please take me within the center of the Earth,
that's connected to the center of the Heavens,
where grows the Flame of Eternal Light.

My Loving and Compassion seeks the mergence of that Light
in my own heart now and throughout my day.
Once lit, I carry it with me throughout my entire day.
I carry it to all I come present with, merging my Divine Light with theirs.

Together, we carry the Light to the next, and the next,
until the whole Universe is a Flame with the brilliant blaze
that dissolves and consumes the ego of disharmony and
any vibrational frequency that does not serve Loving,
Taking it up to the Highest Realm of Light to be released and dissolved,
in service to the evolution of consciousness of all mankind.

I know this to be true because it has been created here
with the Divine, in the Grace of Now.
We are Loved in the Highest and in The Allness of the God Force.
Peace. Be Still.

And so it is.

JANUARY 17
One Consciousness

By Shalini Breault

Angels of Creation and Protection,
thank you for allowing us to be in the flow of life
with ease, love, kindness and support for each other.

Angels of Transformation and Power, thank you for our uniqueness.
As we have grace and courage and allow ourselves to be free
we know we are in your loving arms!
We know you are with us every step of the way!
We all are a piece of a puzzle – the Universe.
Our unique creations, voices, talents and gifts
all contribute to one masterpiece - consciousness!

Angels of Abundance, thank you for lovingly taking care of us.
We always have what we need.
We always have access to the abundance the Universe provides.

Angels of Artistic Expression,
thank you for guiding us to be the BEST creators EVER!
Plants have been seeded by you, Angels,
for us to grow into beautiful flowers,
singing and dancing amongst Mother Earth.
Create playtime and guide us to be in the joy of life.

Angels of Light and Peace,
thank you for allowing us to shine our light to the world.
It's this light which sparks, ignites and connects us.
PEACE!

January Chapter Sponsor – Rev. Jennifer Shackford

JANUARY 18
Cosmic Grace

By Ann Phillis

Deep within the cosmic space
Of living light, the utmost grace.
The heavenly worlds do shower their love
Upon all in their care, planets and stars.

Our little world shines in their wings, their embrace
The angels of Sirius make all things blessed.
But we must choose, day in, day out
To be part of this change, this love and new life!
For it is not them, but us, that hold the key
To manifest peace and world harmony.

We, the angels and humans merged
The body of spirit, made of body of earth.
Alive we are on every plane
Of conscious choice - this is how we create change!

Do not step back from the need of the hour
We stand on the brink of all that empowers.
Accept the demands of body, spirit, light
Balance is the key to angels' delight.

Awaken your soul to love's pure power
The light in your heart will flourish and flower.
The Angels of Sirius, flowing living, loving light
Nourish all in their care - be with them tonight!

January Chapter Sponsor – Rev. Jennifer Shackford

JANUARY 19
Archangel Gabriel
Depths of Presence and Love

By Kimberly Marooney

Gabriel, Help me dive beneath the shallow layer of illusion.
It feels like a flotation device that keeps propelling me up to the surface
when I long to remain in the depths of your presence and love.
My mind lives on the surface, constantly making up scenarios of disaster.
They are no more real than the movies I like to watch.
Are they merely self-entertainment?
Yet I believe them to be true because they come from my mind!

No more.
You are the reality my soul longs for.
Yours is the eternal love that my heart craves.
Help me to cut the jacket away that inflates with fear,
self-importance and stories.
Let it rise to the surface on its own. I choose you.

I desire to live in truth and peace with you
all the days of my life and for eternity.
Take me deeper into the truth of who I am in you.
Take me deeper into this experience of peace.
Hold me. I am yours.

Guide me.
Reveal the vision of how you would have me live –
what you ask me to do - and who you would have me serve.
I am yours in love.

JANUARY 20
A Prayer for a Fresh Start

By Tracy Quadro

Angel Metatron,
you are the all-powerful Guardian
of all possibilities to come.
You hold the promise that starting over brings –
the countless paths of "what if I try this instead," and "let's do it!"

With your guidance and wisdom,
may I see each stop sign or apparent roadblock
as a green light for new adventure,
and a step in the right direction.
Please nudge me to move from "now what?" to "what's next!"
And please remind me that changes are commas, not periods;
way stations in which to read the map,
refuel, buy some snacks,
use the restroom and then once again
take to the road to where we want to be.

Sometimes we hit rock bottom because there is nowhere to go but upward. On our way up, we are bound to meet our best path along the way. Imagine the possibilities when the slate before you is clean! Full of nothing but open opportunities and the promise of something better developing from all you have learned on your way down.

January Chapter Sponsor – Rev. Jennifer Shackford

JANUARY 21
Morning Guardian Angel Prayer

By Stacey Wall

Dearest Guardian Angels,
Please watch over me and keep me safe.
Help me to embrace this day and the endless possibilities it offers.
Illuminate all of the good that comes my way
and help me to stay in a place of gratitude,
realizing that my life overflows with abundance and beauty.

Guide my footsteps so that I stay true to a path
that is good and right, and designed especially for me.
Give me strength to make choices that are in my highest good.

Let me truly live my Divine purpose.
Help me to serve in some way today.
Let me use the gift of this day to help someone heal.
Let me be God's hands, His heart, His voice in this world.
Let me live my life as an expression of the Divine in physical form.

Help me do my part to heal our beautiful planet.
Help me spread love and joy today.
Help me always to be kind, compassionate, patient and understanding.

Angels, thank you for staying by my side,
guiding and protecting me now and always.
I am grateful beyond measure.

And so it is.

January Chapter Sponsor – Rev. Jennifer Shackford

JANUARY 22
Archangel Jophiel
Prayer for Creativity

By Cynthia Helbig

Archangel Jophiel

May I be an instrument of your beauty on Earth.

Help me to release any blocks or fears that I may have about my creativity.

Please wrap me in your golden wings
so that I may hear your voice in the stillness.
Gently support me so that my imagination is inspired.
Grant me strength, courage and the energy
to bring forth my own unique creations into the physical.
Remind me to celebrate my achievements with love and joy.

I give thanks for your love and support
as I manifest my inspired creations of beauty easily and effortlessly.

And so it is.

You can also ask Archangel Jophiel to help you to

- Slow down and breathe
- Align your energies with heaven
- Centre your thoughts in joy and blessing
- Unleash your inner wisdom
- Create Beauty wherever you may dwell on earth.

JANUARY 23
My Intention for Change

By Karen Cowperthwaite

I am seeking change now.
What shall I become?
Building a new piece, so powerful,
I have much to offer, much to love.

Archangel Raphael, I seek to understand who I am,
guide me to what is true.
Wrap me in your loving care,
lift me up so I can see.

Connect me to my purpose,
help me clear the way.
I am ready to accept this challenge,
honor me with all the strength I need.

The blessings of a new year bring intentions of renewal and transformation. Allow your angel team and guides to lovingly create infinite possibilities for the changes you wish to create. My "go-to" angel for growth is Archangel Raphael. During a meditation class, his comforting words allowed my fears of ending my career as a teacher and use my gifts as an angel whisperer and healer, to shift. Surprisingly, I did not take his message to heart, virtually forgetting it altogether. So Raphael sent another messenger in a dream that night. My departed father came forward delivering these exact same words, "You are so deserving." He knew I would believe it if my Dad said it. And I did!

JANUARY 24

An Angel's Message of 365 Days of Change

By Jennifer Parr

Change is inevitable. Each day we wake anew.
No matter what yesterday has brought, today is new.
Rolling tides will come.
Small, flat, calm ripples will gently, playfully wash ashore.
Other days may bring an all-encompassing twister,
engulfing, spinning, a vortex moving with such velocity
that all you can do is surrender and allow it to lead you where it must.

Remember, you are loved beyond measure.
Change is an act of love. Change will push you, direct or redirect.
The universe will only provide that which you are strong enough to endure.

You are strong, courageous and powerful.
With change, you can begin anew.
No matter what yesterday has brought,
today can be a fresh, clean slate, a new beginning.

The universe has a plan and you, my child,
are a perfect piece in this puzzle.
You are needed here, on planet Earth, for a very big reason.
You have a purpose, a mission.
We need you and the special gifts that only you carry.
With each change comes lessons, growth and blessings
that lead you one step further on your path.

Embrace change and allow it to fuel
the blossoming on your divine, golden journey.

January Chapter Sponsor – Rev. Jennifer Shackford

JANUARY 25
A Prayer for Light Workers

By Rev. Vicki Snyder

Calling all angels!
Surround, protect and fully support all the light workers
from every town, state, country and continent.
Bring them together in spirit to do the work of the angels.
Use their light to brighten the entire universe for all to see.

Let their common goals unite and make a true difference in the world.
It's time the outcome of your desires be seen and felt by all.
The world is ready for peace, love and oneness for all.

These light workers require you
to continue to breathe life and love into them
so they may continue with your mission and the mission of God.
When these light workers are down,
feeling tired or have a low supply of energy,
provide the nourishment they need to continue.

Help them be role models, for all to see
how best to handle life's ups and downs.
Demonstrate for them that they can survive
and see that their commitment to light and love is recognized.
Give them signs that they are successful.
Fill their hearts with love so they may continue to spread more love
and rid the universe of any fear.

JANUARY 26
Prayer to the Angels for Balance and Light

By Jan Harper

I ask my inner angel self
to meet me tonight
as I go inward further and further,
guiding me to bring balance
and light to my infinite soul.

As I draw the invisible cosmic light of awareness
to the infinity of my soul,
letting this light expand my physical body
making me feel more open and porous.

Help me feel this light radiate
thru the spaces between the atoms
and molecules in my body
making me feel more spacious, light and diffused.

Expanding me into the outer reaches of space
while at the same time helping me feel
the awareness of being centered
and balanced in my infinite inner soul.

JANUARY 27
Mother Mary Prayer for Life Purpose

By Debby Tamborella

Mother Mary,
I look to you as the epitome of motherhood –
nurturing, caring, selfless.

You withstood heartbreak with dignity and faith.

I see light blue butterflies that show me you are here,
surrounding me with your love and encouragement.

Through your serene grace and wisdom,
guide me to see the light I bring into the world.

Help me to realize my strength is my vulnerability,
which allows others to see and learn from me
and, that through my wounds,
I can show others how to heal themselves.

And so it is.

JANUARY 28
Ask, Believe and Receive

By Susie Robins

Dearest Angels,

ASK

Please be with me throughout this day
and help me stay centered in your love, light and energy.
I ask for your divine healing on all levels:
physical, mental, emotional and spiritual.
Please help me to stay positive, helpful and
guide me in seeing the best in others.

BELIEVE

I believe and trust in your divine presence
and am grateful for your behind-the-scenes help
so that I may experience your divine healing, peace and joy.
I let go of my past and release any fears and worries to my future
so that my prayers may be heard and answered.
I trust that everything is working out for the highest good of all.

RECEIVE

Thank you for your healing of my body, mind and spirit.
I AM healthy, whole and complete.
I am grateful for your guidance, support
and synchronizing my life for the best possible outcome.
I AM safe, supported and abundant.
Thank you for knowing exactly what I need
and for the everyday miracles of your love and light.
I AM happy, joyous and free. So it is. All is well.

January Chapter Sponsor – Rev. Jennifer Shackford

JANUARY 29

Angel Ezekiel's Wisdom for the New Year

By Tammy J. Carpenter

Your angels are here,
surrounding you and uplifting you.
They are near and dear to your heart
and have your best interests in mind.
Do not trouble yourself with earthly worries today.
Be light! Be joy! Be love!

Angels are near
and all you need to do is to ask for assistance.
Live life fully, as you are a unique and beautiful soul.

This is a new day unlike any other.
A new year with the opportunity to get it right.
The angels have seen you with a new light,
a new passion to help those around you.
They believe in you and the important work that you do.
They believe in your loving message and your pure intention.
Be open to receive their guidance and love.

Be not discouraged as there is time yet
to have a positive impact on the world.
Allow the angels to assist you and help carry your load.
Now is the time to discard any fears or hesitation.
Ask your angels to illuminate your path.
Then take the next step with great anticipation.

JANUARY 30
I Relax into the Knowledge, My Abundance is Divine

By Rachel Cooley ATP® and
Kimeiko Rae Vision ATP®, The Angel Warrior™

Dear God, Angels, Archangel Ariel and Archangel Barachiel,
Thank you for your continuous support and supply of blessings
for both myself and my family in all areas of our lives.
We are so grateful!

Please help me to speak and think positively and powerfully
so that I manifest and experience even more abundant blessings
in all areas of my life.
Help me to create the perfect vision of what I know
is already there in spiritual truth.

Thank you for continuously delivering your guided messages,
so that I clearly understand and know all that you are guiding me to do,
through my thoughts, feelings, hearing, and vision.
Thank you for increasing all forms of financial flow,
so that I can prioritize my spirituality, self-care and high quality foods.
Thank you for the time and energy to prepare and enjoy them all.

Help me to truly know that having my needs met is an act of generosity.
As I provide for both myself, and my family, I am free and motivated
to assist others in the world in need of my support and love.
Thank you!

JANUARY 31
Prayer to Manifest Your Best Year Yet

By Karen Paolino Correia

Dearest Angels, Infinite Spirit,
I recognize this moment as sacred.
I am asking for your help, guidance and intervention
so I can own my power and choose to release and let go
of any thoughts, beliefs, feelings and all that
no longer serves me for my highest and greatest good.

I am choosing to be re-birthed into a new beginning.
I welcome in this New Year with positive thoughts, faith
and the knowing that miracles are possible.

I choose to believe that I am never alone,
I am so loved and I have infinite divine support all around me, always.
Please show me undeniable signs, miracles
and confirmation of your presence so I can increase my faith.

As I fall asleep tonight, I welcome the divine to enter.
Heal me and clear my mind, body and spirit
so I may awaken to feel myself re-birthed into a new beginning
where I manifest a year better than I could ever imagine.

May it be filled with joy, love, peace, harmony and prosperity
(and anything else you choose to affirm).
Thank you!

And so it is.

FEBRUARY

Asking the Angels
Trish Grain, RM,
ATP®, UK

My journey and how I came to work with Angels started out because of a back problem. It was so debilitating that I felt that I'd had the rug literally pulled from under my feet. For the first time I was the one being cared for, instead of taking care of everyone else.

One minute my life was ticking along fine the next my life felt out of control. It was also a lesson for me in that I had not been honoring my body's needs and that I was, in fact, on the wrong path.

From a young age I had always been interested in all things Psychic and used to have intuitive hits, but once I had a family I never had much time to explore in more depth the spiritual or psychic side of life and there weren't many good books around at that time.

The only angel I was taught about at school was Angel Gabriel and that was when we did the school play, so I never really thought about angels.

Then I had problems with my back that became debilitating and I was exhausted with pain and couldn't walk very far. I was in and out of hospital and, after having a spinal injection for pain, I was able to take a trip for a few days in a cottage with my husband. At this point in time I was praying for help to get better.

We were both outside one day, the day was warm and the sky blue and the clouds floated by. It was a peaceful day with just the two of us. As my husband looked up to the sky, he told me to look up and from high above a very large white feather was floating down. It seemed as though it was dancing and circling as it descended and we couldn't take our eyes off it. We watched and waited until it finally came to land gently at my feet and we both said *"this is some kind of message"* as it felt that it wasn't just an ordinary feather falling from the sky. We kind of knew it felt special.

My back problem became worse eventually requiring major back surgery. I was in intensive care for about a week and was still praying for help and protection. I was a long time getting better. I eventually found an amazing woman called Karen Stratton who was a Reiki Master and went to her for a treatment and the first treatment I had with her just blew me away.

I had my first encounter with an angel. The angel was so beautiful and I felt such peace. She and I stayed in a beautiful garden for quite some time as she spoke with me telepathically. That experience that day opened my psychic and spiritual pathway.

After the session Karen asked me where I went to. At first I thought she might think I was a bit nutty but I said you won't believe this but I have just met an angel. From that day I continued to get much better in every way. I signed up with Karen to teach me Reiki. From there things started to happen and then a book I never ordered landed on my doorstep. The book was called *Ask Your Angels* and I still treasure that book today, to remind me how far I have come.

I was eventually led to Diana Cooper, the U.K's most well-known angel teacher to train as an angel therapist and then went on to train with Doreen Virtue in angel therapy when she came to Glastonbury in England. The angels have opened many doors for me leading me to many spiritual teachers, including Elizabeth and Cathleen, your authors of this anthology.

I feel that the angels are guiding me, protecting me and healing me. They have helped me to take this work out to help others and with each step over the years, this has led me to where I am today with a centre called Angel Radiance. It's a centre mainly for women and children where I continue the work of the angels. Angel Radiance reflects the heart and soul of my work and my profound gratitude for the wisdom and knowledge I have gained over the years. It is my hope to pass this on through my healing work, with angels and workshops, so that you can nurture your own inner light.

It's been an amazing journey over the years of self-development and healing. At the time I couldn't see it but my back problem was a blessing in disguise. It taught me that I wasn't done and I had another purpose in life to fulfil. I trust and look forward to where the angels will guide me next on my pathway.

The prayers I offer in this book have been received by me as channeled messages from the angels. I hope they bring the love and light of the angels to you each day.

Trish Grain, RM, ATP®is a Reiki Master, Angel Therapy Practitioner® and Heal Your Life® teacher with a diploma in Hypnotherapy/Psychotherapy, Certified in Counseling. Her own path of healing led her to the work of Louise Hay. The Heal Your Life program she offers is based on Louise Hay's philosophies of self-love and the use of affirmations to transform your life. She studied with and was certified as a ***Heal Your Life*** teacher by Patricia Crane. In 1988, Louise Hay personally chose her to lead the Love Yourself, Heal Your Life workshop nationally and internationally.

Trish is also certified to teach Relax Kids, classes that help children improve listening skills, attention, confidence and focus by calming the mind and allowing them to develop positive feelings and self-esteem. Many of her certifications have come through training she has taken with many incredible spiritual teachers and healers including spiritual author and healer Diana Cooper, angel expert Doreen Virtue, author and past life regression expert Dr. Brian Weiss, Relax Kids founder Marneta Viegas, and author and angel practitioner Karen Paolino Correia.

Trish is the founder of the Angel Radiance centre in Barnsley, South Yorkshire, UK where she offers angel workshops, healing sessions and hosts visiting spiritual teachers. Her website is http://angel-radiance.com.

FEBRUARY 1
Prayer for Healing

By Trish Grain

I invite in the highest vibration of light of the angels
I ask Archangel Raphael to shower me with his gentle healing rays,
On my physical, mental, emotional and spiritual bodies.
I ask for healing and trust that you will take care
of my well-being and lead me to wellness.
I thank you for guiding me to the people who can help me,
I thank you for the healing already given and
for the blessings already in my life.
I accept your healing now and so it is and so be it.

FEBRUARY 2
Imbolc Prayer

By Cathelijne Filippo

Beloved Archangel Ariel,

Bless me with the quickening of Goddess energy during this Imbolc,
when the seeds of life are planted within the earth and within myself,
bringing hope for a new time of blossoming and growth.
For as within, so without.

Help me to care for the deep seeds of my thoughts and feelings,
to create new loving behaviors and manifestations in my life.
Help me to open to the light and inner fire of the Goddess,
creating healing, revitalization and a stirring of life within.

May I be blessed by the energy of Mother Mary,
helping me to connect to the energy of the wise woman within,
bringing her energy into all new projects and intentions.
Healing my body and soul,
embracing me and making me whole.

Dear Ariel,
help me to be reborn today,
leaving behind the old and outmoded,
embracing the new and powerful me,
as I merge my mind and heart into the unity of my soul.

So be it.

February Chapter Sponsor – Trish Grain

FEBRUARY 3
A Prayer to Archangel Michael for Protection

By Audrey Simmonite

Archangel Michael,
I stand before your blessed, shining presence
and ask for the protection of your cloak of brilliant purple
to surround and protect us from all the negative forces
which attack us at this time of dark shadows.

May your blazing sword of fire protect us
from all our enemies seen and unseen
who bring down fear and conflict upon us
and that the evil deeds they so cruelly pursue and impose,
be returned to them for the rightful justice and retribution
to be imposed from the highest court on the astral plain.

I pray also that you grant me the wonderful gift of wisdom
and the strength and guidance to walk in your footsteps
seeking only truth and honour as I humbly follow your true path.

Archangel Michael,
I dedicate my time here on earth
to passing on the wonderful message
that your love, protection and strength are always near.

Amen

FEBRUARY 4
Sparkling Heart Blessings

By Eve Picquette

Today I want to live the prayer of St, Francis –
Where there is darkness – (let me sow) light.

I ask the Angels of Unconditional Love
to sweep away all my concerns or negative energy with their wings.

I breathe deeply and relax for a moment.
I picture a beautiful crystal heart in my hands.
In it I place all the things I want for this day –
health, happiness, success, an abundance of all good things,
happy loving relationships, kindness, opportunity and assistance,
discernment and compassion,
beauty, fun, laughter -
all the things that bring me and others joy.

I see the beautiful crystal heart open like a flower
and I lift it and blow all these blessings onto my path
like tiny sparkling gems of light.

I ask Loving Angels
to guide these sparkling blessings wherever they need to go –
to the people, places and events on my path
so that I have happy, uplifting interactions with all I meet
so that I see everything with the angel's eyes of love
so that today I truly will spread love's light.

February Chapter Sponsor – Trish Grain

FEBRUARY 5
Prayer for Transition

By Rev. Jennifer Shackford

Transition is difficult.
The period of time between an old chapter closing
in one's life to a new one opening.

God and Angels, I call upon you now
to release all past guilt, mistakes, regrets to you.
I release them all in knowing that I had to experience all
to be in my present and future.
Without my experiences, I would not have paved the way for my future.

I am open to the new challenges ahead of me,
In the clear knowing that they are for my highest and best.

I give up all to you.

Direct me to the next chapter; I am strong enough to overcome all!

I will be patient through this transition and all will happen in divine timing!

FEBRUARY 6

Prayer for Healing and to Let Go of a Difficult Situation

By Linda Goodings

Dear God, Jesus and Archangels Raphael, Michael and Raziel,

Thank you for allowing me to let go of all of my worries, stress and pain
and to put faith in your hands in regard to (…this situation/ person).
With this next breath, I fully surrender this situation to the Divine.

Thank you for letting me know
that I deserve your Divine intervention and guidance.
I will step back and allow divine light and the love of Jesus to come streaming
through me and this situation, so that it can be fully healed right now.

Thank you, Archangel Raziel, for balancing the karma within this situation
in all directions of time, in this or any other lifetime, for everyone involved.

Archangel Michael, thank you for dissolving any psychic attack energy,
cords, and fear-based energy coming from me and this situation.
Thank you for protecting and shielding me, allowing only light and love.

I am willing to forgive myself and everyone involved in this situation
so that I may be at peace.
I ask for blessings for everyone involved.
I wish this healing be for the highest good of everyone involved.

Thank you God, Jesus, and Archangels for your
loving support, guidance and healing.
Amen.

February Chapter Sponsor – Trish Grain

FEBRUARY 7
Angel Prayer for an Inspired Life

By Suzanne Gochenouer

Dear Angels,

Light my world with wondrous inspiration in every part of my life.
Feed my soul with the blessing of an enquiring mind,
a generous heart, and an inspired life.
Show me how to use those gifts to make this world a place of peace and harmony.

Guide me to share my creativity with others,
who like me, desire to change the world where it is dark and cruel,
bringing light and grace to all who need it.

Guide me to use words that will change lives,
to perform deeds that comfort the lost,
to share love with those who have none.

Make me an instrument of change
for those who fear they will never be inspired.

Share with me the courage
to allow an abundance of inspiration into my life,
and to recognize it in all its glorious aspects.

Amen, Amen, Amen.

Thank you, thank you, thank you.

FEBRUARY 8
Blessed Miracles

By Lisa Clayton

Believe in your ability to create blessed miracles,
each day, through Angel's Divine Love.
Still your heart as it is a sacred and holy place,
where miracles can happen with clarity and deep awakening.
As you experience others' resistance and deep-rooted fears,
let your heart light shine so that it brightens
to heal, love, guide and be in service for evolution.

Go forth and trust.
Our daily infusions of Divine Love guide you.
Love is always the answer.
Forgiveness is as necessary as breathing.
Surrender is as necessary as eating.
Trust is as necessary as sleeping.

Go forth with confidence as you see with clarity
and experience the miracles of trusting, believing and surrendering
to Divine Love by listening daily to your heart's voice.
You are a powerful miracle worker.
Each action you take and each thought you vibrate with Divine Love
magnifies and expands into blessed miracles.

You are ready, Beloved!
Your soul wings are golden and your heart is full of our love.
Keep your eyes on the sky, hands on your heart,
and feet grounded on precious Mother Earth.
Feel the vibrations of love infusing your heart for the birthing of new miracles.

FEBRUARY 9
Bringing in the Light

By Daniel Hyman

I invoke 7th dimension all that is love,
all that is light that I am one with, that is one with me,
to flow to me, through me, with me and from me
into my crown, my third eye, my throat, my heart,
my solar plexus, my sacral, my root and foot chakras.

I invoke my entourage of beings that are 100 percent love and light
to come be with me, to guide me, helping me move forward on my journey
to reach and exceed my destiny with love, light, happiness, joy, and balance,
with flow, with ease, with fun, with prosperity, with abundance,
in the quickest and shortest amount of time that allows for
perfect mental, physical, and spiritual health.

I command my I AM Presence to release and let go
of all that no longer serves me and as I let go to
see, learn, and know the lessons and the teachings of all
that is being released with love, light and forgiveness.

I command my I AM Presence to be open, unattached, disciplined
in order to take, follow, and stay on my path
without fear, without doubt, without hesitation till I leave this planet.

I Awaken now

FEBRUARY 10
Healing Through Dreams

By Gina Barbara

I pray to the Angels,
that in my dreams
your gentle whispers of guidance
come through your silent speech.

I pray that as I dream,
your words of wisdom come through me,
so that I may use these through my day;
knowing this, my heart opens
to the still small voice inside of me,
allowing such spaciousness.

I pray that as I dream,
the love of you connects me
through the light beyond any darkness,
so that my dreaming spirit awakens.

I am so much more than I could possibly imagine,
as in my dreams I bring through the colour of my life canvas.

With the light of you, to see me through,
the dream and dreamer awakens!

FEBRUARY 11
Prayer to Heal a Broken Heart

By Rev. Vicki Snyder

With these words I pray and ask for healing of my heart.

I ask you Archangel Raphael to surround my heart
with the most beautiful emerald green color.
Let this healing color swim through and around my broken heart.
Let the tears flow to release all the hurts and disappointments.
Allow my heart to expand in this healing color of green
and to beat with the constant thump thump,
like a drums sound of life and of love.

I offer these words to you, Raphael
in hope that you may create a sense of peace
and acceptance within my heart
of those things I cannot change.
Help me release those things that create hurt and sorrow.

I ask you to help me to nurture a strong heart
that enables me to live my life in the most courageous ways;
to rebuild my trust in love.
Give me strength to fight this battle of heartache
and to win against the darkness that sets in.
Let the light shine again and for hope to prevail
that yet again my heart will beat with the sound of love.

FEBRUARY 12
Deserving of Love Prayer

By Elizabeth Harper

Open my heart, Archangel Chamuel
to the universal spring of divine love.

Let me be willing to embrace love in all forms,
to release judgment of myself and others,
and bring love into every aspect of my life.

Give me the power to accept love,
even when fear emerges.
Give me the strength and the courage,
to keep my heart open to the essence and generosity of love.
Give me the devotion to continue in the name of love
in everything that I am and do.

Archangel Chamuel, above all
guide me to love myself.
Help to realize the importance of self-love.
Open my heart to the loving kindness
of my spirit and soul,
and help me to know and love my own angelic self.

Thank you.
And so it is.

FEBRUARY 13
A Prayer for Healing from a Relationship Break-Up

By Jennie Degen

Dear Angels
As you know, I have experienced a heartbreak.
The pain is unbearable;
I feel like I am crawling out of my own skin
and that a part of my soul has been ripped away.

Please help me in my time of need.
Please lift this heavy burden
and help allow my heart and soul to heal.
Show me how to go about my days
knowing there is life after love.

Show me that I am worthy and deserving
of a new beginning and a new me.
Please show me the lessons learned
from this relationship so that I may grow.

And most importantly,
please help my soul to open up
to whatever the future has in store for me.

Thank you.

FEBRUARY 14
Prayer to Archangel Chamuel

By Cathleen O'Connor

Beloved Chamuel,
Bring your love and light to my relationship.
Help my words to be kind,
my thoughts responsible,
my actions honorable.
Help me to remember that love is a mirror
reflecting my own shadow and light.

Help me speak my truth in loving and gentle ways;
and give me the boundaries to know when to keep silent.
Help me to know my own needs and ask for what I want,
and to keep my expectations realistic.
Help me learn to give and receive in balance,
to be cared for and to care, to be alone and to be together.

Remind me to hold my values dear,
to forgive with an open heart so that any hurts are quickly healed,
and to stay in the present not in the past.
Allow me to see my relationship as new each day,
and give me the grace to know that my happiness comes from within.
Help me keep my desire alive through presence,
and a willing, grateful heart so this relationship
can continue to grow in love and light.

Shower this relationship with the blessings of patience, joy and laughter
deepened by the gifts of fidelity, longevity and friendship.
And so it is.

February Chapter Sponsor – Trish Grain

FEBRUARY 15
Prayer for a New Relationship

By Sharina

Dear Angel DARACHIEL

You always know my troubled times and are always there
when I need a word of cheer,
someone to praise to give me hope,
or brush away my tear.

You know when I need your comfort
of an understanding heart,
to give me strength and courage,
to make a fresh, new start.

Thank you for always caring and giving me such great happiness,
thank you for never running away when I needed your help
and thank you for being my guardian angel.

*PLACE 6 small pink crystals or pink items on a white cloth, light 6 pink tea candles and then visualize yourself embracing your new partner as you say this prayer on the night of the waxing moon.

FEBRUARY 16
Archangel Jophiel's Message of Light

By Bobbe Bramson

Your true nature is to shine.

It takes a lot of energy to block the rays of that Glorious Shine.
That Light is brighter than 10 billion stars and beyond your imagination.
You have no idea of the absolute brilliance of your wattage.
You are all Radiant souls who have put yourself on dimmer switches.
You are Divine Love burning bright … yet you hide the Light.

Decommission the dimmer switch.
Lift the ban on full-out shining of the Light.
Let it rip!

February Chapter Sponsor – Trish Grain

FEBRUARY 17
Prayer for the Downhearted

By Trina Noelle Snow

On the wrong side of the door with just the clothes on your back,
when exhausted, depressed--perceiving nothing but lack,
when friends you've confided in are on the attack,
Believe!

When the waters run swift and are perilous to tread,
the dreams that you drive cannot see the road ahead,
and the thoughts of tomorrow are nothing but dread,
Believe!
When your body is tired and your heart is so scarred,
when love that you gave returns mangled and marred,
and your heaven seems barb-wired, battered and barred,
Believe!

When you are screaming you just can't go on,
children are hungry cries that can't wait for the dawn,
know beyond good sense that your battle is won,
Believe!
Hold onto the truths that your angels aren't far,
and the radiance within you does construct the stars.
This tide breaking takes you beyond where you are.
Believe!

I've known all too well of the pain that you hold.
Let go of slammed doors, lost love and feeling too old.
Of infinite sovereignty we are created —Our heads high, we must hold
And believe!

FEBRUARY 18

Prayer to Archangel Chamuel for a Soulmate

By Rev. Vicki Snyder

Dear Archangel Chamuel,
I pray to you - please assist me in finding my perfect soul mate.
I am open to receive the love that is meant for me.
I have worked diligently to unlock my heart
and am able to give and receive love now.
I long to have a life partner who will support and love me in all I do;
I also want to return this support and love.

Let me encounter my soul mate and allow peace
to come to both of our lives the moment we meet.
I know that all healing comes through love
so let us both continue to heal on our path together.
Let us come from a heart centered loving place,
in trying times and happy times.

Never let us forget the feeling of joy and love, and how we began.
Help us to learn and grow as a couple;
be willing to change for the betterment of our partnership as a whole.

Wrap us in your beautiful pink wings
and pry away the cage that locks our hearts away.
Permit our hearts to soar and unite as they beat as one,
filled with loving pink light.
Of infinite sovereignty we are created –
Our heads high, we must hold and believe!

February Chapter Sponsor – Trish Grain

FEBRUARY 19

To Archangel Raphael Who Fills My Dreams

By Audrey Simmonite

Through mists of time and endless space
My journey long and seeking grace

I feel you take my hand with love
And show me wonders from above

On wings so soft and gold tipped white
We rise and see with pure delight

A place where miracles and joy are there
And sweet angelic voices fill the air

Now gently back and safely home
Angels watch till my work here is done

February Chapter Sponsor – Trish Grain

FEBRUARY 20

Chiral Connections
On the Love and Loss of a Soulmate

By Diane Hiller

As twin souls we met through synchronicity
A soul contract long planned as our destiny
on roller coaster ride of passion so strong
with conflict and disharmony too often prolonged

We learned lessons of love over those many years
Estranged when you died, it was now crystal clear
I needed more answers than I could ever find here
So I sought shamanic counsel and through her you came
with a nine page letter that really changed the game

Regret and reflection of how we both played our parts
then led to the journey to rejoin our hearts
So marry did we in shamanic ceremony
Unbreakable is the bond of this matrimony

Our love in this life was not meant to be
You are now a partner and guide that looks over me
The songs, signs and omens do come hard and fast
when I have been low and questioned my path
Love after life has become a work of service
You there and me here our souls' sparked with purpose
Keep moving, you say we have places to go and little time for rest;
I honestly can't wait to see what comes next.

With gratitude, love and light I invoke your name
My own personal angel; in my heart, forever your flame.

February Chapter Sponsor – Trish Grain

FEBRUARY 21
Awakening

By Ann Phillis

Ethereal light, pure and bright,
Effusive, radiant, flowing life.

The angels are here, they uplift my being,
They teach and nurture, love me with healing.

I open my heart! Then do I know,
The deepest love, of the universal flow.

I stand now in service,
Awakened and whole,
My soul, incarnate,
My wings are glowing.

FEBRUARY 22
Prayer to Find True Love

By Tracy Quadro

I know you're out there!
I know there is someone out there
who brightens my world and lightens my load.
That person is my friend, my ally, my confidante,
my partner, my companion, my love.
We are ready to find one another,
so close we can feel one another!
Our hearts are connected,
and we're already a part of one another's life.

Angel Raphael,
healer of the mind and body and mender
of all things not yet in their proper place,
please bring my soulmate and me together at last!
We are ready, willing and able to join our lives together.
We need your help to make that happen.
Please put us in the right place at the same time!
Open our eyes to one another and kindle that spark in our hearts.
Please grant us the wisdom to reach out, smile,
hear the beating of one another's heart
and recognize ourselves in the Other's soul
with a playful twinkle in our eyes.

Whisper in each of our ears
that THIS is the ONE we've been waiting for.
Gently nudge us toward one another with the sudden revelation,
"oh.. there you are... I've been looking for you..."

February Chapter Sponsor – Trish Grain

FEBRUARY 23
Prayer for Attracting Love

By Julie Geigle

Archangel Metatron,
At times I feel so lonely and isolated.
I long for romance and love. I fear this will never happen.
Please help.

I take a deep breath and connect with
my unending flow of love and boundless joy.
As I tune into this energy my soul emerges,
And I am bathed with peace and tranquility.
I begin to remember the powerful creator that I am
and my ability to choose again.
The love that I am so desperately seeking outside of myself
does not exist because I am not separate from that love.
I am that love.

As I turn inward my Soul reminds me
that I already have that which I want.
The beauty of love emanates from my soul.
I become like a love magnet, attracting many opportunities
and experiences to share my love with others who are like-minded
and overflowing with this magnetic energy.

I am love. I am loved.
I am fulfilled and connected with all that is.
The Universe, God and the Angels have heard my call
to experience myself as love; and people and opportunities
are being put into place NOW for this truth to be revealed.

FEBRUARY 24
Love

By Lisa K.

Love is in the air;
Love is everywhere,
if only you can see how much we, your angels, LOVE you!

We sprinkle your path with angel dust of sparkles and whimsy.
It brings you magic in our working to make your path light and breezy.

Never let your awareness cloud,
for when we are around, and we always are,
you will expand with happiness and especially love.

When you do this, you will experience more love from others around you,
even those whom you didn't think loved you at all.

– Your Angels

FEBRUARY 25
Email to the Angels

By Lynn Waddington

Dear Angels,

Help me to trust that you are always there.
Help me to live and grow in grace under your guidance.
Help me to understand myself and others.
Help me to be compassionate and kind.
Help me to be tolerant and forgiving of myself and others.
Help me to hear your guidance and act accordingly.

Thank you for all of these things.

FEBRUARY 26

Archangel Zadkiel
Prayer for Forgiveness

By Jillian Leigh

Dear Archangel Zadkiel,
I call on you to surround me in the purest white light.

Hold me in your loving wings.
Help me to let go of past negative experiences
that hold me back from my highest potential.

Guide me to release all transgressions.
For without you, I am but a wilted flower
yearning for nourishing rain.

With you I am a beautiful flower in bloom,
opening my gifts for all to know, feel and see.

As I call on and work with you,
I know I can shake off all negative energy
that I may have absorbed during my day.

I know you will send all negative thoughts, energies,
feelings and words to heaven for transmutation.

I am at peace now with a light, loving heart.
I thank you for your love, guidance and assistance.

And so it is.

February Chapter Sponsor – Trish Grain

FEBRUARY 27

"Love is the magic!" "The magic is remembering the love!"

By Starlight

We are living everyday surrounded by magic and love
but we have forgotten where and what it is!
Now is the time to remember!

Open your heart and breathe in the magic and the love of remembering!
Slow down and see the beauty that is everywhere!
Slow down and look for the little wonders that are everywhere!

On the street!
In your back yard!
Everywhere you are there it is!
In the city!
In the country!
Where you would never expect it, it is there!

Love is the magic!
The magic is remembering the love!
Breathe and Enjoy the Magic and the Love!
Remembering!

Say below affirmations 3xs breathe deeply after each quote.
"Today I open my heart to all the magic that surrounds me!"
"Today I open my heart to all the love that blesses me!"
"Today I open my mind, body, heart and soul to remembering!"

February Chapter Sponsor – Trish Grain

FEBRUARY 28
Prayer for Loving Your Self

By Karen Paolino Correia

Archangel Chamuel, Blessed Mother Mary
and my dearest Guardian Angels, please come to me now.
Surround me in your unconditional love
so I can remember what it feels like to be loved
just the way I am, with no conditions or expectations
(pause to breathe and receive).

I realize how hard I can be on myself
and I would never talk to others the way I talk to myself.
I ask that you nudge me and remind to catch myself
when the unloved parts of me are calling out for attention and acceptance.

I also ask for the miracles of healing.
Please erase and heal any hurtful words or actions
that were said or done by others that still affect me today.
Help me to remember beyond any doubt that –
"I am loved, no matter what. I am perfect just the way I am
and there is nothing to fix, just more of me to love".
Join me dear divine helpers. Embrace me, as I wrap my arms
around myself and proclaim…"I love me and I am so loved"!
(Pause, repeat and experience).

Help me to see, feel and know how beautiful I am from the inside out
and to deeply understand that I am doing the best job I can
with what I know in every moment and I am always learning and growing.
But most of all, help me to love myself as much as you love me."
And so it is!

February Chapter Sponsor – Trish Grain

FEBRUARY 29
Prayer for Leap Year

By Cathleen O'Connor

Dearest Angels,

With gratitude I welcome this extra day –
a new day full of possibilities and potentialities.

Guide me to use this day as the precious jewel it is.
Let me not rush through it, ignoring its gifts.

Instead work with me today to remind myself of what is most important:

A Grateful Heart
An Open Mind
A Compassionate Touch
A Deep and Joyful Laugh
This is a day filled with Blessings.

Help me to see the opportunity to again set intention.
Remind me that my intentions and actions create the day after next –
and the one after that, and the one after that.

Let my intentions be made with a clear mind and heart,
with consciousness and presence,
so that my tomorrows (my next todays)
are filled with the love and light of Divine grace.

And so it is.

February Chapter Sponsor – Trish Grain

MARCH

Healing with the Angels

Suzanne Gochenouer

I began working closely with the angels after a head injury left me in chronic debilitating pain throughout my entire body. The migraine that lasted every hour of every day for 18 months inspired my close connection with the angels.

I have always loved anything to do with angels—books, movies, songs, or art. Beautiful artistic and written representations of angels moves me in ways that lights something deep within. In my childhood, I felt there was nothing more exciting and wonderful than having my own personal Guardian Angel. There was no warmer comfort than knowing that my personal angel watched over me at night. But for years, the Guardian Angel prayer was the extent of my communication with the heavenly hosts.

Over time, my connection with the angels strengthened, yet I didn't ask for specific help from them.

In the past twenty-five years of coping with pain, sometimes struggling to find the energy to do just one thing each day, I've called on the angels. My journey with these messengers of Light began with inviting Archangel Raphael to pour God's healing love and grace over me as I lay sleepless each night. I asked him to share with me what I needed to know to begin my healing journey.

Archangel Michael began showing up to bring me strength for the battle against my disabling pain. He slowed my breathing, reminding me to breathe deep into the pain, rather than attempting to escape it. When I could finally do that, I was able to move above the pain and do the things I had to in order to survive. With his help I went to work each day, even when I could barely draw a breath without excruciating pain.

Archangel Gabriel brought me the message of hope for a life worth living, even in suffering. He helped me move forward, never giving up, even when I could see nothing past the physical disaster my life had become.

From Archangel Uriel, I learned to see the gift in the pain. He walked with me as I created a deeper connection to Spirit, and gained understanding of how I would serve the world through this experience.

After I left my stress-filled job and created a business of my own, Archangel Metatron inspired in me the belief that I would have enough. He led me to discover and understand new ways of living in the energy around me.

As my health improves, I feel the angels moving in and out of my presence all the time. Where before my injury they had been distant, glorious creatures, they are now my constant teachers and protectors. They work with me in my Reiki practice. One client, who is sensitive to energy, asked if I am aware that there is a dome of Light surrounding and encompassing the small valley I call home. She would have been most surprised had she sensed the four angels who plant their swords in each corner of my property on nights when there are disturbances in the energy. And woe to any tailgater, as my traffic angels stand on my back bumper, armed with flaming swords. Within moments, the hurried drivers fall back to a safe distance.

I delight in working with my angels to find each step of my life path, and to hold healing energy for the planet and everyone on it. I ask their opinion and advice for nearly every moment of my life. And I rejoice in their help, as I become more intuitive, and more loving, in my encounters with their high energy.

When offered the opportunity to share an angel prayer with you, I knew it would be my favorite one. Since I love my home, and my friends love spending time within its energy, I treasure each moment there. And I want it to be safe and secure at all times.

Each time I am about to leave the house, I offer this prayer to the angels of earth, air, water, and weather. I begin by touching my stove, which represents the hearth, and the heart of my home. Then as I stand at the door and look out at this piece of earth where I'm blessed to live, I ask the angels to protect my home at all times. I hope you will enjoy calling on your angels to surround your home and loved ones with protection and love.

Suzanne Gochenouer co-authored four books in the Celebrating 365 Days of Gratitude series, has been published multiple times in the Long Ridge Writers Group *Writer's eNews,* and the *Mount Saint Joseph Ursuline Associate Update,* and others. In 2013, she made the shortlist for the *Words with Jam* First Page Competition. Suzanne recently added publishing to her toolbox, acting as editor/publisher of a book of poetry and art, Now and Forever by Mary W. Sublett. She worked with the enhanced-novel publisher Noble Beast, in the role of book producer.

A U.S.A.F. veteran, she also spent twenty years with an aerospace company, working on classified government contracts. A head injury caused chronic migraines, sparking her interest in aromatherapy, Reiki, and all forms of healing energy. Leaving the corporate world to create an aromatherapy business allowed her time to write and help other writers.

A member of The Professional Writers' Alliance, Suzanne enjoys working with everyone who loves words. Certified as a coach and as a ghostwriter, Suzanne is passionate about helping writers define and reach their goals. When not reading, she writes, edits, and coaches other writers. She posts weekly to her website, www.TransformationalEditor.com.

MARCH 1
Angel Prayer for Home Protection

By Suzanne Gochenouer

I'm on my way out again, little house.
But I'll be back as soon as possible.
Angels, please protect my house and my property,
my neighbors' homes and properties,
and my entire neighborhood,
while I am gone and at all times.
Protect us from the force of the weather.
Protect us from those with dark intent.
Protect us from injury and disease.
Amen, amen, amen.
Thank you, thank you, thank you.

MARCH 2

Archangel Michael Prayer for Protection and Cleansing

By Elizabeth Harper

Archangel Michael,
I call upon you to cloak my energy field
with the deep blue violet ray of protection.
Create a reflective surface to shield me from all negativity and darkness.
Safeguard my aura allowing only light to enter.

I invite you to draw upon the power of your sword to sever
any unhealthy cords that no longer serve me.
Completely clear my energy and cellular bodies
of all physical mental, emotional, and spiritual attachments
from both this and previous lifetimes.

Gently dissolve any obstacles that might stand in the way
of me living at the highest vibration of light.
Infuse my heart with the strength, courage
and power of unconditional love.

Guide me to forgive and to accept forgiveness,
and may this and my love for humanity
strengthen my boundaries, and bring me peace.

Archangel Michael,
I am willing to accept and I am thankful for
your protection, support, and guidance.
And so it is.

March Chapter Sponsor – Suzanne Gochenouer

MARCH 3
Relationship Prayer

By Rev. Jennifer Shackford

God and Angels,
I know all relationships are put into place for a reason and a lesson.
Help me to understand with an open heart and mind
when a relationship has run its course.
Give me the strength to not hold on to a relationship
that is no longer for my highest and best.

Allow me to disconnect, send them love,
thank them for teaching me along my journey
And move forward positively.

I am grateful for the time they were part of my life
And the contributions made in alignment of my soul's path in this lifetime.

Thank You!

MARCH 4
Light of My Soul

By Ann Phillis

From the womb of time, I rise like a flame,
My wings full of light, my heart ablaze.

I open my arms, radiant I am!
I lift my gaze, impervious to pain.

I see the horizon, my life flows on,
I stand in my soul, I am whom I am.

Strong, peaceful, clear, in love,
I am the light of my soul in my heart!

MARCH 5
"Angelized!"

By Lisa Clayton

All is taken care of when you ask us to help you.
Let us "angelize" your heart and soul vision.
The sun of abundance and love shines upon you
even through the thick fogs of life.
Clear the foggy lens you have been using
for your vision of your life's purpose on earth.
Give yourself the clear vision of your heart
and listen closely to its messages.

You have the inner beauty, grace, passion
and, most of all, Angel Love to see clearly.
Today, feel the golden light
from the multitudes of Angels surrounding you.
Feel our golden essence and vibration
in every chakra of your body
and every light chakra above and below you.

Feel your cellular composition
changing and tingling with the golden essence of our love.
Feel the vibration of your spirit and soul
taking you to a new level of pure, unconditional love.
This incredible infusion of golden love essence
will forever keep you walking the true path of your soul's blueprint
as you open your heart wider and wider to Angel Love.

You are being "Angelized," aligning your human experience on earth
to your soul purpose, as it travels on the wings of Eternal Love.

March Chapter Sponsor — Suzanne Gochenouer

MARCH 6
Create

By Lisa K.

Spring has sprung within you.
Inside, you are filled with the entire seed of the Universe's potential.

You can create anything, with anyone, or alone, together with us.

You may have reached the end of your New Year's resolutions list,
or just started to work on it.

We are here to cheer you on.

You can move forward with ease,
knowing that we support you in your endeavors,
to create whatever your dreams may be.

So, go forth and know that we support and assist your every heartfelt desire.

– Your Angels

March Chapter Sponsor – Suzanne Gochenouer

MARCH 7
Archangel Gabriel

By Trish Grain

I call upon the energy of Archangel Gabriel

Your beautiful, gentle loving energy
to help me raise my vibration,
to be more loving and compassionate.

I ask that you surround my children and all children,
keeping them safe and protected at all times.

I also ask that you help me to nurture my own inner child.

I ask for your divine messages filled with divine love.

I ask you to show me the way forward to live my soul's purpose.

March Chapter Sponsor – Suzanne Gochenouer

MARCH 8
Angel Prayer for Manifest Intention

By Bobbe Bramson

Dearest Angels, beloved messengers of the Divine,
I come into your holy presence
with wishes and intentions that are near and dear to my heart.
Fill me with hope, inspiration, and a sense of deservedness,
so that I may indeed fulfill them.

Give me clear vision
that I may see through any self-imposed illusions of limitation and lack,
and hold me within your embrace of unconditional love, as
I make the changes I need to make and find the courage to transform.

Walk with me, dear Angels, and illuminate my path,
whispering words of loving encouragement and infinite possibility
so that I may remember my magnificence.
Shine your Light on every shape and contour of my desire so that
I may recognize it when it appears, and give me all of the crystalline
focus, perseverance, and devotion needed to make it so.

And when I have done all that I can,
I pray you will enfold my intentions within your angel wings
and uplift them into the highest vibration of my good.
In that moment, I will bless and surrender them up to God
for the attainment of their Divine Perfection.

Thank you, Beloveds.
With grace and ease, Amen.

March Chapter Sponsor – Suzanne Gochenouer

MARCH 9
Archangel Chamuel:
Prayer for Self-Love & Love

By Cathelijne Filippo

Beloved Archangel Chamuel,

Thank you for your ever-present loving energy.
Please envelop me in this gentle vibration today.
Help me to truly and unconditionally love myself.
Help me to accept my flaws and embrace my strengths.
Help me to make positive changes from this place of loving acceptance.
Let me see myself with the eyes of love,
So that I can see my Inner Light shine through.
I know I am a part of the Divine and as such am perfect just the way I am.

Dear Archangel Chamuel,
I know that I can only share true love with others, if and when I love myself.
So help me to form meaningful bonds with others from this place of self-love.
And help me to heal my heart centre completely,
so that I am free to give and receive love.
I now love myself.
I am open to love.
I am worthy of love.
My heart overflows with love.
There is enough love for everyone.
For love is all there is, in truth.

So it is!

March Chapter Sponsor – Suzanne Gochenouer

MARCH 10
Prayer of Gratitude to the Angels

By Melanie Barnum

Today, I give thanks for the abundance of blessings I have been given.

I thank the angels and the universe for bringing to me all that I need.
I pray to receive a steady financial abundance,
so that I may have everything I need to help me succeed
and allow me to assist others as well.
I ask for the financial freedom to pursue my goals
and the goals of my family and loved ones.

I thank you for the motivation to continue in positivity to reach my greater good.

I pray with gratitude for guidance to be ready and able
to be exactly who I'm meant to be, exactly who I'm supposed to be.
I joyfully thank the angels who are helping me
to become happier and healthier than ever before.

I am blessed and I ask that my blessings are shared
with all who need them, to allow them to also reach their true potential.

I pray to hear your messages and to recognize when you are there to help me.

I pray also to understand the wisdom of the angels
and the universe
and to follow their guidance.

Thank you today and every day.

March Chapter Sponsor – Suzanne Gochenouer

MARCH 11
Archangel Uriel's Prayer
for Personal Power & Manifestation

By Coryelle Kramer

Archangel Uriel light of the Universe
and child of the God/Goddess.
Shine your light upon me; illuminating my path
to the creation of the life that I wish to manifest,
through which clarity and certainty reside.

Assist me in releasing the bondage of
limited thoughts, sight, emotions and beliefs
that are holding me back from my Divine right
as a creator of my time on this planet.

Rest your transfiguring light upon me
so that I may mold negative into positive,
find light in the shadows of the past
and know tranquility in my heart.

I am ready to be with you in the light of Universal Consciousness,
that will bring with it the knowing that all things transpire for a reason
and from that knowing I will find peace within myself.

I walk with you as a child of worthiness,
and as a creating artist of this life I am living,
and a living, breathing representation
of the God/Goddess force of all things.

March Chapter Sponsor – Suzanne Gochenouer

MARCH 12
Angel Prayer for Earthly Guardian Angels

By Emily Gilghrist

God Bless our Guardian Angels on Earth,
Ones cleverly disguised in dresses or shirts.
Little ones singing a song joyfully,
Neighbors and friends who help unselfishly.
Devoted spouses all wanting to please.
Our brothers, our sisters, our pastors, our priests.
The endless array of suffering souls who look
to the Heavens and beg to go home.

God Bless our Guardian Angels on Earth.
The soldiers who fearlessly watch over all,
safeguarding our homeland, our freedom, our flag,
selflessly giving without ever a lag.
Daughters, sons, grandchildren, to add just a few
to the endless variety of Gifts sent by You,
to protect and to guide us in all that we do.

God Bless our Guardian Angels on earth,
Ones who have watched over us since our birth.
The mothers, the fathers, the teachers, the nurse.
Fill them with white light raining down from the sky
and energy drawn up from the earth.
To converge in the heart to give them the courage
to carry out your work.

God Bless our Guardian Angels on Earth.

March Chapter Sponsor – Suzanne Gochenouer

MARCH 13
Call Upon Archangel Haniel for Life Purpose & Unity

By Odalys Villanueva

Archangel Haniel,
clear my heart of old patterns that no longer serve me.
May these old patterns depart from me
for new positive patterns to come along.
Open my heart for the new positive, loving,
and grateful patterns in my life.

Connect my heart with my life purpose and divine truth.
I call upon Archangel Haniel for my inner wisdom to be clear
so that I can hear, know and trust my divine and joyful life purpose.

May this place of divine truth lead me to gracious experiences;
experiences of true freedom, peace, and love,
where I can be connected to my whole being and to others.

Let this place of wholeness be the unity with Mother Earth and all of us.

March Chapter Sponsor – Suzanne Gochenouer

MARCH 14
Friendship with a Guardian Angel

By Rev. Vicki Snyder

Oh my friend,
you are always there when I need you.
You take on my hurt,
you support me,
you I can always count on.
You are my best friend.

It is a one sided friendship
yet you give so tirelessly and without question.
I call on you at all times and you are right beside me,
lifting me and pushing me to go on.
I feel your guidance and accept your help.

I trust you without experiencing you with all my senses.
So I wonder about you and this is what I imagine.
I cannot feel you, but you would feel warm, soft and cuddly.
I cannot hear your actual voice, but I hear your gentle, sweet uplifting thoughts.
I cannot smell you, but you smell like wonderfully warm baked cookies.
I cannot taste you, but you taste like a nice cool glass of water on a hot day.
I cannot see you, but you have a smiling happy face with compassionate eyes.

You are pure love in all the senses.

Using all of your senses,
how does your guardian angel look, feel, smell or taste?

March Chapter Sponsor – Suzanne Gochenouer

MARCH 15
Prayer to Love, Accept and Embrace My Soul

By Karri Ann Gromowski

Guardian Angels, thank you for walking beside me every moment
along this, my Soul's Journey. Enfold me in your loving embrace.
Help me to always feel safe, protected and loved today and for eternity.

Claire, Elohim of Purity & Archangel Raphael,
Awaken my heart to the Love, Divinity, and Light of God, that I Am,
knowing I am blessed, deserving and open to receive miracles.
Infuse pristine, White Light Energy into my cellular DNA
to cleanse, purify, and attune to my Soul.

Archangels Jophiel & Ariel,
Shower me with your beautiful confetti flowers,
opening my eyes to the Beauty I Am.
Harmonize and Balance my mind and emotions.
Integrate Confidence, Courage, and Acceptance for Whom I Truly Am.
Strengthen my Spirit to unveil a joyful, free expression
of my evolving Soul's True Essence.

Archangels Raziel & Michael, Angels of Atlantis,
Lift my Veils of Illusion, Illuminating the depths of my Soul.
Energize me within your waterfall of effervescent, Rainbow energy.
Surround me with the Gold and Silver Violet Transmuting Flame,
upholding and supporting me in the fifth dimension
while transmuting and raising my frequency.

Angels, Help Me to Embrace Life, Live Now, and Let My Soul Shine!
And So It Shall Be.

March Chapter Sponsor – Suzanne Gochenouer

MARCH 16

Healing Generational Suppression of Women

By Julie Geigle

Archangel Metatron, I ask you now for healing
of generations of women suffering in silence,
tolerating abuse and mistreatment from their partners.
I allow my breath to serve as a gateway
to connect me to my mother, who connects with her mother,
connecting mothers everywhere.

I allow their pain to become mine
and in this act of allowing, the pain is transmuted into love.
With another cleansing breath, I feel a deep healing within my soul.
My voice emerges strong, certain and BOLD.

The Divine Feminine rises up as I step into
the Divine Goddess that I came here to be.
I am now an unstoppable force of truth and integrity;
cleansing, clearing and releasing all suppression
in generations past, present and future.

I now find it easy to stand up for myself.
I know exactly what to say and when to say it.
My feet are firmly planted on the ground
rooted in truth and integrity.
I speak one word at a time living my life with honor and dignity.
Fear reigns no more as I join together
with women across time and space to heal.
Freedom rings in my heart today. ♥

March Chapter Sponsor – Suzanne Gochenouer

MARCH 17
A Prayer for Healing

By Tracy Quadro

Dear Angel Raphael,
Healer of the Universe,
please transform the hurt and sickness inside me
into healthy understanding.

On days in which the pain seems too much to bear,
please touch my heart and head and help me find my strength.
When my body is broken, please wrap me in your arms of love
and put me back together.

When I reach into the void and feel alone in my suffering,
please extend your open hand and clasp mine to prove that I am never alone
in this universe full of powerful, gentle and benevolent Spirits.
May your constant attendance focus my ability to heal myself.

And when my sickness is not of the body, but of my heart and mind,
and I feel lost or unable to cope when times are dark,
please bring the light of your love and comfort.

Please open my eyes to the beauty surrounding me,
and remind me to look in the bright places
for the steadfast joy in my life that sometimes seems obscured.
And through your guidance,
may I bring your healing to the world,
and all around me.

So mote it be.

March Chapter Sponsor – Suzanne Gochenouer

MARCH 18
Archangel Chamuel
Prayer for Self-Love

By Michelle Mullady

Archangel Chamuel,
I call upon you to envelop my energy field
with the pink angel light ray.
Please dissolve all thoughts and feelings of self-hatred,
self-condemnation and low self-esteem
that I carry from painful past experiences.

I ask you for assistance in loving and accepting myself,
my opinions, beauty, emotions,
my faults, imperfections, and flaws,
my strengths, humor, wisdom,
as well as my peculiar and unique way of seeing the world.

Help me to love and approve of each and every part of myself.
I desire to know at the core of my being
that I am worthy, valuable, and lovable.
May your healing light of unconditional love
enter every area of my reality and fill my heart and soul.

May the magic of love always move me
to radiate warmth and caring to myself.
Let it be done according to God's Holy Will.
Amen.

* As you say this prayer, place your right hand over your heart center and allow yourself to draw in energy, from the angel of unconditional love to warm, balance, and heal you.

March Chapter Sponsor – Suzanne Gochenouer

MARCH 19
Prayer for Reluctant Warriors

By Kimeiko Rae Vision ATP®, The Angel Warrior™

Dear Angels,
Am I hearing you correctly?
Are you whispering to me that **now** is my time to shine?
Please help me to be courageous
in the face of all perceived danger, real or imagined. Now!
Let the vibration of this prayer wash over my fighting spirit
like music to my ears.
Let comfort be the rhythm, soothing be the harmony,
and be as welcomed and familiar to me as my favorite song.

Angels,
please tickle me and make me smile by showing me small signs,
medium signs and BIG SIGNS that you love and support me daily,
and that my every step is Divinely placed
on God's highest path for me.

Please make the signs so enjoyable and so clear
that my Divine mission becomes unmistakable to me.
Thank you for strengthening my ability to speak up for myself and for others,
turning my insecurities into surprising blessings for us all.

I am ready now.

Please stand by my side as I embody God's plan
as the Angel Warrior that I am.
I accept!

March Chapter Sponsor – Suzanne Gochenouer

MARCH 20
Equinox Prayer

By Cathelijne Filippo

This Prayer is for the Spring Equinox in the Northern Hemisphere;
If you live in the Southern Hemisphere, read the Equinox Prayer on September 23.

Beloved Spugliel, Guardian Angel of Spring,
Bless me with the energy of spring;
the promise of a new day,
bringing abundant beauty and vitality.

Let me clear the cobwebs in my mind,
let me purify my emotions,
and let me take extra good care of my body
as I enter springtime.

Dear Spugliel,
May I blossom like a spring flower turning to the light.
Shower my new intentions and projects
with the energy of love and empowerment.
I water the plants of these intentions with love, positivity and gratitude,
as I embrace my ability to create and renew.

Thank you for all new life in spring:
the blossoming flowers, singing birds, playful lambs and rays of sunshine.
Let me channel the passion, change and positivity of spring into my own life
and that of those around me.

So be it.

MARCH 21
The Gratitude Prayer

By Joe Randazzo

Dear Great Mystery and Great Spirit,

Thank you for the gift of life and each and every precious breath that I take.

Thank you for each and every miracle, big and small, that surrounds me.

Thank you for the outermost reaches of all space and time.

Thank you for Father Sun and Grandmother Moon and the star nations.

Thank you for the angelic realm, and their quiet guidance, protection, and love.

Thank you for beautiful Mother Earth.

Thank you for Her life sustaining waters, winds, and soil.

Thank you for the marvel and mystery of every animal, and insect.

Thank you for the humble majesty of every flower and tree.

Thank you for the joy and privilege of being part of all creation,
the collective life flow, and energy,

And thank you for each and every blessing,
those known, and those unknown,
already on their way!

March Chapter Sponsor – Suzanne Gochenouer

MARCH 22
Archangel Uriel Inspiration Prayer

By Cathleen O'Connor

Dear Archangel Uriel,
Inspire me!

Inspire me to live with purpose.
Inspire me to live with passion.
Inspire me to live with compassion.
Inspire me to live with forgiveness.
Inspire me to live with joy.
Inspire me to live with love.
Inspire me to live with acceptance.

Inspire me to live with presence.
Inspire me to live with gratitude.
Inspire me to live with hope.
Inspire me to live with integrity.
Inspire me to live with responsibility.
Inspire me to live with vision.
Inspire me to live with wisdom.

Inspire me to live with courage.
Inspire me to live with tolerance.
Inspire me to live with curiosity.
Inspire me to live with enthusiasm.
Inspire me to live with generosity.
Inspire me to live with humility.
Inspire me to live with grace.

Inspire me! And so it is.

March Chapter Sponsor – Suzanne Gochenouer

MARCH 23

Enjoying Life with a Divine Sense of Humor

By Christina Scalise

"Angels, please help me find the best way
to deal with this tough situation."
I hear nothing. I see nothing. I sense nothing.

I start to stress and make plans...and God smiles.
I ask for signs from my Guides...and hear a chuckle.
I pray for the Angels to help me...and they dance and they laugh.

"Are you there? Are you listening? Do you hear me?"

I ask again for a sign...and my favorite song begins to play on the radio.
I smile...feel the rhythm of the music...and start to sway.
Oh, what am I so worried about anyway?

Yet, I ask for a sign once more...and the sun and clouds form a smile.
I request confirmation...and suddenly, a feather falls from the sky.
I demand proof beyond a shadow of a doubt...and feel bird poop splat in my hair.

"Message received."

"Angels, please give me the strength to find humor in all situations,
the ability to laugh at myself and enjoy life with a divine sense of humor. Thank You."

May your days always find humor, your eyes always sparkle...
and a bird not poop in your hair - Christina

March Chapter Sponsor – Suzanne Gochenouer

MARCH 24
Angel of God – A Morning Prayer

By Betty Sue Hanson

Angel of God,
my guardian dear,
through whom God's love
permits me here.

Ever this day
be at my side
to light and guide
to rule and guard.

AMEN

Dear Angels,
please guide, surround,
protect and direct me today
to do God's work.
Please get me everywhere
safely and soundly.

These are prayers of intention and connection to your angels to be used daily.

MARCH 25
An Angel by Your Side

By Anna Taylor

Every moment we are alive,
an Angel is always with us.
Every time we ask for help,
an Angel fulfills their purpose.

Every time we feel alone,
an Angel whispers, 'I am here'.
Every time we pray for peace,
we rest in an Angel's wings.

Every time we follow our guidance,
an Angel relaxes.
Every time we choose happiness,
an Angel celebrates.

Every time we have the courage to fly,
an Angel flies beside us.
Every time we sing and dance,
an Angel plays more music.

Every time we say 'I love you' and mean it,
we become Angels ourselves.

MARCH 26
Rose Healing

By Ann Phillis

I hold you close. I pour love into your heart
Through the petals of the rose, on wings of love.

We are angels of harmony, resplendent in the light
Engaged with the Earth, through flowers of delight!

Rose petals shimmer as we descend our embrace
This is how we reach all, with love's pure grace.

A revolution of heart is happening now
On Earth as in heaven, it is cosmic power.
The veil is lifting between worlds of light
Between worlds of matter and conscious choice.

We, the angels of evolutionary flow
We come in our millions for the time it is now.
See us, know us, we are in every flower
We are of every forest, every rock and rain shower.
Seek out the rose, the garden, loving nature
For where you feel love, it is there we empower!

Step into our love, allow your consciousness to know -
Let us fill you, nourish you, shower spirit's grace to all!

March Chapter Sponsor – Suzanne Gochenouer

MARCH 27

Healing Prayer for –
'Bringing Light to Grey Days'

By Gina Barbara

I pray to you Angels above,
bring through your light and purity of love.

I ask for your healing in the shady parts of my life,
so that the cloud of greyness lifts
and the rays of sunlight shine upon me.

I ask this to be so,
opening my heart to the beauty and warmth
that you offer with your radiant glow.

Replace my fear, with love,
so that I may embrace all that is,
and allow healing to lovingly take place.

I let-go of my will to thy will
and open up to receiving all the colours of the rainbow
to heal my life, others and the Earth.

I give thanks for what I have received.

MARCH 28
Angel Prayer for Self Love

By Keysha Sailsman/Alberga

Dear Angels
Teach me to know I am a beautifully embodied Spirit with unlimited potential.

Please help to increase my self-awareness each and every day.
Fill my mind with positive, loving thoughts and remove all fear and self-doubt.
Put me in perfect alignment with my Spirit
and help me to live life from my authentic self.

Through the process of forgiveness, feed me with
the best medicine life has to offer – "self love"
by showing me how to forgive others and in the process set myself free.

Please reawaken my soul with your
Angel touches, kisses, whispers and guidance.
I call on you to plant the seed of unconditional love within my heart center.

Cleanse my body (in particular my heart), mind, spirit and aura
of all negative thoughts about myself.
Teach and show me how to value myself and not seek approval from others.
As the seed of love germinates, let the birth of an Angel
come forth in me to shed light on the world.

Thank you for healing me through this time in my life.
Thank you for your love, support and guidance.
Infinite love and gratitude.

And so it is.

March Chapter Sponsor – Suzanne Gochenouer

MARCH 29

Archangel Zadkiel: Prayer for Heart Centered Transformation

By Cathelijne Filippo

Beloved Archangel Zadkiel,
I call upon you to fill my heart with the Violet Light of Transformation.
As I breathe into my heart, may it be filled with this Light
As I breathe out, may my aura be filled with the Violet Ray.
I now place within my heart all issues that need transformation,
namely: (fill in your words)

I ask you to blaze the Violet Flame through these issues,
turning my heart into an alchemical cauldron of Light.
By doing so I now let go of all that no longer serves me,
making room for positive change within my being and within my life.
I now place within my heart all those people and circumstances
that need my forgiveness,
namely: (fill in your words)

I forgive all those who have hurt me in the past, including myself.
Help me let go of criticism and judgment
as I open up to unconditional love and understanding.

Dear Archangel Zadkiel,
I am willing to be a vessel for positive transformation and change, and I am deeply
grateful for your help in learning my life lessons with ease and grace.
And so it is.

MARCH 30
A Prayer for Creative Growth

By Tracy Quadro

Angel Uriel, set me aflame!
You bring your torch of creative thought to those of us
who struggle to understand the depth of the abundance of the universe.
You help us to appreciate the changes we endure on a daily basis...
the weather, the movements of the earth
both subtle - *slowly creeping magma*
and intense - *cataclysmic eruption...*
and the things that move us, from gravity,
to earthquakes, to the songs of our souls.

All is growth, all a continuation
of the creative force that put us here.
The passion of the Creator to add, to enhance,
to improve, is also within each of us.
I ask you to please stoke the fire in my belly.
Breathe gently on the smoldering embers of my creative soul
and ignite me to new life.
Show me that I *always* have the time to set free
the playful muse inside me.
Kindle in me the thirst for knowledge that will lead me
to the answers that I and others are awaiting.
And please guide me toward the wisdom that will spark my expression
in a way that will touch others and lead them to their own
unique experience of the Truth.

MARCH 31
Prayer for New Growth & Manifesting Miracles

By Karen Paolino Correia

Dearest angels,
just as the seasons inevitably change,
I realize my past is behind me and I cannot change it.
My desire is to live my life fully in the present
and to move forward to experience a new beginning
better than I could imagine.

I am asking for help and healing,
to accept and let go of all that no longer serves me.
I am ready to plant the healthy and empowering seeds of my past
along with the seeds of my desires to create a life
filled with love, joy, fulfillment and prosperity.

I come to you now dear angels and I share my deepest desires
(be as specific and detailed as you share with the angels).
Help me to believe and have faith in the truth of miracles,
especially when I doubt and I don't trust that my dreams are coming true.

I ask with gratitude that you guide and direct me from this moment forward
with profound and undeniable synchronicities, coincidences and miracles
so I can recognize, trust and clearly see my souls path illuminated before me.

I am open, worthy and I now become a magnet
drawing all the help and support I need and rightfully deserve
to live my personal heaven on earth with ease, joy and grace.
And so it is!

March Chapter Sponsor – Suzanne Gochenouer

April-May-June
The Energy of Resurrection

with **Rev. Kimberly Marooney**

The Energy of Resurrection

By Rev. Kimberly Marooney

Imagine waking up from a dark, cold and lonely night to a warm burst of radiant light and heat? Spring is my favorite time of year because that is what happens. The dark of night and light of day are equally balanced at the Vernal Equinox.

The veil between the heavens and earth is lifted making it possible to receive the energy of pure potential and creativity into our consciousness and lives. Just as day and night are in balance, we are called to bring our earthly self and spiritual consciousness into balance.

Millions of angels surround the Earth bathing us in energy of renewal so palpable that we can feel it! This infusion of energy calls seeds to burst forth and sap to rise up trees. Likewise, we receive an infusion of radiant God-union calling us to burst forth from our shell of illusion and rise up in a luminous new life of destiny.

Archangel Raphael oversees Spring as the angel of brightness, beauty, healing and life. With the returning sun of spring, Raphael embodies God's healing power to unite our heart, mind, and emotions with soul using the vibrant force of the planet to quicken our healing.

My most important and powerful breakthroughs followed an intense period of inner inquiry as I worked through painful and challenging situations in life. We all suffer. What turns suffering into golden epiphanies of realization is the willingness to let old ways die, making room for rebirth. Each breakthrough brings more freedom, peace and love to our hearts.

The awakening process is massively supported by the influx of resurrection energy directed by **Archangel Gabriel**. Life has a way of revealing the beliefs and lifestyles that are not in alignment with our true Being. Every situation reveals clues. Conflict and resistance, experiences of betrayal and loss, self-doubt and internal battles are sure-fire symptoms that you are preparing for resurrection.

Spring Cleaning with Archangel Uriel

In April, the energy of purification is palpable. It's the ultimate Spring Cleaning. It's painful when you are forced to sacrifice stuff, situations, and relationships. Have faith that light is shining into the darkness. Through the death of ego and the crucifixion of false beliefs, you gain access to the eternal world of your divine nature. Sacrifice is the transmutation of separate will into sacred light of Oneness.

Archangel Uriel is guiding you to confront old beliefs about yourself, values and reality so a glorious new self can be reborn. Uriel responds to your prayers for help. You have never been alone or abandoned. Not for a single second in all eternity. Angels have been with you always, loving, guiding, healing and nurturing you through the experiences of life.

Each experience is part of a Divine Plan guiding your life. Uriel works closely with your Guardian Angel, your soul and Gabriel helping you to awaken to the truth of who you are. You are a magnificent Child of Light.

If you feel agitated and anxious, clean something! Your home is the outer expression of your inner state. Ask Uriel to guide you in clearing away the stuff and connected beliefs that are overwhelming. Get rid of old clothes that don't fit, aren't you, and don't look great on you.

Clutter and grime at home, work, and in your car affect your consciousness. Clutter feeds a sense of overwhelm and helplessness. Grime holds underlying beliefs in place of unworthiness and poverty. Clean with Uriel by your side to feel more peaceful, open, and receptive.

Resurrection with Archangel Gabriel

April's spring cleaning opens space for May's infusion of resurrection energy bringing the remembrance of your divine qualities and gifts. Your true Being shines through the veil, touching your heart and infusing your life with radiant beauty, resources, and wisdom.

Archangel Gabriel rolls away the stone of limiting belief so you can rise up in soul infused God luminosity, bringing your inner light to the outer world.

- What are your divine qualities and gifts?
- What are you good at?
- What comes naturally?

Align your life with your newly discovered truth, then determine what needs to change. Use the resurrection energy to support and assist you in making things new in all areas of life. When you feel a surge, ask Gabriel to help you draw the burst of energy into creative projects and healing endeavors. This is the most powerful time of year to experience Oneness.

Meditate often to be immersed in divine white Light radiance and ecstasy. The heavenly host of angels surround and escort you into the Presence of Divinity where your soul qualities are revealed.

"The New You" with Archangel Jophiel

Once you've been up to the Heavens, June brings the descent of the Holy Spirit into body, mind, emotions and life. The divine transmission to begin your mission flows into your heart, imbuing you with the spiritual gifts needed. You are charged by divine spirit to create heaven on earth. Your mission is the combination of your unique soul calling and life purpose. The influx of energy empowers you to consecrate your life to the expression of your sacred mission.

- How will you step forth in your radiant new light body?

Archangel Jophiel walks with you, illuminating your powers of co-creativity with Spirit. Jophiel helps you to live in a soul infused state of Oneness, functioning fully and consciously in both worlds.

Who is the new you?

- What do you love to do?
- What is your soul calling you to be?

- What makes you shine brightly?
- What brings a surge of joy?

I love dressing for how I feel. When I come alive within my soul, then choose clothes and makeup that express my experience, I feel hot and juicy, supported, connected, and powerful. Try it!

Remember, you are loved and appreciated. You are supported. You are worthy. Live each day guided by your heart, choosing love, cherishing your connection with people, Spirit, and Love!

Rev. Dr. Kimberly Marooney is a beautiful spirit who lifts up the souls who come to her, deepening their hearts to know the Divine Creator within. Hundreds of thousands of people worldwide have benefited from her gentle guidance into personal experience with angels and Divine Love that heals everything. As one student said, *"When Kimberly opens her mouth, lives change."*

A pioneer in the fields of Angelology and Spiritual Transformation, Kimberly felt alone on the leading edge of evolution for much of her life. The first person in the world to earn a Master's degree in Angelology and a Doctorate in Spiritual Psychology, many of the best-known angel experts including Doreen Virtue have sought to learn from her.

In addition to her scholarly knowledge, Kimberly devoted 15 years to deep, cloistered, intensive meditation. Kimberly emerged with the ability to go to the deep places of pain that most people can't, in very gentle ways that result in profound healing. And the realization that she is never alone, she is eternally in the embrace of The Divine.

By following inner guidance, this gifted mystic has authored a dozen books including bestselling *Angel Blessings Cards*, and founded *TheAngelMinistry.com*. Most recently, Kimberly introduced an *Angel Reader Certification* program and *Bring the People Back to My Love*, a new rosary for the Children of Light. Learn more at http://KimberlyMarooney.com.

APRIL
Angels of the Rising Light
Ann Phillis

The touch in the caress of the lightest breeze. The dancing sparkle in the golden sunlight. The extra brightness in the blue, blue sky. The pulsing life force that hugs me in the tree...*APRIL!*

My childhood was lonely, challenging, uncertain and scary, but I was graced to live in the grounds of a large house with a huge garden, and that is where I found solace. This was my childhood salvation, where I felt nurtured, nourished, embraced. This is where I sought comfort, where I prayed for help. This is where I first met the angels.

I couldn't see them then as I do now, but I knew there were living, loving beings around me. I felt their gentle embrace as I lay in the branches of my favorite jacaranda tree. I felt their kisses in the sunlight, their joy in the breeze. They gave me hope. They lifted my gaze to believe in tomorrow. They soothed my fears and troubled heart. They gave me calm when all around me was uncertain. I have never forgotten this beautiful place, this tree in my garden of solace. I still go there in my mind, into the soft lilac of the flowers and the feathery green of the leaves. Into the peace and embrace of the angels wings, where I feel their whispers of love.

The sense of this livingness all around, this living light and loving hug from beyond our physical world, has never left me. It sits in my being as a deep knowing and truth, which has never wavered in my heart. A knowing that nature is greater than the beauty of leaves and flowers, mountains and pastures, rivers and oceans - that she is the splendor of living light manifesting with joy in our world! That our physical life and all our experiences and expressions in this world are the colorful clothes of our soul. That everything is the living expression of a greater oneness, a coherence that unites every atom of our world into the unfolding splendor of life itself. Life with purpose, evolving into greater love, service and brilliance. Life physical, interwoven with the spirit divine. Life in the flow, in partnership with the angels!

The living light flows from the One Heart of cosmos, through the loving heart of our Mother Earth, infusing all life with light. Every day this pulse brings life's vitality from our Sun. Every year this pulse flows through the Earth and our being, through the eternal heartbeat of the seasons that take our consciousness from stillness to growth, from fruit to harvest. It is the great angels who guide this flow, each day sprinkling sun-kisses on all life, each season nourishing our life's journey, leading us ever closer to the light.

In this gracious flow of life through our year, April is my favorite month. That's because it is filled with the ecstatic love of the rising light! The light that rises from the deep heart of our Earth, where it has infused in the still point of the December Solstice, then bursts out through the Earth and our bodies at the Easter full moon festival. This light is pure sparkling effervescence that energizes new life and awakens consciousness, to bear fruit for the harvest ahead. The seed bursting through the soil, opening out to the Sun! It reminds me of the uplifting joy I felt from the angels in my childhood, when their whispering embrace brought hope to my heart.

The angels that flow this living light give us this hope. They lift their wings and our consciousness soars. They move their wings and our vibrations rise. They hold us in their embrace and we emerge out of past heaviness, able to see our lighted path ahead.

Who is the greatest angel of this living light? The Spirit of Resurrection! The Spirit of Resurrection is an angel of the cosmic heart, bringing pure life force to us and to Mother Earth, resurrecting true life, uplifting us to soul! This is a great cosmic angel of utmost grace and pure life force - shining and shimmering in pearlescent light. An angel that has come to counter the forces of materialism that constrict the flow of heart and dam the flow of consciousness, until stagnation and death result - the death of spirit, death of heart, crushing inspiration and hope

I invite you to let this rising light, this angel of resurrection, infuse you with living light this April, and all year round! Celebrate and sparkle; let your heart sing and rejoice! For in the love of this living light, we walk the path true to our soul, our heart. We become one in heart and body with the angels' flowing living light. We become one with all life, with the One Heart, and with our Mother Earth.

As you read these inspiring prayers, let the angels uplift you. Let them lift your consciousness and raise your spirits, show you the light that surrounds and fills you, enfold you in their embrace and nurture you. Spread your wings and let your soul soar, and keep your feet on the ground so you can bring light to our world! This is life in the angelic flow of the heart. This is life in the living flow!

Rise in the light, dear angels of April!

Ann Phillis is an author, soul seer, angel clairvoyant and Earth lover. A passionate change-agent, global activist and spiritual mentor, she has immersed in the western esoteric heart wisdom for 35 years, and is an ordained priest in that lineage. She is totally committed to the living light of heart, the awesomeness of awakening consciousness through life's kaleidoscope of lessons, and the magic of inspiriting positive change into all we do!

Ann is unwavering in her belief that when humans and angels work together, we become an unstoppable force for good. We inspire and manifest positive change in all areas of worldly activity, and truly evolve to peace. Even though we are in the midst of challenging global transformations, she holds great hope for our future because together we are this force for change, and we will create the sustainable, equitable and healthy world we all seek.

Ann shares her love, hope and vision through www.NourishingSoul.me, where she offers meaningful insights, soul wisdom and practical how-to's that empower you to be in the flow of angels and soul while standing strong here, in our world. Walk your heart path. Become that united force for good, and make your difference on our beautiful Earth!

APRIL 1
Emergence

By Ann Phillis

From the dark I emerge;
From the womb of my Mother,
Mother of Earth, Mother of Heaven.

Nourished and whole,
Free and strong,
Enlivened and sparkling,
I am ready to grow!

My soul soars with love,
My wings spread with grace,
I stand here on Earth,
Sharing blessings, in my place.

Radiant heart,
Now, I am that,
A radiant human,
My wings flow with love.

APRIL 2
To the Angel of Light

By Inger Marie Moeller

I have searched for You throughout my life
for comfort, for peace, for love and joy.
I have looked for Your smile in every face
for Your grace and compassion
in mothers eyes
in childrens laughter
in flowers bloom
In sunset colours
and rainbows light
In the snowcapped mountains
and rivers wild.
I have searched for Your wisdom
in endless words
in the beauty of art
and musical tunes

I found You in a moment
when everything was still
my mind had stopped its searching
my heartbeat was at rest
and everything inside me
was one with all of life
and there You were beside me
- we had never been apart

April Chapter Sponsor – Ann Phillis

APRIL 3
Message from Heaven

By Rev. Jennifer Shackford

My dear, I am at Peace.
I am vibrant and full of the strongest, brightest light!

Do not weep tears of sadness for me and my life.
I have fulfilled my soul's path and helped you along yours.

We are always deeply connected because the love we share is everlasting!
I will continue to be by your side
waiting for our souls to be re-united once again!

I need you to keep loving and embracing life!
I will send you back signs so you will know without a doubt I am there!
Be open to the signs and you will see them!

I love you!

APRIL 4
A Prayer for Growth

By Lisa K.

This month take to heart all that you are seeking.

Allow yourself to become like the bud of a flower;
take in the nutrients from the soil of the earth,
the fresh water from the spring rain,
and the wonderful rays of the sun.

You are setting the bed for growth
by nourishing your soul with spiritual thoughts from heaven above;
ensuring that your body is fed with fresh food and water,
and your mind is grounded in good thoughts.

With all of this, your budding flower will open,
with grandeur and great abundance!

– Your Angels

April Chapter Sponsor – Ann Phillis

APRIL 5
Prayer to the Angel of Grace

By Helen White Wolf

Angel of Grace, I surrender into your heart
all the moments of time, carried deep within me
where I have been unable to forgive myself, and others,
those moments in which I have felt wounded
or I have caused wounding.

Angel of Grace, I give to you my unwept tears,
the fathomless longing of my heart for peace and redemption,
the stony hardness of my self-punishment,
the pain and shame of my forgetting.
That in your light I may be healed, through your tender heart
I may feel again the warmth of unconditioned love.

Angel of Grace, I invite your sweet mercy
into the hidden abyss within me, the void of my loneliness
and separation from God, Myself and all beings.
For it is but a single wound, played out
in the apparent multiplicity of creation.

In the depths of your holy and compassionate heart,
may I remember and return home to the centre that holds nothing out.
The sacred circle whose circumference is infinity.

From this timeless place
may the light of Grace touch with the deepest tenderness
and transform the suffering of all living beings.
Amen

April Chapter Sponsor – Ann Phillis

APRIL 6
Prayer for Guidance

By Elizabeth Harper

Angels, open my heart,
so that I may easily feel your messages of support.

Expand my mind,
so that I may know the right choices to make.

Guide me to listen to your gentle whispers,
so that I might hear your words of wisdom.

Help me to see the light of your love,
so that I can share in your vision.

Angels, guide me to be aware of your presence,
so that I can implicitly trust the guidance I receive from you as the truth,
and as my truth.

Thank you.
And so it is.

APRIL 7

Angels of Atlantis: Prayer for Spiritual Integrity

By Cathelijne Filippo

Beloved Angels of Atlantis,

I now call upon you to reconnect me to the age of Golden Atlantis,
When humans were Masters and Healers walking hand in hand with Angels.
Please cleanse my Soul from any impurity and karma,
Caused by misuse or abuse of my spiritual power in the past.
May I walk my spiritual path with the highest energy,
Choosing love over fear and light over darkness.

Dear Angels of Atlantis,
Please reawaken me to my spiritual powers.
Safely open my Higher Senses of clairvoyance, clairaudience,
clairsentience and claircognizance.
Please awaken the Wise One within me.
May I always heed its wisdom and act according to my inner knowing.
May I always be connected to my angels and spirit guides of 100% Light,
As I walk my true Path in Life

I now give my Higher Self complete sovereignty of all I do, think and say,
Helping me to always choose wisely for the Highest Good of all.
As such let me be a Light Worker true to the purity of Golden Atlantis.
Keep me firmly on my path of Light,
With joy in my heart and a lightness of being.
So be it.

April Chapter Sponsor – Ann Phillis

APRIL 8
Angel Prayer for Self-Confidence

By Suzanne Gochenouer

Dear Angels,

Instill in me a humble self-confidence
in the skills and passions with which I am blessed.

Help me recognize the gifts I can share
with those who search for new ways to connect with themselves,
with Mother Earth, and with their angels.

When I am unsure, bring me the knowledge and strength I need
to step forth in my personal power.

Help me keep my feet on the ground and my heart in the heavens,
so I can be present in this world
while remaining fully connected to the spirit of unconditional Love.

Share with me the understanding
that while I am blessed with many gifts,
the more I share these gifts, the more they grow.

Amen, amen, amen.

Thank you, thank you, thank you.

April Chapter Sponsor – Ann Phillis

APRIL 9

Claiming My Divine Right as a Multi-Dimensional Being

By Daniel Hyman

I now invoke all that is available to me in 100 percent
love and light for the highest good of all.

I now invoke and command my I AM Presence to come forth and take charge.

I invoke the divine light being within,
I invoke my awaken christed-self,
the god, the goddess, the divine child within.

I invoke all that I am, all that I was, and all that I shall be
on all levels claiming my divine right, my power as a multi dimensional being,
bringing forth and reawakening any and all wisdom, knowledge,
gifts, power, love, light, passions, and energies
that are of 100 percent love and light for the highest good of all
and are aligned with my current mission and purpose
in this lifetime from all lifetimes on all
planets, stars, solar systems, galaxies, dimensions and realms
here and now into this physical human body.

I ask for all that I do to serve as a vessel for the highest good of all
and to be in service to Mother Earth.

And I know all is already done and granted as I ask from my heart
and for knowing what is in my heart I am grateful.

Thank You, Thank You, Thank You!!!

April Chapter Sponsor — Ann Phillis

APRIL 10
Peace and Protection Prayer

By Robyn Clark

There is a place in heaven
where angels gather round
to hear the calling from your heart
when peace needs to be found.

If you listen, you will hear
gentle whispers like the wind,
messages of love
and the truth that lies within.

It's like a warm embrace,
sometimes a tickle on the ear,
signs will be shown
when your guardians are near.

Swap your fear for love
as you walk within the light.
You are forever protected,
every day and every night.

APRIL 11

i wish

By Asher Quinn

I wish you every kind of joy
I wish you were not so far away
I take you to be one of a kind
A rare fragrance that cannot be defined
I understand your sleepy soul
I planted fruit trees for when you get old
Let's meditate on where we go from here. . .

I wish you every kind of love
Be drinking from your golden cup
I wish you a Zen garden for your mind
And that your conscience will learn how to be kind
I left a message with a trusted friend
We'll start our journey when it looks like journey's end
We'll catch a night-train into the wild unknown. . .

I wish you every kind of peace
And every kind of emotional release
Let's wait until the storm has passed
Until the thunder-clouds make way for the stars
I dreamt about a railway-station scene
A place where I had never been
And there I saw you wait for me
And then one day we saw it for real

I wish you every kind of grace
A good journey into inner space
A sanctuary for your higher self
A connection to your spiritual wealth
Some magic for your eternal child
A gateway to a hundred thousand smiles
I hope my love can set you free
And I wish you were here with me

April Chapter Sponsor – Ann Phillis

APRIL 12
Archangel Raphael

By Trish Grain

I invoke Archangel Raphael's beautiful healing light.

I ask that you fill my body with your emerald green healing energy,
helping to heal my heart, mind and emotions,
bringing peace, balance and harmony.

I ask you to help lead me to the right people
who can help me with my health issues
and to get the treatment I so need.

I trust and have faith that you will help me find
what I need to become healthy and vital once more
and to help me take my power back.

Thank you, Archangel Raphael.

APRIL 13
I Declare

By Julie Geigle

I declare…
Miracles are a daily occurrence in my life.
Doors are beginning to open
and I am greeted with unexpected surprises.
Money flows to me easily and effortlessly.
The cells in my body are being regenerated, recharged
and rebooted for my own well-being.

Love begins to blossom and bloom from my heart
and touches all I come into contact with.
Angels surround and uplift me daily
as they walk this journey with me.
All limiting belief systems fall away
and are replaced with prosperous, powerful belief systems
that connect and align me with the infinite perfection of my Soul.
Peace, harmony and love course through my veins
filling me with a sense of connectedness to all.

My success is assured as I tune into and honor
the voice of my soul, the whisper of God.
Blessings abound in my life as miracles are unleashed
in all directions of time and space,
past, present and future.
I declare all these things and more as I open to receive
the love and guidance of God, the Angels, the Ascended Masters
and Beings of Light who are my constant companions.
And so it is.

APRIL 14
A Prayer to Mend a Quarrel

By Tracy Quadro

Angel Raguel,
Friend of the Spirit, Mediator of Broken Bonds,
please bring me back to the middle ground with my fellow traveler.
Teach me to see the "other" as just another essential part of myself.

Hold up the mirror before me that shows me as I am,
with all of my incredible fragments of Spirit attached in a unique way
that have been given to me and only me,
and help me to make peace with those fragments.

Then to look beyond myself, and see those same fragments
in a different arrangement, in others.
And especially show me how those pieces of us interlock
all of us, everywhere
to make the whole of the Universe.

Smile your large infectious grin and make me forget
what all the fuss was about and open my hand and heart,
even when my feelings have been scraped and bruised.
Please help us become whole once again.

When a loved one is estranged, when pride blocks an extended hand, when turning away turns to walking away, the life energy attached to that friendship seeps from our hearts and leaves us feeling depleted.

April Chapter Sponsor – Ann Phillis

APRIL 15

Calling on the Archangels for Abundance

By Samantha Honey-Pollock

Are you with me now, dear angels?

Thank you for this:
(name a wonderful thing you appreciate in your life right now.
It needn't be big, just special to you, for example:
A loving family. A good breakfast. A sunny day...)

And for this, dear angels: (name money worry)
I request your attendance and help.
Please guide your shining grace and sweet vision to this issue.

Please assist me to bring this situation to a positive, uplifting solution.

Jophiel: Archangel of Beauty,
shine your feminine caring and understanding here.
Michael: Archangel of Protection,
please make it all okay, or better than okay!
Raphael: Archangel of Healing,
please help my mind and spirit heal.
Please give me now the strength,
and any other gifts you think I will benefit from,
to journey through and above this.

I am open and ready to accept your gifts.
Thank you, angels!

And so it is.

April Chapter Sponsor – Ann Phillis

APRIL 16
Golden Angel Flow Glows

By Lisa Clayton

Stay in rhythm and harmony with the Flow Glows
coming from the Golden Angel Realm,
sometimes fast and sometimes at standstills.
Move into action during the rapid flows.
Rest, meditate and reflect during the slow flows.
Be at peace with both flows.
Embrace these flows, as it is important to balance
the energies coming in to your heart and soul.

Listen closely. Our messages will go deep into your heart's core.
There will be new souls appearing in your life
to receive the messages of your heart.
Rejoice! Create a living from your heart.
Source is in you, your Higher Self, your connection to Divine.
Following messages within you,
your Higher Self and Divine are the keys to wisdom and grace.

Expanding your heart comes through embracing change.
Change accelerates your evolution.
Divine collaboration with us moves you forward
into providing your beautiful heart gifts to the world.
Follow the voice of your heart. Feel its breath. Hear its song.
Use its eyes to see passion, peace, and prosperity.

Abundance glows in the rays of sunshine
when the eyes see what the heart reveals.
Embrace Angel Flow Glows! They are flowing to you now.

April Chapter Sponsor – Ann Phillis

APRIL 17
Prayer for Remembrance of Self

By Cathleen O'Connor

Dear Angels,

Help me remember who I am,
a luminous emanation of Divine love and light,
a unique, unrepeatable event in time and space,
and a gift to the world at exactly the right moment.

Help me remember that I am made of starlight;
that to not shine hurts the very heart of the Divine;
that I was put here to do what only I can do.
Give me the courage to stand in my purpose.

Help me not get so distracted by the busyness of daily life
that I fall asleep to who I am and why I am here.
Awaken me each day to my true reality
that of a spiritual being having a physical existence.

Remind me that I am held in the Divine Mind and Heart,
and that when I am unkind to myself I pierce the very heart of God,
for I am not separate from All That Is,
and the love I give myself is an honoring of the Divine love I am given.

With deepest gratitude I thank you for your unconditional love.
It brings abundant blessings that fill my body and soul with joy.

And so it is.

April Chapter Sponsor – Ann Phillis

APRIL 18
Angel Prayer for Living the Good Life

By Michelle Mullady

Much-loved Angelic Beings,
I pray to you for the faithfulness I need
to know that heaven on earth is a possibility
which I can adopt and manifest into my reality.

Help me work through
the reservations, uncertainties and pessimistic beliefs
that represent my sense of severance from the Divine Source.
Remove the blocks and barriers I have built up
during this lifetime and all others.

Allow nothing to stand between me, and God.
Assist me in claiming harmony, wholeness, delight,
fun, love, success and health as my birthright as a cherished child of God.
Support me to accept all goodness,
and enjoy my kingdom of paradise thoroughly.

Thank you angels!
Thank you! Thank you! Thank you!

As you say this prayer, get comfortable, close your eyes and breathe softly for several minutes.

April Chapter Sponsor – Ann Phillis

APRIL 19
A Prayer for Self-Acceptance

By Anna Taylor

Thank you God and all the Angels,
especially Archangels Jophiel and Chamuel
for being here with me.
I call upon you now to embrace me with your healing love and light
as I begin to embrace all that I am.

As I breathe deeply,
I invite you to open my heart to even more love
and to help me feel worthy and deserving of all blessings.
Thank you for uplifting my thoughts
so that I can think kindly of myself
and make clear decisions for my highest good.

Thank you for inspiring me to appreciate my body as the gift it is,
for helping me feel comfortable in my own skin
and for guiding me towards choices that support my health,
vitality and joy in this lifetime.
Thank you for reminding me of my Divine perfection
and for helping me to accept myself in all ways.

I now open my eyes to see myself as you see me.
I am loved and loveable just as I am
and everyone and everything around me is a reflection of this truth.
For this and so much more I am so grateful.

And so it is.
Amen.

April Chapter Sponsor — Ann Phillis

APRIL 20
Prayer for Physical Healing

By Rachel Cooley ATP®

Dear God, angels and archangels,
Thank you so much for being so strongly present with me right now,
especially Archangels Raphael and Michael.
Please surround me in this moment
in your beautiful and powerful healing lights.
Please bring health, vitality and wholeness
to all areas of my body, mind and spirit.

Archangels Raphael and Michael,
please fill and surround the _____ area(s) of my body
with your emerald green and royal purple lights.
As I breathe in and out I fully receive
your healing energies in my cells and DNA right now.
May my dear guardian angels also add their
unconditionally loving white lights to surround my body as well.

Dear archangels,
please release from me my fears, worries
and concerns regarding my health right now.
May you bolster my faith, strength and courage.
Please also shield me in your protective
royal blue and purple light, Archangel Michael.
I am so grateful for my physical healing in perfect divine timing,
for my highest good!
Thank you and so it is!

Amen.

April Chapter Sponsor – Ann Phillis

APRIL 21
Angel Prayer to Find Lost Objects

By Patty Nowell

Archangel Chamuel,
I come to you now, hurried, frazzled, and frustrated
at having misplaced (*insert your lost object*) again.
I've checked all the places I've found it before,
but I'm in such a hurry I may have overlooked it.

Please help me to slow down, take a deep breath,
and surround myself in the beautiful pink light of your love.
Let me feel your presence as it calms my spirit.
Open my mind, my heart and my senses
to the energy of (*name of your lost object*) and its location.
Slow me down so that I can feel, hear and know your guidance.

Help me to be gentle with myself in this process.
Help me to forgive myself for misplacing (*name of your lost object*),
which makes me feel disorganized and imperfect.
Heal my heart and my soul around these feelings.
Fill me with the radiant light of your love.
Teach me to apply that love to myself.

I am so grateful for all the items you've helped me find before,
and for your assistance in finding (*name of your lost object*) now.

Archangel Chamuel,
Make me a clear and open channel to receive your guidance.
Show me where to find (*name of your lost object*).
Thank you.

April Chapter Sponsor – Ann Phillis

APRIL 22
Calling in the 7 Powers Prayer

By Kari Samuels

I give thanks to the Divine for giving me the love,
healing and protection from your angels.

I call upon Archangel Michael to release me from my fears,
so I may courageously live my heart's desires.
I call upon Archangel Uriel to transmute my feelings of shame and guilt,
so I may love myself with compassion.

I call upon Archangel Gabriel to assist me in speaking my truth,
so I may share my unique message with the world.
I call upon Archangel Raphael to imbue me with your light of healing,
so I may feel vibrantly healthy.

I call upon Archangel Jophiel to show me the world through angel eyes,
so I may see myself and others with beauty.
I call upon Archangel Jeremiel to give me the gift of spiritual vision,
so I may have crystal clarity about my soul's purpose.

I call upon my guardian angel to wrap me
in your loving wings of protection,
so I may feel your love and be love.
I ask for all beings to know and feel the love
of angels and experience your light.
Thank you for being with me, and my loved ones always.
Amen.

April Chapter Sponsor – Ann Phillis

APRIL 23

Archangel Chamuel's Prescription for Relief of Perfectionism

By Bobbe Bramson

Dear One, When you awake each morning, call on me
and let the radiance of God's love for you fill your beautiful heart.

Hear this truth:
You are worthy, beloved, cherished and adored, always and forever.
Cease comparing yourself to others,
for as God's *perfect* expression of Love,
there is only joyful anticipation
and delight at what your next creation will be.

No one before or ever hereafter will express your Essence as you do.
Please do not withhold your gift for fear of making mistakes;
these are not only allowed but necessary
to help you grow into the fullness of your being.

To heal, say aloud and often:
"I do hereby revoke the lie that says I'll never be good enough.
Instead, I adopt the truth of my perfection *right now* in this moment.
There is nothing to prove, no requirements to be met, no 'perfect' way.
It is safe to begin now, and I trust my path will open before me.
Today I choose to take it easy on myself.
Instead of pushing, I will allow.
Instead of critiquing, I will praise.
Instead of controlling,
I will ride the wave of inspiration and see where it leads me.

And so it is."

April Chapter Sponsor – Ann Phillis

APRIL 24

To the Greatest Angel of All: Mother Earth

By Inger Marie Moeller

Mountains and valleys, water and air
rivers and oceans, streams in Your hair
flowers and treetops, birds in their nest
butterflies dancing, elephants rest
Mother Earth, a home you give
from Your love we all can live

Fairies and angels, devas and men
bees making honey, flutes blowing zen
buffaloes roaming, ants crawling by
lions in sunlight, eagles fly high
Mother Earth, a home you give
from Your love we all can live

Crystals and silver, oil as Your blood
gold as Your treasure, diamonds flood
thunder and lightning, rain falling down
crickets are singing their praise to Your crown
Mother Earth, a home you give
from Your love we all can live

Dolphins and whales, corals, blue dream
icebergs and ice bears, swim like a team
This is my prayer, to God and to You:
"May all what You give, be given You too"
Mother Earth, a home you give
from Your love we all can live

April Chapter Sponsor – Ann Phillis

APRIL 25
A Prayer to Appreciate My Contributions

By Kimeiko Rae Vision ATP®, The Angel Warrior™

Dear Angels,
I allow/accept/invite your support
in making appreciation an easy habit for me.
Yes… you can nudge me to notice my own accomplishments.
I appreciate myself now.
Angels, please make it easy for me to appreciate the natural gifts,
God-given talents and blessed experiences that I already acknowledge
and those I have yet to claim or discover.

Help me to know that I deserve to truly and easily
embody my magnetic presence
as I draw happy, helpful, balanced people into my world
in steady, friendly, refreshing streams.
Help me to notice that as I receive love,
support and energizing appreciation,
I am truly a joyful and balanced giver.

If there are souls in the world, at large, who need my wisdom or my service,
please allow my powerful angelic influence
to flow forth (as needed, where needed)
from my Divine consciousness, with ease and grace.
And now… help me to STAND on my own two feet,
smiling my casual confidence and genuine gratitude
with really cute, comfortable shoes!

Amen!

APRIL 26
An Angel Prayer for a Blissful Life

By Michelle Mullady

Beloved Angels of Love and Luminosity,
I invoke your power to unlock the gate of my higher mind
and let the healing magic of divine light flood my inner being.

I am open to receiving the miracles of the Holy Spirit
as I move along my path.
I thank you for the gift of life and I wholly surrender
to your love, truth and splendor.

May the golden rays of heaven cover
and penetrate every aspect of my world.
Let me live in the awareness of limitless joy.
Please inspire me, fill me with happiness,
and completely align me with my Soulful Self,
so that I might experience an existence
of blissful prosperity and abundance.
And so it is.

Amen.

For best results, recite in front of an altar with a lit candle, on holy ground, or outside in a sacred space that you create.

April Chapter Sponsor – Ann Phillis

APRIL 27
Now the Future

By Ann Phillis

Let the past be gone, the future our power
Angels of life, awaken us to the hour.

Take away death - death of spirit, death of heart
Open our consciousness, grateful for life!

Bring our hearts into the age of love
Bring our minds to the path that is just.

Awaken our souls to shine every day
Angels of peace, life's power here to stay!

April Chapter Sponsor – Ann Phillis

APRIL 28

Archangel Jophiel ~
Prayer of Illumination

By Carolyn McGee

Archangel Jophiel,
angel of beauty, light of God,
illuminate my mind to see the gifts in everything.
To accept peacefully, easily and fully the loving lessons of life.

Open my eyes to realize the grace, beauty and love
in all that I see with my eyes and my inner vision.

Open my ears so that I may deeply experience the joy of all I hear;
the simple beauty of silence, the laughter of children,
the song of the birds or a whispered prayer.

Open my feelings that I may profoundly acknowledge
the love in all I encounter.
As we are all God's children, help me to see the beauty and good
in everyone and everything.

Open my heart to feel the love of God, in myself, and in every experience.
Help me to find joy and wonder in every aspect of daily life.

And so it is!

APRIL 29
The Earth Angel's Prayer

By Rev. Sheri

Make me an Angel, full of Love and of Peace.
Make me an Angel to help those in need.
May the prayer in my heart always be
make me an Angel on Earth; let it be.

Make me an Angel, to teach and to lead.
Make me an Angel to strengthen the weak.
May the power in my words always ring
make me an Angel on Earth; let it be.

Make me an Angel; help me remember and light up our world.
Make me an Angel; please help my wings to unfurl.
And, may the Divine in my soul always sing
make me an Angel. Make me an Angel.
Heaven, make me an Angel on Earth; let it be.

APRIL 30
Archangel Raphael's Healing Love

By Kimberly Marooney

Archangel Raphael,
Breathe healing love into my lungs.
Quiet my emotions and mind with eternal peace.

Illumine my heart with Divine Love
so the brightness of Spirit shines through my eyes.
Help me to see the beauty of my soul, my body, and my being
to find deep appreciation for who God created me to be.

Kindle the flame of the Divine that dwells in my soul calling me to Oneness.
In you, I receive waves of Love from God
allowing me to feel how loved and treasured I am.

With your guidance and love, I can let go of the past and forgive.
You hold me in compassion that heals my deepest wounds.
Hold my hand and walk with me during difficult changes.
You remind me that I AM a Child of Light.

You whisper in my ear that I AM loved and worthy of goodness.
You comfort my heart and nourish my soul with Divine Truth.
Thank you for helping me to see the radiant beauty in my Self.
You make it possible to love my Self.

Awaken my soul's gifts making me a vessel for your healing energy.
I feel deep gratitude for your healing touch.

April Chapter Sponsor – Ann Phillis

MAY
Out of the Blue
Lisa Clayton

My unique connection with the Angels started early for me when I was six years old. One of the assigned chores on our family farm was to gather our dairy herd for milking time. I vividly recall one memorable cloudless, hot summer day when I received my first "out of the blue" Angel message. I secretly took a break, lying down in the cool, green pasture grass making Angel wings and daydreaming. I asked God why am I here? I didn't feel comfortable in this human form and felt out of place. I often heard voices in the wind and received messages through my heart that I didn't understand. Was I an alien visitor here or an earth angel without wings?

Before I opened my eyes during this daydreaming inquisitive state, I felt an unusual, cold breeze suddenly swirl around me, almost spinning me upward from the pasture field! When I looked to the sky, there above me, "out of the blue" was a beautiful angel cloud. I remember repeating over and over, "I will always believe in Angels." A calm and confident energy infused me that day which was very difficult for a six year old to communicate to anyone, especially to grown-ups, so I remained silent for years about my connection with Angels. During my upbringing on the farm, I kept my eyes glued to the sky and found feathers and pennies on the ground that I knew were gifts from my Angels.

Throughout my life, Angels have blessed me with good health and successful careers. From starting my life service as an elementary school teacher to becoming a professional training consultant, I founded my own human development business, Source Potential. Each time life presented changes; I always trusted my intuitive guidance and "out of the blue" signs. Shortly after birthing Source Potential, I traveled around the globe many times with my corporate clients, functioning at a fast and furious pace with much financial success. During this extremely busy time, there also came an empty, internal feeling in my heart nudging me to meditate and connect more frequently with my Angels. It was easy to ignore the internal nudging, as the next big deal kept pulling me fast forward.

In 2008, life in the successful fast lane came to a screeching halt. The economy crashed and overnight all my Fortune 500 clients ended contracts. I spun into survival-panic mode to find new clients so another successful cycle would appear. I drained my savings, family inheritance and retirement to keep my business afloat; yet it was continuing to fall apart with a looming bankruptcy and giving up my beautiful home in Half Moon Bay, California.

As I was sinking in my deepest despair, I tuned into an "out of the blue" Internet radio-talk show regarding Angels. Dr. Kimberly Marooney was the guest speaker. I listened intently to every word she spoke about becoming an Angel Minister. Her voice sounded like an Angel and she gifted me with an Angel Blessing card! I reached out to Kimberly after the radio show and synchronistically we connected. I was immediately enrolled in the Angel Ministry program. This event definitely was not part of my business plan, yet I trusted it was another significant sign from my beloved Angels.

I was officially ordained as an Angel Minister in 2011. I rediscovered my intuitive relationship with the Angels and experienced a renewed heart opening. However, I was still struggling financially and was five days from foreclosure of my home. In the middle of the night, my bedroom filled with white light and this message came forth: "Take the lead now! Trust us to show you the way." The next day, I cancelled all my appointments and started calling people for help. "Out of the blue" former neighbors listened to my story and generously, with no questions, paid my arrears to save my home, all within 24 miraculous hours.

Now, my direct connection with the Angels is just like that summer day when I was a young girl. I trust and follow the Angels' "out of the blue" guidance every day; giving me my inner GPS system for joyfully living life with passion and purpose.

Lisa Clayton is a master teacher, professional facilitator, intuitive coach and spiritual leader who helps individuals reclaim their passion, power and potential through individual or group counseling sessions in addition to motivational workshops and seminars. Throughout Lisa's career, there has been a consistent thread woven throughout her teaching, facilitation, leadership and coaching which always stands out…her passion and love in helping others develop their talent and potential and applying immediately to their personal and professional lives.

Founder of Source Potential (www.sourcepotential), a human development company Lisa offers a unique learning approach with application techniques for corporate training programs and deployments worldwide for Fortune 500 companies to the small business owner. She firmly believes in guidance from the higher realm and the intelligence and power of the heart. Most recently Lisa was led to find fulfilling corporate work with a growing Senior Living organization and fulfilled a personal interest for providing intuitive services by joining the Angel Ministry.

Lisa completed her ordination as an Angel Celebrant through Gateway University of Higher Consciousness and Spirituality and conducts intuitive angelic readings, counseling and workshops as well as home and office blessings, wedding ceremonies and life passages. Her website is www.lisaclayton.com.

MAY 1
Beltane Prayer

By Cathelijne Filippo

Beloved Archangel Uriel,

Bless me with your light during this peak
of spring and beginning of summer,
when Earth energies are so strong and active.
Infuse me with abundance and fertility on all levels.
May the Divine Feminine awaken within me
the manifestation of growth and renewal,
and may the Divine Masculine dance with her to complete her.

Sweet Archangel Chamuel,

Open my heart to love, like the petals of a delicate flower.
May I reawaken the love for self and others,
as I unite within me the Divine Feminine and Masculine energies.
As I am balanced, so will my love life be in divine balance.

Dear Archangel Nathaniel,

Ignite within me the flame of passion,
that I may be passionate and joyful in all that I do.
Help me to bring ideas, hopes and dreams into manifestation now.
And let me walk my path of Light with joy and grace.

So be it!

MAY 2
Tickle My Heart

By Lisa Clayton

I ask the Angels to tickle my heart today.
Open my heart chakra wide
and expand its energy and light to your golden wing tips.
Place my smiling heart in a boat
with God steering through earth's ocean of love and peace.

Help me offer my open and willing heart to you, beloved Angels,
so I can experience spontaneous delights within my soul.
Reveal the information needed to receive the essence of love from my soul.

Connect me with the messages of love, light and joy
that are available from the Divine Source,
so I may be a channel for others to radiate their heart light to the world.

May amazing grace and healing light
from Archangels Michael, Gabriel and Raphael
bring forth the healing force of forgiveness for trespasses
that have found hiding places in my own heart, some deeply buried.

I ask that my heart be freed of these perceived betrayals
and wounds that are holding me back
from pure and unconditional loving
of all human, animal and nature spirits on our beloved planet.

I ask the Angels to tickle my heart today
with joy, laughter, compassion and kindness,
so I can radiate love and light to all.

May Chapter Sponsor – Lisa Clayton

MAY 3
Prayer to the Aloha Angel

By Kia Abilay

Dear Aloha Angel,
Your loving nature fills my heart, body and soul.
I hear the whisper of aloha in my ears.
Angelic presence vibrates in me the breath of life
and welcomes me into your realm of maluhia (peace).
I can relax and be calm in your gentle touch.

Freshness of the morning air sways in my energy field
eliciting my splendor of lokahi (harmony).
The movement and story of lovely hula dancers' hands
gestures to me – reminders of your everlasting presence.
Your companionship makes me smile and I feel pa'a (secure).

Beautiful flower leis garland me
and sooth my mind with sweet fragrances.
I breathe it in…

Mahalo (thank you) for your cleansing rain.
I bathe in your affectionate charisma and am blessed
with the brilliance of the rainbow in the sky
that lightens and vibrates my chakras.

Mana (Divine essence) surrounds me with love.
Inhale and exhale…
ALOHA

MAY 4
Archangel Chamuel

By Trish Grain

Dear Archangel Chamuel,
the Angel of Love.

I ask that you surround me in your cloak of delicate pink,
the vibration of love and joy.

I ask you to expand the flame of love in my heart,
so that I may touch other people's hearts with compassion and love.

I ask that you send healing to those people who are grieving
and in pain and ask for forgiveness.

Help them in difficult relationships and help them find compassion.
Enfold them in your wings and pour love into their hearts.

MAY 5
Prayer to Ramaela, Angel of Joy

By Bobbe Bramson

Dearest Ramaela,
I would love for joy to be my default setting,
but my lineage has taught me that joy is something
best avoided or denied altogether;
that way I won't be hurt when it gets wrenched away …
better to not feel it at all.

Please unravel the anti-joy code written on my DNA.
Let this pattern end with me, that my ancestors may also be liberated
from their chains of suffering.
I long from within the deepest part of my soul
to reconnect to the sweetness of a joy-filled life.
Did God not feel joy at His creation?
Whom am I, then, to not cultivate my own beautiful Garden of Joy?

My heart is willing, Ramaela.
It is my mind that needs reassurance.
So coax me gently down your many paths of pleasure and delight,
keeping me company, that I may feel safe as I journey.

Awaken me to the good and the true, the Light-filled and blissful.
Teach me to be comfortable
with the flutter of happiness and the grace of flow.
Wrap me within the warmth of your splendor
and enfold me in your aura of lime-green, peach and violet.

Thank you for rescuing me, Ramaela.
I love you. Amen.

May Chapter Sponsor – Lisa Clayton

MAY 6
A Mother's Love

By Lisa K.

A mother's love is unconditional.
When a mother loves her child,
she is always surrounded by angels.
Love is where the heart is,
and a child is in a mother's heart forever.

We cannot explain to you how powerful unconditional love is,
for it is what created the universe.
Unconditional love is not costly,
it is purity of feeling which you all have within you.

You were born from love.
It is the energy of creation,
of All That Is and where we came from.

Just know that we will,
and always have, loved you unconditionally,
no matter what you do,
what you say,
whom you're with,
or what decision you've made.

We will never leave you.

– Your Angels

May Chapter Sponsor – Lisa Clayton

MAY 7
Archangel Raphael Prayer to be Joy

By Lori Kilgour Martin

Archangel Raphael, I call upon your nurturing guidance
and to offer my gratitude for your continued support,
bringing me to this day and this moment.

Help me uncover the pearl of joy within,
to accept and know this wondrous gem is my true essence,
so that I may be the embodiment of Divine inspiration to all I meet.

I am with you, beaming with delight in your magnificent presence.
Walk with me on a healing journey
to a magic forest where the Unicorns reside.
There is a tree waiting just for you, its leaves are in full bloom,
sparkling with beads of diamond and rainbow light.

Feel the warmth from the sun and
lambent moonlight rays emanating through you.
Love from God, Mother Earth and
the Elemental Kingdom is enfolding you now.
My angel wings forever round,
your soul opens to joy, held safe and sound.
Oh Beautiful One, where your heart resides,
love surrounds, my angel wings forever round.

Archangel Raphael, I feel the radiant light flowing through me;
its gentle energy is uplifting.
I am ready to be joy and dance in joy with all of life.
From the deepest place in my heart, I honor you.

May Chapter Sponsor – Lisa Clayton

MAY 8
Angel Prayer for Problem Solving

By Suzanne Gochenouer

Dear Angels,

Help me strengthen my intuitive gifts
so I may solve each challenge that comes my way
by moving higher into my soul purpose.

Show me how to see, hear, and understand
the signs and messages that you bring me
as I work through problems and questions in my life.

Give me the courage to move confidently and quickly
through any dark times and stress that visit me.

Guide me to face life's challenges directly,
and to work with all the angels to resolve these challenges,
not only for my own higher good,
but also for the higher purpose
of everyone my decisions will affect.

Share with me the wisdom and clarity I need
to move through life with grace and compassion for all.

Amen, amen, amen.

Thank you, thank you, thank you.

MAY 9
A Prayer to Heal from Grief

By Julie Geigle

Archangel Metatron,
Let me find comfort
within your golden, magenta wings of love
soothing my grief and anguish.

Lift the veil so that I may see beyond
the limitations of this physical world
calming the cries of my heart and illusions of my mind.

Allow me to let go of my attachment to "form"
and embrace "formlessness"
securing my connection to my loved one,
beyond our physical bodies.

Deep in my soul is a place of knowing that
passing from this Earth dimension only means an end to "form."
I remember that our souls are connected
through all eternity, time and space.
As this truth rises up within my being
it brings me a sense of peace and comfort.
Opening a divine connection with my loved one,
that death can never erase.

Thank you, Archangel Metatron,
for helping me to remember that life really is everlasting.
By the grace of God it is so.
Thank you. Thank you. Thank you.

May Chapter Sponsor – Lisa Clayton

MAY 10
Prayer for Mothers

By Rev. Jennifer Shackford

God and Angels, please provide strength,
confidence and independence to all Mothers,
whether they are adoptive mothers, animal mothers, or biological mothers.

Provide them all with the divine guidance needed in difficult situations
and decisions regarding their children.

Fulfill them with peace, love and joy in their hearts,
even when their children are at a difficult time and place,
without a doubt in their mind that YOU are watching and protecting them!

Remind them in difficult times concerning their children to turn to
Mary, The Blessed Mother, for guidance and support!

MAY 11
Angels Sent from Mothers Heart

By Inger Marie Moeller

Angels sent from Mothers Heart
spreading as a wing of light
flying, flying, flying high
with Her Love, with Her Peace
Her Compassion and Her Grace

Oh Angels sent from Mothers Heart
take us home, take us home
flying, flying, flying high
take us home, take us home
to Her compassion and Her Grace
to Her compassion and Her grace
to Her compassion and Her grace

Mothers Heart

May Chapter Sponsor — Lisa Clayton

MAY 12
A Prayer for Single Parents

By Rev. Vicki Snyder

Guardian angels please watch over all the single parents.
They work so tirelessly to provide for their families.
Help them to see they can fall back on your love and your angel wings,
to comfort them through their hardest days.

Give them your support
as they handle family issues as a single parent.
Help them to know they are not alone.
Permit their days be simple and bright.

Let the drama,
that could adversely affect their abilities
to parent positively, steer clear of them.
Keep negativity away.
Whisper in their ears so they know they are not alone
in a job that can be scary and lonely at times, with much responsibility.

Allow them to stand tall, proud and feel you next to them,
supporting and guiding them.
Charge these solo parents with the strength and energy of two parents,
so they may best raise and influence their children to be productive adults.
Let their hurt and disappointments be replaced with joy and wisdom.
Provide an extra dose of courage so these parents
and their children may face all life throws at them.

Most of all allow peace to enter the home and fill each person.

May Chapter Sponsor – Lisa Clayton

MAY 13
My Mission of Heart

By Ann Phillis

In the heavenly realms I live and flow,
Here on Earth I stand and grow.

I blend my wings with earthly delight,
I share love with all, through my heart.

My wings, my grace,
I flow, I embrace.
I stand solid and firm,
I know what is right.

I am here as a messenger,
Full of light!
I am ready to serve,
My mission of Heart.

MAY 14

A Prayer to Archangel Ariel for Garden Blessings

By Belle Salisbury

Archangel Ariel, guardian of Mother Earth
I call upon your blessings
that my garden will give birth.

Bless each seed lovingly placed
that it will sprout and grow with God's good grace.

Bless the soil that embraces each seed
with nutrient and goodness
that will provide what it needs.

Bless the rain as it falls from above
with purity and cleansing
as my garden grows with love.

As the sun beams with its warming light
bless the sprouts' growth
as they reach their greatest height.

Bless the Harvest when my garden is ripe.
Remind me of the miracle
that allowed my garden to take flight.

As I prepare to enjoy the fruit of the Earth
I pause for a moment
to thank God for my garden's birth.

May Chapter Sponsor – Lisa Clayton

MAY 15
Angel Prayer for Grandmothers

By Cathelijne Filippo

Beloved Angels,

I am so grateful for my very special Grandmother.
Thank you for all the lovely moments we have shared
and for the love that is forever sealed within my heart.

Dear Angels,
Please wrap your magnificent wings around my Grandmother's soul,
protecting her always.
May she forever be at peace as the light guides her,
and may our loving connection stay strong through time and space.

May all grandmothers in this world and the next be honored and respected.
May their great wisdom guide the next generations
towards more love, peace and compassion.
May we care for them as they have nurtured us,
and may we listen to their wisdom as we embrace the Wise Woman within.

So it is!

MAY 16

Message from the Angels for Courage and Perseverance

By Ingrid Auer

You sometimes feel desperate when things do not work out
the way you want them to, or problems seem insoluble.

You wonder if it is worth fighting,
or whether it would be better to surrender.
In many cases, it is the happy medium that brings you forward.

Feel inside you, and find out why a certain situation stagnates,
and hold on to your wish with gentle determination.

Therefore, do not give up or see yourself as a victim,
but also do not try to force things.
Courage and perseverance are qualities that help you reach your aims,
or solve your problems.
Just like us – if you ask us.

Affirmation:
I courageously accept my life with all its challenges.
With all its consequences.

MAY 17
Angel Prayer for Forgiveness

By Michelle Mullady

Beloved Angels, please help me to see things differently,
to behold the innate goodness in others, awaken me to compassion.
I am willing to discover how to set myself free.
I choose to return to Love.

Rather than hold on to resentment and pain,
I take the first step in forgiveness and actively become willing to forgive.
I surrender, despite my resistance,
all feelings of retaliation, revenge or repayment.
I acknowledge and accept a clearing out
of the energetic ties that have bound me.
I claim unconditional love as a feat of courage and empowerment.
The act of forgiveness now liberates space within me
and opens a portal to the Divine.

Heavenly angels, I am willing to accept the miracle.
Provide me with spiritual strength.
I am willing to forgive them all. And I ask to be forgiven.
I thank the True Source of Light, for expanding me,
for assisting me to evolve, for bringing me closer
to the divine power in my heart that flows forth from my soul.

I surrender all struggle to divine love.
I surrender all people to divine love.
Heal us all at this moment.
Thank you. And so it is. Amen.

May Chapter Sponsor – Lisa Clayton

MAY 18
To Remove what I *Think* Are Obstacles

By Kimeiko Rae Vision ATP®, The Angel Warrior™

Dear Angels,
When I feel I have bitten off more than I can chew,
help me to realize that what appears to be a back-breaking obstacle
is really my next amazing opportunity for a breakthrough.

Archangel Jophiel, your name symbolizes "The Beauty of God."
Please beautify my world and help to keep my mind,
my thoughts and my words
clear of shortcomings, disappointments or fears.

Archangel Chamuel, your name symbolizes "The Eyes of God."
Please help me to trust my spiritual sight even more
than the physical eyes I use to see the world around me.

Angels, with your help and God's will,
I promise to look for what is good and beautiful in both myself and others.
Please help me to stop looking for signs of disappointment
in other people's eyes, actions and speech.
I am open to receive rewards for every sign of disappointment that I miss.
Please allow me to see that I am, indeed, on the right track.
Help me to know that what appears to be massive, unmovable boulders
can be flicked away like itty bitty pebbles!
Help me to turn all of my mountains into molehills
and see my future as bright as it truly is!

Amen.

May Chapter Sponsor – Lisa Clayton

MAY 19

Archangel Metatron:
Prayer for Powerful Presence

By Asia Voight

Archangel Metatron,
I call upon you to bring powerful presence into my life.
Guide me to remain fully grounded
and be a messenger between worlds like you are.
Hearing Divine wisdom is my soul's desire
and yet I become unbalanced and distracted.

You, Metatron, succeeded in wholly embracing
earthly energy with heavenly energy.
Teach me your wisdom.
Reroute my body's aura to accept perfect balance
of high and low frequencies.

Metatron, clear my cellular memory of persecution fears
in this life and all lifetimes of being
a sage, seer, medium, channel, wizard and witch.
Allow me to have compassion for those in my life
who do not understand my spiritual desires, and not be guided by them.
Escort my direction so I may find a powerful balance of spirit and earth.

Archangel Metatron, I welcome your strong presence
so I feel safe to be completely spirit-filled in my physical body
and capable of holding my soul in a centered state.

May Chapter Sponsor — Lisa Clayton

MAY 20
Angels Are Everywhere

By Helene Kelly

Angels are everywhere. If you just look you'll see them.
Though they rarely wear wings or a halo,
they show up shining wherever we go.
There's the grocer who says, "Wow you really look great!"
on the day when you're feeling so blue,
or the gal who can tell you the right road to take
when you're lost and have not got a clue.

The baby who smiles in response to your face
'stead of giving a lip quivering frown.
When you trip, the guy next to you catches your arm
and up-rights you before you fall down.
Angels aren't only in heaven above,
they're the people all 'round us who act out of love.

There's the young kid who chases you right down the street
Yelling, "Hey! You forgot your change!"
and the writer who touches the depth of your soul
by sharing his most secret pains.

A stranger simply says "hello" and somehow
you've just found your life-long best friend,
the person who sees you through all of life's strife's
and supports you right through to the end.
Angels aren't only in heaven above.
They're the people all 'round us who act out of love.
Angels are everywhere there is love.

May Chapter Sponsor — Lisa Clayton

MAY 21
Seeking a Patch Of Sky

By Maddy Vertenten

No matter what is swirling around you,
no matter the conditions, circumstances,
other people or loneliness,
you can always turn your face to a window or to the sky
and know that you are very small.
That the Universe is vast.
That there is more possible in this life
than one can possibly imagine.

It is a way of letting go. Giving up control.
Trusting something larger. Seeing angels.
Feel yourself tethered to exponential power,
grace, wisdom, consciousness.
Sometimes life feels cluttered and full,
and you have only a moment
to seek your patch of sky.

If you are able, take this outside, down a street or a path.
Move your body, bringing more oxygen in through your lungs
and new energy into your bloodstream,
allowing it to bring you to a place of surrender and gratitude.

This practice is vast indeed.
It honors the beauty in all time and space.
It celebrates your place within that resonance.
It attunes you to your angels, and deep within.

May Chapter Sponsor – Lisa Clayton

MAY 22

A Full Moon Prayer to Archangel Gabriel

By Ellen McCrea

I call upon you, Archangel Gabriel, to shine the full moon's light,
onto the hidden things that I am ready to have shown to me.

Assist me to release from my life emotions, behaviors,
and expectations that do not serve my highest good.

May my soul lovingly receive your help as I call upon your strength
to triumph in the work that is required of me.

Attune me to the angelic messages that you'll bring forth in my dreams.

The energy of the full moon is blessed and potent in its vibration upon my body.

I am ready, bring forth the light, together we will release the darkness.

With a grateful heart, I thank you for your assistance.

MAY 23
A Prayer to Ease Grieving

By Tracy Quadro

Dear Angel Azriel,
my grief is profound.
I have lost what is closest and most important to my life,
and I have thereby lost a part of myself.

I feel myself wandering alone with my pain,
unable to find my way forward.
I can't relieve the ache inside of me.
Please help me to gracefully let go of what I can't change,
and to have faith in what's to come.
Stretch out your hand to me and light the way ahead.

Remind me that there are many surrounding me
who are ready to ease my sadness
and give me comfort and warmth.
Remind me that all things pass,
and for every valley of our life,
a following peak will lift us up
from darkness and into the Light.

And at the end of my life,
please show me the way to the next.
Carry me through the passageway
to the great beyond with your smile,
impart to me the grace, hope and optimism
of that which awaits me in a Universe of eternal joy,
and the excellent adventures I will encounter there.

May Chapter Sponsor — Lisa Clayton

MAY 24
Never Alone

By Lisa K.

Just as we will never leave you,
neither will those you love who have left the physical world.

We are all here in Heaven looking down upon you,
sending you our love and supporting you every step of the way.

We watch your struggles and your triumphs, your loves and your hates.

Through it all we still love you and stand by you even when you think you are alone.

So don't be afraid to let us know when you need us most.

We will call upon a legion of angels
and your loved ones in heaven to be there for you and give you assistance.

– Your Angels

MAY 25

Prayer for the Fallen Soldiers and Families

By Rev. Vicki Snyder

Dear angels,
I ask for you to support and guide the fallen soldiers and families.
These soldiers gave unselfishly for our safety and defended our rights.
Please return them to perfect health and happiness
in the heavenly dimension they now reside.
Help them find peace in your wings,
love from your heart
and joy from your strength.

Be of assistance to them as they continue
to guard and protect their friends and families;
show them they can still offer protection from the heavens.
Their work is not complete
and they can still assist their loved ones by doing good deeds for them.

Help the fallen to hear the prayers of their families
and to provide healing to them as they grieve their loss.
Offer the families a bright sun to shine down on them,
warm them and feel the love that never dies between them.

Watch over their families and let them feel all the soldiers rally around them
to push on with their hopes and dreams.
Let the memories fill the families
and offer comfort
as they start on a new chapter in life.

May Chapter Sponsor – Lisa Clayton

MAY 26
Daily Prayer to all Beings of Light

By Ms. Linda Xochi Avalos

I call on the white light of the
Holy Spirit, Ascended Masters, Archangels, angels and Elementals
to guide me this day.

Open my eyes to the truth of who I am
and the beauty the Universe/God/Goddess has created.

Remind me on this day, to be loving to both myself and others.
I place my family, friends and loved ones on your altar
and give thanks for all that I have NOW.

Thank you for my answered prayers as I begin to acknowledge them,
as I let go of all false beliefs, fears and worries.
My concerns I give to you and I pray that from this day forth
I am open to receive HEALING and LOVE.
And so it is!

Amen

MAY 27

An Angel Prayer for Mothers

By Debra Snyder

Beloved Angels and Guides,
please surround the mothers of our world
with your unyielding Love and protection.
Allow them to never feel alone on their journey.
These amazing women are the ones who care for our children
and the most vulnerable in society without compliment or complaint.
Grace them with abundance, patience, and knowledge.
Please support the energy of compassion and understanding
as they guide their families each and every day.
Grant mothers strength as they face the hardships and fires of Life,
yet allow them to be gentle with themselves and others.

Angels, I ask you to envelop their hearts, minds and bodies with your pure radiance,
so they may accept their own Divinity as they walk this Earth.
When they cry, may their tears be cleansing.
When they laugh, may the laughter be robust and free.
Allow these incredible women to live without fear,
always knowing the Light of their heart will point the way Home.

By the grace of Heaven, so it is.

Amen.

MAY 28
Always By Your Side

By Caitlyn Palmer

Know that I am always here
to help, guide and cheer you on!
Call on me when your heart is unclear
and I will help until your problems are gone.

All you must do is look into your heart
and hear my special song,
Then you will see that we're never far apart,
and that I was here all along.

While I cannot participate in your every milestone,
I will help you find the strength within.
You may have forgotten, but I have always known,
that your strength and beauty go beyond your skin.

Do not fear death and cling to life in terror,
because when it arrives, we will fly off together.

MAY 29

Angel Prayer for Healing Mother Earth

By Michelle Mullady

I call on Archangel Raphael, the Earth Angel Sofia,
and all Healing Angels, to bring healing to
our beautiful home, Mother Earth.

I send forth a golden spiral of healing light
and gleaming love from my heart to seep in,
bless and restore the health of our planet for all life
in its many forms on the land, in the sea, and in the air.

I send forth that golden spiral of healing light
and gleaming love from my heart to hold our world
in this loving healing consciousness, inviting the angels
to speed and ground the healing rays upon the Earth
to bless all humanity.

I pray for the awakening of the human race and the dawning of a new era
of peace, health, and harmony on our planet.
I pray for the upliftment of every member of humankind
into the realm of Divine Agreement
that we are all godly in creation, whole and holy, loved and loving.
I pray for perfect spiritual attunement to resonate
between Earth and her human children.

Amen.

May Chapter Sponsor – Lisa Clayton

MAY 30
Mother Star

By Ann Phillis

Gentle light of the healing night
Twinkling stars in the darkness so bright.

Angels on watch, Mother's embrace
Caring, flowing, healing with grace.

Replenish my cells, my mind, my heart
Fill me with love that I may start
My new day, my new path, my new life in your heart
Renewed, revitalized and with re-awakened hope!

MAY 31

Archangel Gabriel
Remembrance of My Divine Gifts

By Kimberly Marooney

Archangel Gabriel,
Bless me with your Presence.
Infuse my heart with the remembrance of my divine qualities.
Open my eyes to see the gifts that God has given me.
Wake me up to the talents that make me unique.
Roll away the stone of limiting beliefs that keep me captured in suffering.
Fill my heart with experiences of Grace.
Into Thy hands I commend my Spirit.

Everything worthwhile in my life has come through my Lord.
I surrender the ways of my mind and personality.
Thank you for holding me in the remembrance of Divine Love.
Thank you for the moments that reveal lack of faith.
In those moments I am reborn in you.
I am reborn in your sweet tender embrace.

Your courage and strength flow through my veins.
Your loving forgiveness redeems all.
Guide my thoughts, words, deeds, desires and feelings.
Walk me in your ways. Walk me in the magnetic power of pleasure.
Teach me the pleasures of love, joy, bliss, ecstasy, devotion.

Help me to trust completely.
You are truly my source for everything.
I am your hands and heart in this world.
Your eyes and ears. Your vessel.
Guide me now. I'm listening.

May Chapter Sponsor – Lisa Clayton

JUNE
Angel Connections
Julie Geigle

I grew up in a large family of six and from the moment I was born, I knew I was not like everyone else. I tried everything I could to fit in, to no avail. As a child growing up I was labeled "hypersensitive." I didn't quite know what that meant, but I did know that it made me different and I didn't like being different. I was also painfully shy. I used to view my sensitivity as a curse. I felt lost and lonely.

When I was 30 years old, my father died of lung cancer. In my anger and grief I began talking with him as if he were still here. In the beginning, I thought I was just making up what I thought my father would say. After a while, I began asking, "What if my father's spirit was here and he could communicate with me just as he did when he was alive?"

Then I stumbled upon John Edward's TV show "Crossing Over", or so I thought. I have now since realized there are no accidents. Each one of us has a whole team of angels working with us, helping us to remember the amazing spiritual beings that we are and why we came here to this planet. One night, I had this overwhelming desire rise up inside of me while I was watching the show and I said to my husband, "I want to do that. I want to talk to the dead and help people." I didn't know at that moment when I spoke those words that I was answering the call of my soul and my life would never be the same.

My dad's death literally changed my life's path, and what I found through this loss is that we're all gifted. We all have the ability to talk to the spiritual realm and loved ones who have passed. If you take time to meditate daily and engage in that higher vibrational frequency it opens a portal, a gateway if you will, of guidance and love from beyond. It creates a direct connection to a plethora of angels, spiritual masters and beings of light that are here to help. And help they do. I also discovered that being sensitive is a gift not a curse. Learning how to ground and clear myself daily helps me to stay balanced and harmonious, and truly connected to the angels and beyond.

In 2005, I was called to travel to Brazil to see the healer, John of God. While I was there I had a visible surgery for migraines performed by Dr. Augusto through John of God. Unbeknownst to me this trip was to be yet another turning point in my life. Two years later, I ended up leaving teaching and opened *Heaven Sent Healing*. To my delight during my healing work with clients, Dr. Augusto began to pop in to do psychic surgeries for clients who needed more physical healings. I felt truly blessed to work with such an evolved spiritual master.

Several years later, I began studying "The Law of Attraction" and received the call from Spirit to go even deeper and began trance channeling Archangel Metatron and other spiritual beings. We began with a small group in my home and now we have an international radio show and have touched thousands of people across the globe. Three years later I was called again to Brazil for a second trip to become an approved and certified guide. I now make this sacred journey to The Casa four times a year, bringing people from all over the world for a spiritual transformational healing from John of God.

I now know that when a desire seems to burn like a fire in my soul that it is simply confirmation from the angels that I am moving into something divine, that I am being CALLED. I now recognize that feeling, and can sense the buzz of "angel activity" around me almost as if they are all a flurry with excitement and anticipation.

I have learned to surrender my will to God, trusting that I am here to help humanity and now when the CALL comes, I answer.

Julie Geigle is an International Psychic Medium & Certified Guide for The Casa, assisting people on a spiritual healing journey through the John of God experience. She holds a Master's degree in Education and is a Spiritual Healer, Teacher and gifted channel of Archangel Metatron. Julie also holds certification in hypnotherapy, meditation & Reiki and is an Ordained Minister.

In 2012, Julie created "Inner Circle" because she wanted a place for people to go to connect with like-minded souls and get the help and support they needed on their spiritual journey. She is also the host of several radio shows featured on Blog Talk Radio, W4WN, and iHeart Radio.

Julie is a 4th generation psychic and began to embrace her gifts once her own father passed in 1996. She has a very calm, soothing voice and soft, angelic presence. She tunes into messages from the angels and her guide, Archangel Metatron, easily and effortlessly to guide and direct you in your life. She specializes in Psychic Business Consulting. http://juliegeigle.com

As a "tested & approved" member of Shay Parker's Best American Psychic directory, Julie is honored to have received the "Awesome Accolades" award for 2014. Most of the Angel prayer contributors for June are from this esteemed "Best of the Best" directory. http://bestamericanpsychics.com

JUNE 1
A Prayer for Healing Communication

By Julie Geigle

Archangel Metatron,
I call on you now for your assistance
in healing my communication with others.

Please surround me with a beautiful cloak of love
knowing that I am fully supported in all that I say and do
here and beyond.

I now visualize my throat chakra opening
and any blocks to my ability to respond lovingly and appropriately
in my relationships with others is now dissolved and released.

Any interference to communications
is now healed in all directions of time and space.

I step into my power and trust that
perfect words will come to me at the perfect time
to allow me to express my truth perfectly
with all those I come into contact with.

Thank you, Archangel Metatron,
for your wisdom, your love and your guidance.
I trust and remember
that everything is always in divine and perfect order.

By the grace of God, it is so.
Thank you. Thank you. Thank you.

June Chapter Sponsor – Julie Geigle

JUNE 2
A Prayer for Peace

By Joy Elle

A child of innocence
A vision of remembrance on the other side of the world
Gazing in wonder through flashing lights and thunder
Blazing through the fields; sounds of a war ringing through
Is there peace for me and you - in this life?

This is a prayer–A prayer for peace; This is a prayer–A prayer for peace
This is a calling to Angels Above; Oh hear us calling–Send us your love.

We can reach anything we believe
Let us teach; We will achieve.
These are the lives of our children; These are the souls of our Universe
This is our chance - Our chance to bring peace.

This is a prayer–A prayer for peace; This is a prayer–A prayer for peace
This is a calling to Angels Above; Oh hear us calling–Send us your love.

Remember the beginning; Let this be an ending
Speak your voice - Let it be heard
We have a choice to affect the whole world
Let it be now - It takes you and I
And together the world will survive.

This is a prayer–A prayer for peace; This is a prayer–A prayer for peace
This is a calling to Angels Above; Oh hear us calling–Send us your love.

I pray . . . I pray . . . I pray for PEACE

June Chapter Sponsor – Julie Geigle

JUNE 3
Angel Prayer for Grounding

By Suzanne Gochenouer

Dear Angels,

Help me plant my feet firmly in this physical world,
even as I stretch my soul into the unending vastness of the Light.

Inspire in me a love of personal development
with which to ground myself within my physical body.

Help me create a deeper connection with this Earth on which I live.

Help me build stamina for the spiritual and physical journeys ahead
by finding sure footing where I stand in this moment, on this Earth.

Guide me as I learn new ways to serve
not only this physical world but also the Light.

Share with me a love of this Earth, and of the Universe,
where all the angelic hosts invite us to live within the Light.

Amen, Amen, Amen.

Thank you, thank you, thank you.

JUNE 4
Mother Ocean

By Ann Phillis

Ah, Mother Ocean!
So pure and abundant,
Full of life force, with angels resplendent!

Awaken your love in my consciousness today,
Let me feel your grace, your endless embrace.

Your power of life, uplifts me to the sky,
I feel so whole, so luminous and bright.

Heal my woes, my fears, my fright,
Strengthen my love, to be with you tonight!

JUNE 5
Angel Prayer for Mother Earth

By Allison Hayes, The Rock Girl®

I call upon the Angels,
with the utmost reverence and respect,
to facilitate the Healing of Mother Earth.

I call upon the Angels,
with the utmost reverence and respect,
to offer Protection for Mother Earth.

I call upon the Angels,
with the utmost reverence and respect,
to help strengthen my Connection to Mother Earth.

I call upon the Angels,
with the utmost reverence and respect,
to assist me in Celebrating Mother Earth.
To Love Her Stones, Honor Her Trees, and Embrace Her Wisdom.
In Deepest Gratitude ~ Blessed Be.

This Angel Prayer was channeled atop Mount Kurama, a Sacred Mountain in Kyoto Japan. When read aloud, and accompanied by the following stones, this can be quite a powerful experience: Celestite for connecting to the Angelic Realm, Rose Quartz for the healing of yourself & Mother Earth and Smoky Quartz for connecting to Mother Earth Herself. Mighty Blessings ~ Allison Hayes, The Rock Girl®

JUNE 6
I Love My Body Prayer

By Michelle Beltran

I love my body just as it is.
My body is aligned and balanced at all times.
I release resistance of any kind surrounding my body now.
My physical body blossoms as I release any resistance.

I am making mental lists each day of all the things I love about my body.
Body balance is my birthright.
Every aspect of my body-every atom-every cell-is whole and complete.
There is profound rejuvenating of all the cells of my body
beyond my comprehension.
Past or unwanted issues leave my body now.
I begin to feel the power that flows through me with this releasing.

Every morning, before I start my day,
I take a few moments to appreciate my perfect body.
I end my day in the same way.
I am _____ and I love my body fully and completely.
As I allow my body to come alive,
I feel an unleashing of magnificent energy.
My body's natural way is one of well-being.
I thank my body now. Vitality exudes from every cell of my body.

There is no need to try to find body balance.
It comes to me effortlessly, with love and grace.
There is a divine plan-far greater than me-
bringing health and well-being to me now.
I trust in this with all that I AM.

June Chapter Sponsor – Julie Geigle

JUNE 7

Direction and Energy from Divine Spirit

By Bob Kenney

Divine Spirit;
Please send us all the positive energy you feel we can hold
to help ourselves and others by spreading your spiritual wisdom and guidance.
Please provide your guidance and direction
to allow us to do our very best to raise the spiritual energy for all.

Please allow us to awaken others to whom they truly are as souls
and help them to ascend in accordance with your spiritual plan.

Please protect all those who walk the spiritual path
from negative energy and harm
and show them your directional light and wisdom
so they do not stray from the spiritual path.

Please give us the courage and strength that is often needed
to continue to spread your loving light throughout the world
and if you so will, allow us to grow in our spiritual work.

Please continue to provide us signs and validations
that we are on the correct path toward your loving light.
Please provide us direction on how to further spread your love and energy
throughout our world so our world can ascend and prosper.

Thank you for hearing our words and please give us, your messengers of light,
the strength to continue on the path to helping others to ascend.

JUNE 8

Archangel Uriel Assist Me to Embrace Transformation

By Jill M. Jackson

I call on you Archangel Uriel as I surrender to the process of releasing all fear.
In this physical 3D reality, many times we allow anxiety, worry,
and concern to step into the forefront of our existence.

Provide me with the wisdom to recognize when my ego self begins to surface.
Just as a caterpillar shape shifts effortlessly to become a butterfly,
I ask for your guidance as I release my lower self's ego
And welcome the emergence of my Light Body.

As I sip the nectar to nourish my soul,
fill me up with your healing energy.
Help me remember what powerful manifestations
I am capable of when I remove my human self.
Please support me as I evoke the recall
that we are all creators in this cosmic dance.

Archangel Uriel,
it is my prayer that you assist me in my awakening
to the realization that there is nothing to fear,
as we are all one collective consciousness,
sharing this physical reality together,
for the mutual benefit of vibrating closer and closer to Source.

JUNE 9
Prayer for Children

By Rev. Jennifer Shackford

Archangel Michael,

I ask that you stay by my children's sides all day, every day,
to protect them from outside influences.

I ask that you give them strength and support during times
when they are struggling.

Thank you for protecting my children, my heart and soul!

And so it is!

June Chapter Sponsor – Julie Geigle

JUNE 10
The Power of 6

By Cher Slater-Barlevi

GOD GODDESS ALL THAT IS,
I call forth my high-self Spiritual Council:
my Teachers, Guides, and Angels:
to help me to align with the vibrations of today,
the power of six: the highest vibration of Harmony;
giving the best that I can be for the good of others and myself.

As I walk in Harmony, I see the Peace in all things.
If there is strife,
I AM committed to finding peace in the lessons I am learning.
I AM committed to the Loving of my Divine Heart.
I will stop, reflect and re-choose when needed.
For I know today is a perfect mirror of this Love and Loving
I am committed to.

I look forward to every precious moment with delight and laughter:
knowing the whole Truth of All is Divine Grace.
I thank all my Teachers, Guides and Angels for this journey
and their presence in the Light
that is ever carrying me with Divine Grace and Ease.
My heart is full to the very brim with Light and Love
and I share it in service to the Divine Being of every one of us.
Peace.
Be still throughout every heart, throughout the world,
throughout the Universe.
And so it is.

June Chapter Sponsor – Julie Geigle

JUNE 11
A Bedtime Prayer for the Children

By Nicolebeth

Close your eyes beautiful child; your Angels are near!
With a flash of light, we flock quiet my dear.....
soon lovely one your dreams will be here!
Your sweet words whisper us in,
like a teeny tiny mouse violin!
A yawn and a cuddle your pillow awaits,
hurry, hurry little one, it's half past eight!

Close your eyes beautiful child; your Angels are near!
Sleep is a journey for the mind and the soul,
with adventures for only you to behold!
Shall we see twinkly stars and big giant moons,
or doggies and kitties holding hands with raccoons?
Soar high in the sky on our big giant wings,
past white fluffy clouds to the Faerie Kings!

Close your eyes beautiful child; your Angels are near!
Our mind transports us free,
as we listen to the gentle flow of the rhythmic sea!
Drift little love for your slumber is here,
your garden of visions opens up so clear!
Until tomorrow sleeping explorer, we bid you adieu,
only to meet once again when the sky turns to blue!

Close your eyes beautiful child; your Angels are near!

JUNE 12

Archangel Michael
Prayer for Inner Peace

By Cindy Nolte

Archangel Michael,

Please surround me with your strength.
Fill me with courage to walk the path that was intended for me.

Help me to see what I need to see.
Help me to recognize and dismiss my fears
and remove all obstacles so I may live a life of passion.

Motivate me when I feel weak.
Encourage me when it is easy for me to give up.
When I am unsure, remind me of my life's purpose.
Remove all negativity from in and around my being.

Keep my vibration high.
Fill me with the light of our Creator from the inside out.
Allow that light to emanate through every pore of my body.
Help me to always be in a state of peace, love and joy
so that I may send those feelings out in to the world.

Allow me to be a messenger
that makes the world a better place
and in turn fill my heart with gratitude
for a life that is exceptional beyond my imagination.

And so it is.

June Chapter Sponsor – Julie Geigle

JUNE 13
Spiritual Prayer for Ease of Change

By Avianna Castro

Beloved Source, Angels and Spirit Guides,
I invite you to deliver energies of love and release
during this time of transition and change.
Assist me in surrendering to the experience and exploration of this journey,
understanding that this growth is essential for my continued awareness.

Disconnect the energies of the past;
eliminating the loops and patterns that are no longer deserving.

Dismiss the desire to control,
understanding that what I want and what is best for my soul
may be two different outcomes in this moment.

Replace reaction with response,
frustration with peace
and anger with compassion.

I am so grateful for you Infinite Spirit,
I know I am completely protected and safe in all situations and
that only love and light energies are surrounding me.
I declare that I am ready for what awaits and
I trust that what I may not understand right now is for the highest good.
I AM at peace, love and harmony at all times.
Om Shanti, Shanti, Shanti

JUNE 14
A Father's Day Prayer

By Joyce M. Jackson

A Prayer from My Father,
Brought on the Wings of Angels

Seeing you through the eyes of love, I came to spur your growth.
I offered to play a role, holding the angels close.

A Prayer to My Father
Sent on the Wings of Angels

I always thought I would be angry, and time would heal the pall.
I never dreamed the angels would heal my heart,
with no human shape at all.

I always pretended I moved on from the trauma
and analyzed it deeply.
I found the answers with angels, embraced in their arms,
revealing your gift while sleepy.

I always knew I would find them.
At first, I foolishly looked with my eyes.
Here with me all along, Angels opened my heart
to the reasons you were my Dad,
hidden until I was ready.

Dad, Thank you for helping me to have the courage and confidence to move forward through this life.

June Chapter Sponsor — Julie Geigle

JUNE 15

Archangel Raphael
Divine Healer of Humanity

By Kimberly Thalken

Archangel Raphael, divine being of love and healing,
I humbly call upon you to heal our souls.

Allow us to experience the power of your miracles
and the healing that's available to all of humanity
and all of the animals that have been divinely and perfectly created.

Help to restore us to complete wholeness and wellbeing.
Through the purity of this healing may it allow us to see the beauty in,
and feel the ultimate joy of, living in balance, harmony,
and as one—as divinely intended.

As my healing contributes to the healing of all
I lovingly invite you into my life
to heal the physical, emotional, mental and spiritual layers of my being,
helping me to experience love in its highest form
and strengthening my connection to the divine.

I pray for a cleansing of my mind and my energy field,
freeing me from all things that do not contribute
to my health, happiness and peace.

In love and gratitude - Thank you for hearing me.

JUNE 16
Prayer for Healing

By Jennelle Deanne

Dear St. Raphael,
your lovely name means "God heals."

The Lord sent you to young Tobias to guide him throughout a long journey.
Upon his return you taught him how to cure his father's blindness.

I now ask of you to heal all those going through tough times.
Allow their grief and tears to turn to smiles and happiness.

Wrap your arms around the hearts of our children
and parents dealing with illness and loss.

Allow us to know that love pursues all and we are all loved

JUNE 17
Archangel Michael's Grounding Light Prayer

By Jennifer Shaffer

Mother Father God and Goddess of the Earth, Moon, Seas and Stars,
I invoke Archangel Michael with his sword of brilliant golden light.
I ask to please cut the cords of any past, present and future energies
from all dimensions in which I may reside, and that no longer
serve my highest good in being of service for the highest good of others.

I ask and visualize your infinite presence of golden love, light and strength
to take my energetic cord deep into the center of our loving mother earth,
wrapping the cord around her axis so I have an anchor for grounding.

I see your light come back as it runs through my left side,
lightening all of my energy centers.
I see your light flow back down through my right,
clearing and illuminating the energy flow going through my body.
I see your golden love, light and strength flow through me
seven times in a circular motion finishing through my crown,
connecting my spirit to my higher self.

Finally, as immense gratitude fills my heart,
I invoke the seven Archangels under Michael's direction
to encompass my etheric body with solid golden white light protection
starting clockwise surrounding seven times,
cloaking the Merkabah sphere I stand in.

JUNE 18
Angel I Am

By Beth Lynch

Today as I wake I thank you my angel for all that is before me.

I Am thankful for your love.

I Am thankful for your light.
I Am thankful for all that is in sight.

I Am thankful for what serves me not to know.
I Am thankful for strength that shows me how.

I Am thankful for good health and humble wealth.

I Am thankful for the hand you extend as a friend.
So today my angel as I journey around the bend,
I Am thankful to see, feel and know – there is no end.

<u>Note</u>: Begin and end your prayer with a few slow, comfortable breaths and a smile.

June Chapter Sponsor – Julie Geigle

JUNE 19
Blessing Archangels Prayer

By Shelley Robinson

Blessed Archangels, messengers of Light,
I humbly call upon you to walk with me through all the days of my life,
giving me hope even when things are hopeless.

Banish the shadows of my doubts
and allow my inner self to shine through,
reflecting the Divine in myself and others.

In your infinite wisdom,
help me to develop my natural talents
while accepting my shortcomings.

Give me the courage to see beyond the mundane and ordinary,
learning to see all that is beautiful and good in this world.

As you love all of humankind,
inspire in me that same level of benevolence toward all creatures.

When I fail, or when I am tired and weak,
lift me up on your wings
and carry me above the clouds of my despair.

I ask you, the representatives of heavenly light,
to share your luminosity with me
and illuminate each step I take on my spiritual journey.

JUNE 20

Prayer to Archangel Uriel for Remembering Your Divine Identity

By Katherine Glass

I call upon Archangel Uriel
and the Angels of Light and pure Love
to encircle me at this time on my journey.

As I stand openly,
in the vulnerability of my human awareness,
I feel and receive all of the comfort, protection and Grace
which surrounds me now and always.

I KNOW that I am a child of the Divine,
a holy creation of that energy and Love.
I KNOW that I never walk alone.

I thank you Uriel,
and the Angels of Light and pure Love,
for lifting my heart and mind
with the wings of remembrance
of my true Divine Identity.

And so it is.

June Chapter Sponsor – Julie Geigle

JUNE 21
Prayer to Celebrate the New Day

By Diana Blagdon

Angel of the morning
Bringer of new light and new energy
Open me to receive all the blessings in today.

Instill in me an attitude of grace and forgiveness
so that I may know the *God-ness* in all that I experience.

Help me to be a humble instrument
of your eternal loving consciousness.

Assist me in my loving service to Spirit

Thank You

JUNE 22
Prayer to Arch Angel Gabriel

By Sharon Pugh

Archangel Gabriel,

I call upon you for direction and guidance in my life during difficult times.
I always know you will be there for me when I lack insight and clarity.

I ask for your beautiful Golden light to enlighten me toward
the path I'm supposed to walk in this lifetime
as I sometimes may not know what is right or wrong for me.

I promise to listen to your subtle signs
that will awaken my soul
and give me the answers I need
to fulfill my soul contract on this Earthly plain.

When I feel your presence in the most unique of ways,
I realize you are wanting me to "wake up"
and be more aware of my surroundings.

Within that beautiful blanket of Gold,
I feel the clarity and wisdom
to find my way out of despair
and into a life of happiness and peace.

You are the Archangel of Messages and Wisdom
and I thank you for being here for me in times of great need.

Amen.

June Chapter Sponsor – Julie Geigle

JUNE 23

Prayer to Strengthen the Connection to God's Light

By Maggie Chula

Dear God, Lift up my heart and my mind
into the vibration of your Divine Source energy.

Help me stay strong and connected to your Light and Love
while working within a world of illusions.
Help me remember the illusions are only as powerful
as the amount of energy I willingly give them.
Let my attention not be focused
on the chaos and doubt they create within my mind.

Help me to instead breathe in the light of your source vibration.
Help my mind center and focus so I can feel
your love and compassion flowing to me and within me.
Help me share my loving vibrational energy with others.
Help me remember I am safe sharing my love and light in the world.

Thank you for restoring peace and calm
to **my mind and my thoughts.**
I focus on my breathing,
bringing your Divine vibrational energy of
Light and Love deeply into my body.

Thank you for helping me to release tension and stress from my body.
I breathe in your Light and Love.

Thank you for strengthening my connection to your Light and Love.

June Chapter Sponsor – Julie Geigle

JUNE 24
Prayer for Divine Surrender

By Sara De La Mer

I call on the powers, dominions and angelic realms
that know, love and do God's will.
Please guide and instruct me clearly as to the correct road ahead.
I invoke the peace which passeth all understanding and offer a calm,
serene mind ready, willing and able to do divine bidding.

I surrender once and FOR ALL the things that stood or stand in the way
and permanently release the ties that bind.
I acknowledge and realize that I do not always know best.
I hereby release diversions, personal will, expectations
and preconceived ideas.
I await divine guidance in whatever form it may come.
I am open, ready, willing and able to serve and
follow God and his higher bidding;
knowing that my best interests are always served.

Everything works in perfect timing for those who
know and love and do God's will.
This I know and acknowledge from the bottom of my heart.
With the help of the angelic realms I vow to remain receptive, malleable
and ready to act at a moment's notice.
I promise to trust and not second guess the universal wisdom.

I call on the empowerment of the Holy Spirit
to bless my requests and light the road ahead.
So be it.

JUNE 25
Solstice Prayer

By Cathelijne Filippo

This Prayer is for the Summer Solstice in the Northern Hemisphere;
If you live in the Southern Hemisphere, read the Solstice Prayer on December 21.

Beloved Archangel Raziel,
Please bless me with the energy of renewal on this summer solstice.
Help me to open up to my fullest potential.
As the rays of the sun shine brightly on the earth,
and my body is filled with its power.
Let me embrace a new passion for life,
extending this to all beings around me.

Dear Raziel,
Bless me with the gift of solar initiation,
opening me up to my greatest, spiritual potential,
enabling me to live a magical life,
as a co-creator on Earth.
Please give me new esoteric insights,
helping me ground them in my life,
enabling me to work with the Spiritual Laws,
manifesting my dreams as I shine ever brightly.

May I now receive the energy of abundance on all levels,
as I anchor my heart's wishes,
so that they may grow towards the light.
May I have the courage to now walk my talk!

So be it.

June Chapter Sponsor – Julie Geigle

JUNE 26
The Most Powerful Prayer is a Smile

By Mary O'Maley

Do it now. A really big smile.
Start your smile at your toes. Feel your legs smile.

Smile from your root chakra as you feel gratitude
for having your daily needs met.
Smile from your belly button as you acknowledge your friends and family,
and the beautiful creative expression of yourself.
Smile from your heart and feel the vibration of joy explode within.
Smile from your throat; sing your joy or laugh out loud.

Feel your face smile;
let your physical and inner eyes be astonished at the beauty around you.
Smile a great big, open mouth smile, all your teeth showing.
Smile from the top of your head.
Experience the Universe and your Guardian Angels smiling back at you.

Smile at your perfections and your imperfections.
Smile because you woke up this morning.
Smile at the trees and birds and the world around you.
Smile at a stranger and wonder if the light from your smile
will make them stand taller and feel better.
Stop many times throughout your day and just smile.

Know that each smile is a prayer;
a powerful and dynamic vibration that is felt, appreciated, and returned.

Thank you.

June Chapter Sponsor – Julie Geigle

JUNE 27

Answering Archangel Uriel's Call to be of Service

By Kimberly Marooney

Beloved Archangel Uriel,
Here Am I.
Here am I in gratitude and devotion.
Here is my love flowing out to you.

Here are my hands and voice in service to your calling.
Here are my actions and energy answering your call.
Here are my heart, soul and ears to hear your call.
I am yours Beloved, use me well.

I release the belief that being your servant means deprivation and poverty.
I know that in you is the wealth and abundance of Spirit and Matter.
I know that you provide the need for a first class
material existence for your calling.

I release the belief that my body is not capable to health.
I release the belief that illness is encoded
in my DNA and health is not for me.
I release the belief that I am not able to be fit, strong, healthy and mobile.
I know that you are calling me to fitness and health.
I deserve a fit, healthy and beautiful body that can travel
and experience the pleasures of human life.
You are calling me to wellness and I say YES!

Guide me Uriel,
give me the substance, the words, the energy to move myself into Truth.

June Chapter Sponsor – Julie Geigle

JUNE 28
A Prayer for Peace

By Gisabel

God, please help me going through my journey
which I want to use to bring Love around me
in order to help my neighbor.
The Love of God that is shining on me,
I want to shine it around because,
that is the way I want to help my neighbor.

In these days where there are a lot of wars in the world,
I want to use the light of God to bring some peace around me.
Although there are many people in the world,
I would like you to shine on every one your light
in order to bring peace all around the world
so that we could live all together in peace
and be close to the love of God.

Please God, allow the world to always be close to you
as it could be possible for you to look after each of us here on earth,
and that way all of us could be part of the same family
which is the family of God
all sitting at the same table which is the Table of God.
By that goal we will be living in peace
and there will be no more wars.

This prayer has been given to me by the spiritual world
and the Table of God during an automatic writing session.

JUNE 29
Prayer to Archangel Michael

By Lorraine Appleyard

Hear me now as I pray to you.

I ask that you comfort me and
ease worry from my mind.

Give me the strength to face my challenges.

Bless me with your healing Light.

Surround me with your perfect love.

Protect me from any negativity.

Release any karmic ties and negative attachments.

Archangel Michael,
I ask you to be with me constantly throughout this day and guide me.

Give me knowing so that I may make the right decisions.

I ask you this with all of me.

Amen.

JUNE 30

Angel Prayer for
Healing and Transformation

By Robin "Raj" Munger

Archangel Raphael
I call upon Archangel Raphael, with his healing staff
I ask to shed healing light upon all of us.

I ask to provide healing for all who are affected
physically, mentally, emotionally or spiritually.

May your healing green light open us up to the possibility
that all wounds illnesses and our own limiting beliefs
be healed and surrounded with your guidance
and transformed and transmuted.

May your light and power illuminate and heal
our animal kingdom, our mother earth
and allow for compassion, kindness and love to be our path for healing.

I ask for guidance during times of change
so we may see it as an opportunity for growth and enlightenment.

May this light multiply and amplify and be shared for all of us
to be happy, healthy, wealthy, whole, body, mind, spirit and soul.

Archangel Raphael,
I am ready willing and able to receive healing.

And so it is.

June Chapter Sponsor – Julie Geigle

July-August-September

The Energy of Manifestation

with **Sunny Dawn Johnston**

The Energy of Manifestation

By Sunny Dawn Johnston

Each of us goes through periods of time where our spiritual growth accelerates at a level that can be hard to keep up with. We ask for it, pray for it even; and then when it comes, we are often challenged to know what to do, where to go, and really… just how do we begin. How to begin to step into the energy of growth and change that we truly desire? How do we allow ourselves to release the old so that we can step into the gift of transformation? How??? That is the million dollar question, and the one that keeps the spiritual growth we so desire just on the other side of our fingertips.

For when we focus on the how, we lose sight of the why. We spend way too much time in our heads and not enough time in our hearts. We get into the energy of "figuring it out" instead of the energy of "feeling it out". We get lost somewhere in the middle and often end up disappointed, disconnected and frustrated. We try to rise from the level of where we are now without utilizing all the support we have within and without of ourselves to reach where we want to go.

The Archangels are beautiful light beings responsible for the "stepping down" of the energy of creation from Spirit into physical form… manifestation. They are dedicated to helping humanity move into the light and are always available to help us when requested to do so. By calling on the support of the Archangels and tapping into the power of our own Law of Attraction energies, we can manifest all that we desire in a relatively short amount of time. All we have to do is ask.

Seven Steps to Manifesting with the Angels

1. Choose one thing that you would like to manifest in your life

    •   It doesn't have to be the biggest thing - just something you want
        to put your attention/intention on at this time.
        o   Career
        o   New Relationships
        o   Health
        o   Abundance

2. Invoke the Archangels — Archangel Jophiel specifically for
    manifestation.

    Invocation: *I invoke the golden yellow light of Archangel Jophiel. Help
    me to manifest beauty within and around me. Jophiel, I know that I am a
    creative being and I ask that you help me to use that creative power in every
    aspect of my life. Please help me to remember that whatever I focus on is mani-
    fested through the vibration of my own thoughts. Help me to align my thoughts
    with who I really am and to see the beauty in all that crosses my path. I will
    remain open-minded and be guided by the light within. With your help and
    creative power, I can and will manifest the beautiful life of my dreams ... and
    so it is!*

    As I invoke Archangel Jophiel, I visualize a golden yellow
    light entering the top of my head and moving down my entire
    body. This vibrating light encases me in a safe and comfort-
    able energy field. I see, hear, feel and know that the energy of
    creativity and manifestation surrounds me and dwells within
    me, at all times.

3. Hand write your Desire or Intention across the top of the piece of paper

    •   The perfect career opportunity for me is coming to me and these are the qualities of it:
    •   The prefect relationship for me is coming to me and these are the qualities of it:
    •   Perfect health is coming to me and these are the qualities of it:

4. Now list 30 – 40 qualities of your Intention …***Ways you want to feel***, specifically.

    •   Describe how you want to *FEEL* in the experience. Think about **why** you want what it is you want, and **describe that in feelings**.
        o   Example: I want to feel like I am appreciated
        o   I want to feel like I am making a difference
        o   I want to feel like I am respected
        o   I want to be feel like I can express my creativity

5. Make 5 copies of this Intention list in order to surround yourself with the energy of your desires.
    •   Place the copies in the five following places:
        o   1 copy in between the mattresses of your bed
        o   1 copy in purse/wallet or bag
        o   1 copy in glove box of your car
        o   1 copy in your office/kitchen or where you spend the most time
        o   1 copy in your Sacred space

6. At ***least*** twice a day invoke the Archangels and read through your entire list to affirm your desire.
    •   NOW, the most important part of this step (next to invoking the Archangels of course!) is to at least once in each day (<u>every single</u>

day), while you read through your list, also take this time to *feel* through the list, in this present moment.

 o Take yourself back to a time in your life where you remember feeling that particular way you have described in your Intention list. Bring the memory up, really **feel the energy of that experience** … and now take a deep breath and breathe in the energy of that experience. Then go to the next one, and **FEEL** the feeling described in that item. You must feel each and every experience on your list!

 o It doesn't matter if the last time you felt appreciated, for example, was when you were Girl Scout at six years old and you helped someone pick up the groceries they had spilled. It doesn't matter how long ago the feeling was; all that matters is that you tap into that feeling again. You want to bring in the energy of that feeling, to be able to then attract it to you again **NOW**.

7. Repeat this technique daily for 30 days minimum, invoking the Archangels every single day. Watch as your life begins to grow and expand as you begin to transform the energy of the old into the NEW and exciting energy of creation, abundance and allowance.

With the help of the Archangels, I used this technique to transform my life from a place of scarcity, fear and hopelessness into one of unconditional love, appreciation, freedom and connection. I know that with the help of the Angels Realm, anything is possible and I believe that you too will experience transformation from the inside out, as you attract amazing miracles and gifts into your life!!!

Sunny Dawn Johnston is an internationally renowned author, dynamic and engaging inspirational speaker and gifted psychic medium. Since early childhood, Sunny has always known she was different and destined to do great things. As a teenager she possessed an innate wisdom, awareness and curiosity of the Angelic realm and Spirit world. While she fought those gifts for many years, Spirit ultimately won and today Sunny is dedicated to teaching others about the Spirit world and unconditional love.

Over the last fifteen years, Sunny has performed thousands of readings and workshops where she's communicated with angels, guides, and loved ones who have crossed over to the other side. The constant theme she receives from all of these divine entities and loved ones is: Love never ends!

Sunny is the author of 6 books and has spoken internationally on the subject of Angels, Mediumship and Healing the Heart. Sunny has been featured on many local and national television and radio shows and has appeared in the award-winning documentary *Sacred Journey of the Heart*. Her most recent endeavor was starring in "A Séance with…" on Lifetime Movie Network LMN. Sunny's latest book, *The Love Never Ends: Message from the Other Side...* was released in October 2014.

www.sunnydawnjohnston.com

JULY
Healing Heart Angels
Cathelijne Filippo

Angels are with each and every one of us. This certainly has been a given in my life from an early age, when my Catholic granny taught me to call on angels before going to sleep. After she fell ill with cancer, granny said she would ask God if she could become my guardian angel after passing away. In later years I felt that she did indeed become my spiritual guide.

Soon after she passed away I cycled past the cemetery and her church. Just as I was about to turn the corner, a car came barreling towards me. The lady driving the car looked almost as if she were in a trance. She obviously did not see me at all! I knew I could not escape the car coming towards me. Then all of a sudden, it felt like a force pushed me onto the pavement. There was no explanation of how I could have gotten there so quickly, and I have always felt it was my guardian angel saving me. I remember thanking my guardian angel and granny for helping me that day.

A few years later, my connection to the angels was further reinforced. My mother had a friend visiting who was a medium. She told me there was a huge blue angel with me and that his name was Michael. From that moment on I kept seeing signs of Archangel Michael around me. I was guided to books about him, churches dedicated to him and by the time I went to university I had begun channeling Archangel Michael. He even gifted me with a radiant blue orb on a picture after channeling him in a church in Italy. Michael has always been a wonderful support to me.

My connection to the angels became even more personal during a lucid dream. While I was in that state between sleeping and waking, an immense golden light appeared in my room. As I slowly opened my eyes, I saw a beautiful angel. She radiated pure love and I remember thinking "this is what heaven feels like." I still remember the deep feeling of unconditional love and joy filling my heart upon seeing her. The memory of it has remained vivid and deeply touching till this day.

All in all, the angels have been a personal support in my life through my teens and university years, but it was not until my dad became ill with cancer that life readied me for professionally working with the angels. I had been meaning to learn healing modalities, but had been procrastinating. Seeing my dad so gravely ill and feeling helpless by his hospital bedside, I decided to learn Reiki to help him during his journey. It was such a blessing to be able to support him in this way and it strengthened our bond tenfold. The angels had told me his healing would be an emotional one and not physical. This turned out to be true. When it was his time to pass away he looked back on his last years as a huge gift, he too felt it had brought us together.

After he passed I created an angel sculpture holding a heart, to honor him and the love we shared. Love once shared, will always remain there in the Spirit. It can never be taken away from us.

I put the sculpture on a website and soon an order came in. The client missed her father too and wanted a *Healing Heart Angel*. As such, my dad's angel sculpture would be the start of the *Healing Heart Angel* sculptures and I have made these for people all over the world ever since.

The angels have been guiding me whilst making these sculptures, and sometimes little miracles or special signs are given to those receiving them. Like the time I made an angel sculpture of two angels with a yin-yang figure connecting them. I later heard the yin-yang sign was on the grave of the client's husband.

This was the start of my working together with the angels. I cut down working hours as a psychologist and made time for spiritual and creative work, which truly feeds my soul. I love working with the angels, whether through art, writing, healing or coaching. I feel very blessed and wish you the same loving connection to your angels!

Cathelijne Filippo is a psychologist, Angel Coach, Angel Healer, Angel Artist and spiritual teacher. Her formal training includes clinical psychology, cognitive behavioral therapy, mindfulness-based therapy, solution focused therapy and Heart Focus coaching. She also has qualifications as a Usui Reiki Master, Angelic Reiki Teacher, Angel Coach and Certified Angel Card Reader®.

In her business *Angel Light Heart* she merges spirituality and creativity to inspire and help others in their personal and spiritual development. She loves enabling others to help themselves and by doing so, helps them grow and transform in order to become stronger and more authentic people. Everyone has a special inner light that wants to shine and the more one lives from the heart, the more that light will reveal itself.

Cathelijne loves writing about angels and other spiritually uplifting subjects. She is the author of the Dragon Oracle, her angel blog and has written articles for spiritual magazines in the Netherlands and the UK. She creates angel sculptures, oracle decks, *Crystal Angel Essences*, gives workshops, consultations, readings and healings. You can read more about her work on her website www.angellightheart.com.

JULY 1

Prayer for Self Esteem and Self-Acceptance

By Cathelijne Filippo

Beloved Archangel Michael,

Bless me with a new sense of self-esteem,
acknowledging my strengths and accepting my weaknesses.
Help me to move out of my comfort zone and step into my power now,
As I start to walk my talk and live my dreams.

Help me to realize that I am a Spark of the Divine,
and as such I am perfect just as I am.
When I strive to grow and change,
I do so from a place of loving kindness and acceptance of self.

Dear Archangel Chamuel,
help me to truly love myself,
realizing I need not change a thing
as I am fine the way I am.
For all is well in my life,
as I give my higher Self the reign from this day forward.

I am a beautiful soul,
with a special mission on this Earth.
The more I live my Divine Blueprint,
the more I love myself and life.

So be it.

JULY 2
Your Heart's Voice

By Lisa Clayton

Trust your inner voice that is connected to your heart.
Can you hear it?
Melt mind chatter and connect,
listen and learn to recognize and honor your heart voice.
The logical world is crumbling and the spiritual world is expanding.

Trust and have faith in the Divine Guidance we send to you each day
and flow into your heart's golden glow.
Structure and rules from old ways are dissolving to the new structure
with flow of love-living and giving in heart-centered communities.

Nothing feels the same.
Nothing is the same as the Divine energetic waves
transform your perceived reality
to the new reality of living through loving ALL.

Learn to listen to your heart's whispers.
Remember, Angels are always by your side
flooding your heart with love and golden light.

Call upon us. Ask us. Trust and believe in us.
We are ALL one. Unity is our mission.

Fall in love with your heart's voice.
Honor it. Believe in its intelligence.
Be in alignment of your heart leading and your mind following.
Angels' guidance will always lead you to your heart's voice.

July Chapter Sponsor — Cathelijne Filippo

JULY 3
Trust & Faith

By Lisa K.

Are you ready to go to the next level?

This month is the month for trust and faith.

Trust that your prayers will be answered.

Have faith that we are here to help you.

You will go to the next level with a little trust and faith.

You do not need much;
so start now with your having a little more trust
and a little more faith.

As you see results begin to happen,
your trust and faith will grow,
and so will the abundance in your life.

— Your Angels

JULY 4
A Prayer of Summer

By Connie Gorrell

Oh, to savor the warming days of summer!
I rejoice at the return of the Light
when Mother Earth is bountiful with color
and bursting with the fruits of her labor.
Today, I breathe in the Light and
release the dark days of winter's repose.
May I be inspired by summer breezes felt lightly on my skin
as if kissed by angels on the wind.

I invoke earth's healing green light of Archangel Raphael
as I am surrounded by lush meadows and rich farmlands,
joyfully immersed in the feel of the earth beneath my feet.

I invoke the luminous white light of Archangel Gabriel
whose messages of brightness guides me on my journey
with the promise of sun-filled days ahead
that will light the path before me in this life.

I invoke the protection and support of Archangel Michael
whose radiant presence is as wide as the clear blue sky
—and as infinite as well.
He lovingly reminds me that the only limitations in this life
are those which I place upon myself.

Let me dance in the days and bask in the glow of a summer's moon
—and know that all is well in my world.
Amen.

JULY 5

Blessed Angels Are
the Ones Who I Call

By Bobbe Bramson

I don't need no superheroes
Leaping buildings at a single bound
'Cause I've got my blessed Angels
Who ring me all around.
Superheroes' X-ray vision may have benefits to impart
But I'll stick with my blessed Angels
Who see straight into my heart.

Any day, any hour, should I need a superpower
Blessed Angels are the ones who I call
In the moment of my prayer
That's the moment that they're there
Yes, blessed Angels are the ones who I call.

I don't need no superheroes
Fighting hard on many fronts
'Cause I've got my blessed Angels who help everyone at once.
Superheroes' heft and muscle takes them mighty far and fast
But I'll stick with my blessed Angels
Who bring changes that will last.

Any night, any hour should I need a superpower
Blessed Angels are the ones who I call
With their wings lit up with fire
They bring all that I require
Yes, blessed Angels are the ones who I call.

July Chapter Sponsor – Cathelijne Filippo

JULY 6
You Are Spirit

By Gayle Kirk

You are Spirit.

You are not your body.
Your body may fail you.
However, the real you - your Spirit - lives on forever.

When you leave this world, you will continue to live on.
Do not fear death.
It is merely a transition into a greater world.

Fear not, for we are with you always.

JULY 7
Archangel Uriel

By Trish Grain

Archangel Uriel,
the Angel of Wisdom.

I ask that you pour your golden, yellow light
into my mind and heart
for all the creative ideas that I need
to help me through a task I have to finish
and to help give me the courage
to trust my own wisdom and intuition.

I ask for your help in guiding me in my decisions and insights.

July Chapter Sponsor – Cathelijne Filippo

JULY 8
God Lends Us the Angels

By Giuliana Melo

God lends us the angels every day
to help us on our earth journey in every way.
All you have to do is invite them in,
and then watch your life change!

They help with everything, if you let them.
They will guide you and support you
and send you the most amazing signs,
coins, feathers, songs and numbers are a few,
and they always guard you night and day.

They help you through trials and tribulations,
tears and smiles, births and deaths.
Their energy is that of love and gentleness
and you will know they are there.

Won't YOU invite them in today?
All you have to do is ASK.

Dear Angels,
Come into my life, into my heart, into my home.
Guide and support me,
send me signs of your presence.
Stay by my side and shower me with blessings,
and the love and light of the Divine essence

Amen.

July Chapter Sponsor – Cathelijne Filippo

JULY 9

Angel Prayer for Compassionate Leadership

By Suzanne Gochenouer

Dear Angels,

Help me be a compassionate leader.

Guide me to discover new ways to share
what I know when someone asks for help.

Remind me to keep my words loving
and to avoid judging what others need
or where they should be in their journey.

Help me live my life as an inspiration
to everyone my energy touches.

Share with me the ability to know what is in the hearts
of those who seek my leadership,
to know when and where to lead,
and when to allow myself to be led by Spirit.

Amen, amen, amen.

Thank you, thank you, thank you.

JULY 10
An Angelic Love Letter

By Emily Berroa-Teixeira

Beloved Angels, I invoke your presence in true celebration and
gratitude of your Divine inspiration and dedication to mankind.
My gentle guardians, your beautiful energies have awakened my soul,
allowing me to experience the enriching colors of life and love.

Your guidance has faithfully led me through many transformations,
supporting each of my dreams and aspirations.
I am infused with the strength, encouragement, and bravery
necessary to exercise my personal power in healthy ways.

Through all moments of time I have sensed your presence
and trusted in your unconditional love,
surrendering my attempts to control,
knowing I will be guided to the most beneficial outcomes.

My beautiful messengers, I am beholden to the powers
that have cleared away binding forces of my past.
Your illumination has provided insight and clarity
which enables me to experience the infinite wonders of love and grace.

Dear Angels, please continue to surround me
with your protection, grace, and inspiration.
Continue to empower me in promoting the harmony and peace
that our world so needs at this time.
Shine your ever-present light upon us so that we may see each other
through the eyes of love and understanding.
And so it is, always.

July Chapter Sponsor – Cathelijne Filippo

JULY 11

Archangel Muriel:
Prayer for Ocean Healing

By Cathelijne Filippo

Beloved Archangel Muriel,
Please bless me with the healing energies of the ocean.
Let its sea breeze clear my mind.
Let its salty water cleanse my aura.
Let the grainy sand ground my body.
Let its ebb and flow, help me to go with the flow of Life.

May I be as joyful as the dolphins,
May I follow my inner knowing like the whales,
May I live from a sense of peace like the sea turtles,
May I be connected to the oneness as every drop of water is part of the ocean.

Dear Archangel Muriel,
Please help us preserve the seas and return its healing blessings upon itself.
Help us keep the ocean clear and safe,
For all the beautiful creatures that call her their home.
Let us respect all sea life, from the smallest plankton to the biggest whale.

Awaken my inner mer-being,
So that I may truly be one with nature,
Ever present and balanced, No matter stormy seas, or rocky waters.
All is motion, all is change.
I move with it like flowing water and know that all is well.
And so it is.

July Chapter Sponsor — Cathelijne Filippo

JULY 12
Infinite Blessings

By Rosemary Hurwitz

Dear Angels,
Thank you for being Messengers of God.
Thank you for showing me how to connect to my Divine within.

For my eyes to see
And my ears to hear
And my heart to feel
And my mind to know
And my belly, to receive your precious
and often whispered messages of wisdom,
hope, love, caution, or urgency.

Thank you for your constant healing presence,
and the many ways you teach me balance.
And when I fail to connect with you
when distraction comes between us,
help me to remember I need only breathe into my faith,
that you are here beside me.

When I find myself in the deeper waters of my consciousness,
let me pass through any fear, and know that your messages of truth
will always point me to more love and freedom.

Continue to lead me in guiding others in all I do and say.
Help me to show my family, friends and even strangers by my example
how available to us you always are.
And so it is,
Amen.

July Chapter Sponsor — Cathelijne Filippo

JULY 13
A Prayer for Presence

By Rosemary Boyle Lasher

Dearest Angel Uriel:
Bless this day!

Know I am truly thankful,
awakening from a restful sleep –
refreshed, alert, and alive!

Allow me to deeply appreciate
all the gifts in my life.

Just for today,
help me set aside computers,
cell phones, social media and TV
so I may restore real life connection
with friends, family and co-workers.

Let me find time to be in nature,
even if only for a few precious moments.

Please surround me, guide me,
ground me and protect me.

I now allow myself
to deeply experience
the fullness of this day
with gratitude and love.

JULY 14

Prayer for Releasing Fears and Worries

By Rachel Cooley ATP®

Dear God, angels and archangels,

I call upon you now to please surround me
with your love, light and blessings in this moment.

Please release from me all of my fears, worries and concerns
that do not serve me right now.

Please replace them all with
your healing, love, light, protection and blessings.

Thank you so much,
I am so grateful!

Amen.

JULY 15

Archangel Ariel
Prayer for Pets/Animals

By Lori Siska

Archangel Ariel,
I ask you today to help me love and understand
the wonders of my pets and all the animals of the world.

Help me to help animals wherever they may be
and to speak on their behalf when they are injured or abused.
Please help our world learn to be respectful and kind to beasts of burden
so that both animals and humans can bring service in the spirit of love.

Help us to not judge others' ways of dealing with animals by criticism,
But, instead, by guidance, that animals are beings like us
who deserve the utmost respect and love.

Help the lost find their way home
by shining a beacon of light above their loved ones.
Please give our animals sustenance
when hungry for food, shelter, or love.

I pray that you heal sick animals,
and for those who have chosen their time to leave this world,
that you welcome them into a new world of peace, tranquility, and abundance.

Finally, please bring peace to war-torn areas where animals are often trapped.

I promise to follow the light of your truth,
to love and to live with all animals in peace and love.

July Chapter Sponsor — Cathelijne Filippo

JULY 16
Angels of Grace

By Ann Phillis

I stand in the fire
Of renewing grace,
The grace of life, where all are blessed.

Heal me, nurture me, hold me in your heart,
Angels of grace, of living light.

Your fiery power fills me with hope,
Your burning light clears all that must go.
You renew my being, so I stand anew,
Ready to unfold my spiritual love.

Love for myself, and this Earth my home,
Love for the future I now behold.
I lift my gaze in your fiery embrace,
Now I see, full of grace!

JULY 17

Archangel Michael
Prayer for Healthy Boundaries

By Cathleen O'Connor

Dear Archangel Michael,
Sometimes it is so hard to tell where I begin and end,
and where the boundaries are with those I love.

I need your help and assistance to remind me
that I am responsible for my own happiness and wellbeing;
that this should be my focus – my healing journey;
that it is not my role to try to fix another.

Surround me and my loved ones with your powerful light.
Watch over those I love. Give them a safe harbor in your arms.

Teach me how to hold a compassionate heart;
to allow others their experience, however difficult it may seem.

Remind me that each life flows according to Divine purpose;
that I can surrender my worries and cares to you.

Dear Archangel Michael,
Thank you for offering your protection, your wisdom and your heart.
You call forth the compassionate warrior within me

Embraced within your wings, I have no fear, only faith, trust and love.
And so it is.

July Chapter Sponsor – Cathelijne Filippo

JULY 18
Pray, Heal, Love

By Rev. Vicki Snyder

Ask the angels for their help

Pray

Pray to the angels to assist you in reaching your life goals successfully.
Pray to the angels to watch over and protect you in all you do.
Pray to the angels for insight into your life purpose and to be guided to it.

Heal

Heal your heart and soul of any hurts that interfere
with you giving love and fulfilling your life purpose.
Heal your communication skills
so you may speak your truth in the most authentic way.
Heal your mental, spiritual and physical body of any ailments
that deter you from living the most happiest and joyful life you can.

Love

Love yourself fully, ask the angels to show you what is lovable about you.
Love others with an open heart that is non-judgmental.
Love your environment, your friends and family.
Acknowledge that you cannot change them and accept them as they are.

Through prayer and healing comes the ability to love in a way
that lifts you higher and brings much more love to you.
Let go of the fear that holds you back and embrace the angels
through prayer, healing and love.

July Chapter Sponsor – Cathelijne Filippo

JULY 19
A Shower of Blessings

By Julie Geigle

Archangel Metatron, I call on you now
to help me keep my vibration high throughout the day,
because I know that when I am able to do this
I open up the flow of blessings in my life.

I now move into the art of allowing
and as I embrace anger, frustration, and sadness
I take a moment to be with that feeling by simply pausing,
stopping whatever I am doing and acknowledging the feeling.

I breathe in deeply from the wellspring of love and light,
and as I exhale, I imagine surrounding these feelings of angst
with the healing energy of love.

As I do this, these emotions slowly detach from my physical body
and lose their power over me.
I continue to breathe deeply and completely,
watching these emotions float away, like a balloon,
and dissolve into thin air.

As my vibration returns to its natural state of order, love and forgiveness,
I am showered with blessings untold.

Thank you, Archangel Metatron,
for helping me to remember who I am and why I came here.
By the grace of God it is so.
Thank you. Thank you. Thank you.

JULY 20

A Prayer to Connect to Your Higher Self

By Tracy Quadro

Dear Haniel,
Angel-Goddess of the Spiritual Self,
please connect me with my Higher Being.
Remind me to call upon you when I lose sight
and feeling for my inner knowledge.
Assist me in meditation and raise awareness of my intuition
and the language of my deepest Spirit within.

Please help me to tune out false thoughts, worries, trivial concerns
and unhelpful obsessions and to make a lasting pathway
into the true vision of my Soul's life journey.
Please teach me to believe my feelings,
to trust my instincts and to have the courage
to sing my own personal life-song, even, and especially,
if I'm the only one who hears it.

Sometimes it's difficult to connect with anything beyond the physical realm of the present moment, as we are so bound up in the concerns of the body and what our base senses convey. The trials of our everyday life distract us from what is most important to the nurturing of our souls connection to our higher selves, communication with our Angels and communion with Spirit. As important as it is to keep our bodies functioning, our souls and minds need tender care as well. - Tracy

JULY 21

Archangel Haniel:
Bring Peace to My Heart

By Lilly Wong

Breathe in, breathe out, reach out.
Breathe in, breathe out.
In the name of Love, open up to receive my grace.

I am Archangel Haniel.
I am here and now, with you, in all of you.
I am here to bless you, embrace you,
and above all…
I am here to repeat your name into the Universe,
So your grace will resonate around you,
Inside you… and beyond you.

You are the most beautiful Soul,
You are Heaven on Earth.

Repeat my name Haniel, Haniel, Haniel…
And your Soul will remember who you are,
And you will be filled with peace.

Do you feel me?

I am here with you!

Ana'a Anamaká
(With our heart in connection with the "Pachamama"
Mother Earth in Light Language)

JULY 22

A Prayer to Enjoy What I Already Have

By Kimeiko Rae Vision ATP®, The Angel Warrior™

Dear Angels,
Please help me to genuinely and happily enjoy all of the things in my life that I can be thankful for right now.

Help me to gracefully receive compliments, happy surprises and assistance from eager helpers who truly enjoy what they do!

Please help me to remember that sometimes it is best to *be* the giver and other times it is truly best for all parties involved for *me* to *receive*, and to *accept* being given to.

I am grateful for your support.
Thank you!

July Chapter Sponsor – Cathelijne Filippo

JULY 23
Prayer to Create the Perfect Day

By Elizabeth Harper

Angels, Angels, Angels,
surround me now with your light and love,
help me to be at one with you.
I ask for your protection and guidance.
I ask to draw closer to your divine angelic light,
to align me with the wisdom of my higher self
and to assist me in creating the perfect day.

Support me as I breathe in light, and breathe out
any tension, stress, cares, concerns, or worries I might have,

Support me as I breathe in love, and breathe out
sadness, grief, loss, fear and any emotion
that does not serve me in this moment.

Open my heart and soul as I breathe in
this light and love into every cell of my being.
And as my heart opens, it overflows with
the beautiful, radiant, living light of my soul.
With the help of you my dear angels, my soul and I unite as one.
I give my soul permission to create the perfect day
one that will serve my highest and greatest good.

I am ready, fully present, energized,
and willing to embrace a perfect day.
And so it is.

JULY 24

Archangel Michael ~ Prayer for Loving Energy

By Carolyn McGee

Archangel Michael,
I ask your assistance in removing any and all energy that is not mine
from my heart, mind, body and soul.

I ask for any negative energy, including fear, anxiety, anger, and regret –
anything that is not of love – to be removed from my energetic body.

Fill my energetic body up with the white light of God
and surround me with your blue light of protection.

If anything is directed towards me that is not of love,
from others or myself,
transmute that energy to love and return it to sender
so that we may raise the vibration of the entire world to that of love!

And so it is!

July Chapter Sponsor – Cathelijne Filippo

JULY 25
Be You, Be Love

By Robert Haig Coxon

©2014 Song Lyrics

Be you,
be you,
be love.

Be you,
be me,
see love.

Awake my Light
through love.

For all is well
in love.

JULY 26
Archangel Jophiel

By Trish Grain

Archangel Jophiel,
The Angel of Wisdom.

Please illuminate my mind with inspiration and higher consciousness,
and pour your beautiful golden light into my crown chakra
of a thousand petal lotus.

As I receive your energy,
it flows down to each chakra,
and as it does so my crown chakra opens up
to more of your divine wisdom and illumination,
helping me to spread your wisdom.

Thank you, Archangel Jophiel.

JULY 27
Simply with Love

By Cindy deJong, DSW, ATP®

As I begin or end each and every day,
I take the time to sit, and to pray.
Sometimes I wonder, "Where do I start?"
Then whispered back I hear, "Just listen to your heart."

Inside my heart is what I know to be true.
It starts with two simple words, "Thank-you"

I send up my prayers; they are always heard -
every thought, every whisper, each and every word.
When I get quiet, I can clearly hear,
a beautiful message, often starting with, "My Dear..."

My heart opens wide. I feel guided from above.
Because the angels are near, embracing me with love.

JULY 28
Prayer for Love

By Rev. Jennifer Shackford

God and Angels,
I ask that you fill my life with loving relationships, including with myself.

Allow me to walk MY path, beat to the rhythm
of my OWN drum easily and effortlessly.
Allow me to see the beauty within myself, my mind, body and my spirit.

I am open to guidance!
I am open to achieving my highest and best for myself!
I am open to happiness!

And So It Is!

JULY 29
Leaning Into You

By Jodi Chapman

Dearest Angels,
Please help me lean into your love, your light,
your strength, your wisdom.

Please help me remember
that I don't have to do this whole life thing on my own,
that I don't have to struggle to the point where I am exhausted
and push to the point where I break.
Please remind me that I can always lean into you,
and we'll walk through each moment together.

Please be the tree that I can lean against,
the ground that I can stand upon,
and the rock that can support me when I need to rest.

Please be the hand that holds my own
and guides me into the light on even the darkest days.

Please help me surrender and be able to trust — really trust —
with every ounce of my being that you are already beside me
lifting me up and surrounding me with your love.

And if my faith ever wavers,
please help me remember that you've never left
and that I can always lean right back into your love.
I'm leaning in, and I can feel you waiting with open arms.
Thank you for that.

July Chapter Sponsor — Cathelijne Filippo

JULY 30
A Prayer for Animals

By Marla Steele

We are united in spirit,
under the auspice of the angelic kingdom,
sending peace, love and protection to all animals on our planet.

We call on Archangel Raphael to assist any animals with
special needs and we observe their perfection now.
We ask Archangel Michael to safely guide any lost or missing
pets back into the loving arms of their families and friends.
With Archangel Chamuel's peaceful presence,
we see the animals passing on to the next leg of their journey,
doing so blissfully and gently.

We give thanks that Mother Mary looks
after our animal welfare organizations
and all of the souls working to provide nurturing,
life-long homes for surrendered pets.

We enjoy seeing our wildlife thrive, living in healthy, balanced ecosystems
with the abundant blessings of Archangel Ariel and the nature spirits.

We are forever grateful to God for gifting us
with these sacred beings of pure, unconditional love.
We give thanks to St. Francis that our hearts, minds and ears
are open to their intuitive whispers and that we may
continue to honor them in the highest and best ways.

We are open and receptive.
We welcome any miracles with a grateful heart.

July Chapter Sponsor – Cathelijne Filippo

JULY 31
Invocation of the Archangels

By Sunny Dawn Johnston

I invoke the blue light of Archangel Michael
to surround and protect me.
I ask him to bring me courage and strength
and to protect me from any negativity, seen or unseen.
I ask that the brilliant blue energy of protection is placed over me
allowing only that which is for my highest good.

I now invoke the white light of Archangel Gabriel
to envelope me in his energy of purity and peace.
I ask that he helps me to communicate with intention,
that which is in my heart,
through my words, thoughts and feelings of light and love.

I now invoke the golden red energy of Archangel Uriel
to fill me with wisdom, clarity and vision.
Help me to soothe all conflict in my life
and replace it with knowledge and understanding of the bigger picture.
I ask that Uriel help me make choices
that are the wisest for my personal journey.

In closing, I invoke the green light of Archangel Raphael
to pour health and well-being into my bodies;
physical, mental, emotional and spiritual.
Help me to allow the healing to be received wholeheartedly
and guide me to my own natural healing abilities.
Thank you and so it is!

July Chapter Sponsor – Cathelijne Filippo

AUGUST
Touched by the Angels
Rev. Vicki Snyder

I am an angel messenger who came to work with the angels in a very simple way. This was not something I planned to do. The angels chose me. I have no huge tale to tell of impending tragedy, of seeing angels or being saved. My narrative is no different from many others who have stumbled into becoming an angel messenger. Therefore, my story is to inspire you, to let you know that you don't have to experience a major life event to begin working with the angels. You don't have to be "special!" My story, I hope, will help you reflect and jog your memory of how the angels have touched your life.

Looking back on my childhood, there was no discussion of angels in my Catholic family. I just believed and knew they existed, that they were there for me whenever I needed them to be. I always felt they were looking over me. When I closed my eyes I would see grayish black shadows move; they grew larger then smaller, it was like shadow dancing. It wasn't until a few years ago that I realized I was seeing angels and this is how they appeared to me. I have always listened to the voice inside that says, "don't go there" or "do this." At times this angelic voice has been louder and easier to hear. For instance, in High School I was in a car with a boyfriend. He was speeding and I was fearful, but I heard the angels tell me "don't worry, you will not die in a car accident." At the time I did not know where this voice inside me came from, but I knew it was very important.

Do you see or hear angels?

Several years ago, the angels guided me to my first angel card deck. However, this deck did not resonate – this may have happened to you too – but it didn't deter me. I was guided instead to another deck and that one allowed me to see, think, and feel each card. It heightened my intuition. I was guided through opportunities just presenting themselves to do angel card readings. This allowed the angels to speak through me and is an example of angel synchronicities, of being guided by the angels.

Are you paying attention to the coincidences in your own life?

One day, while offering readings at a local metaphysical shop, I felt totally invisible, like no one saw me. Even though there were many people in the area I hadn't done any readings and was feeling a little down about the lack of work. I tuned in to get a sense of what was happening. It was then that I realized Archangel Michael, the Angel of Protection had placed a protective dome over me shielding me from the harsh energy present that day. It was an amazing experience for which I was very grateful. I thanked him for having my back and keeping me safe.

Are there instances when the angels have helped, supported and guided you?

Angelic guidance manifests in healing sessions too. After I became more comfortable doing angel card readings, the angels led me to Integrated Energy Therapy (IET), a healing technique that focuses on channeling angelic energy. This opened me up to a new way of working with the angels. Clients reported feeling numerous hands working on them during healing, when really it's only been mine. This is the angels at work. We act together in unison and it is a beautiful gift to serve side by side with the angels.

Do you feel the presence of angels when healing or receiving healing?

In April 2014, I decided to rent my first private office. I was guided to the perfect place and on the day I said "Yes" I was blessed to actually hear the wings of an angel loudly fluttering directly next to me. At first this took me by surprise until I realized what I was hearing. I felt the love of my angels and knew that I was fully supported in this next big step.

Can you sense the vibration of your angel's wings?

So please, take my story and allow it to bring you memories of your own angel interactions, of how they have assisted and urged you to take your next big step. I hope that you can see when the angels have simply touched you too and I trust that you have followed their guidance.

Rev. Vicki Snyder is certified as a Medium, Angel Card Reader, Realm Reader and Spiritual Healer. She is also an Integrated Energy Therapy Practitioner, Reiki Master/ Teacher and Ordained Interfaith Minister with a degree in psychology. Vicki is a member of the Lily Dale Assembly, a well-known 1880's spiritualist community, and as a practicing medium and spiritualist is affiliated with the Mother Church of Spiritualism and Plymouth Spiritualist Church in Rochester, NY.

In her private practice in Pittsford, NY she supports and partners with clients, guiding them to discover and realize their true authentic selves. She offers a variety of services such as spiritual counseling, private readings, parties, message circles, and pet communication, and also participates in local psychic and wellness fairs.

Vicki is a lifelong learner who always searches for new information and skills to share with her clients and students. She teaches classes in healing, mediumship, and Angel Card Reading and facilitates monthly angel card reading practice groups. Vicki's goal is to offer uplifting and empowering messages to her clients so they may find peace in life and reach their personal goals. No matter where you are in the world you can receive her free weekly angel messages on her Facebook page, Divine Angel Messages. http://vickisnyder.webs.com

AUGUST 1
The Four Angel Agreements

By Rev. Vicki Snyder

Call on these four Archangels for help living the four agreements.

Uriel,
I call on you to help me <u>do the right thing</u>,
to admit mistakes,
and guide me to try to do better next time.

Michael,
I call on you to help me to <u>be courageous</u>
and to let go of negativity.
I ask you to use your sword
to remove negativity from me
so I may succeed with this task.
I call on you to protect me as I live my life.

Raphael,
I call on you to help me to be <u>compassionate</u>
towards all creatures on Earth and to help them in any way I can.
Let my healing light shine on all creatures and planets.
Allow this healing light to shine so brightly
that all will be healed from its light.
Help me to be loving and kind and be a role model for others around me.

Gabriel,
I call on you to help me to <u>provide uplifting messages</u>
to all I come across and to leave them better than I found them.
I ask for help to provide the words to offer encouragement to all.

August Chapter Sponsor – Rev. Vicki Snyder

AUGUST 2
Lugnasadh Prayer

By Cathelijne Filippo

Beloved Archangel Sachiel,
Angel of the grain harvest and abundance,

Bless me with your energy of deep blue and purple,
casting your golden glow around me,
as I enjoy the first harvest of summer,
and the fullness of nature's bounty.

As I reflect on the warmth of these last days of summer,
and the abundance of nature at this time,
let me, too, appreciate the abundance in my life,
now that I harvest the fruits of my labours and spiritual work.

Dear Sachiel,
Please let me share my abundance and learning with others,
as I reach up towards the sky,
like a well-rooted tree reaches its branches up to heaven.
Help me to soar high as I attune to the energy of my soul and angels,
bringing this blessed energy of light into all that I do, think and say.

Let me now reap, what I have sown,
enjoying the blessings that come with it,
and learn from the challenges that have led me to where I am now,
on my sacred path in life.

So be it.

August Chapter Sponsor – Rev. Vicki Snyder

AUGUST 3
Awake and Present

By Daniel Hyman

Today I am awake;
I am strong, powerful, fully focused
and aligned with my mind, heart, body and soul.
I am free of all the judgment and pressure from myself and from others.
I am empowered to be in this present moment,
as I know it's this present moment that is the catalyst, creator,
and source for all future present moments.

It is my goal and destiny to live and be in this present moment,
which will open my heart to its true desires by being one
and connected to all things around me, teaching me,
and helping me remember my next steps in my path
to my next moment in my next present moment.

I am aligned in my mind, my body, my heart, and soul with my focus.
It is my focus to be happy and fulfilled, healthy and aligned,
all in the present moment.

I do not need to think of my wishes,
as my true wishes are already within my heart,
and my heart will guide me in the direction so long as
I choose to see the path clearly by choosing to live and be
in the present and in the now.

August Chapter Sponsor – Rev. Vicki Snyder

AUGUST 4
Angel Prayers for Animal Companions

By Karri Ann Gromowski

Dedicated to Shiana

Guardian Angels, Archangel Michael's Protection,
Enfold (Animal's Name) within the safety and comfort of your wings
Surround her/him with your Indigo Blue Cloak of Protection,
infuse Confidence, Perseverance, and Clarity of Communion,
strengthen their Spirit, Enlighten their Soul, forevermore.

Archangel Raphael's Healing,
Enfold (Animal's name) in your loving embrace.
Infuse each cell with Emerald Green Healing Energy
and Violet Transmuting Flame to Align complete and perfect health,
unconditional love and happiness.
Guide my actions to support her/him,
knowing God's healing energy makes
(Animal's name) safe, whole and well, now and for eternity.

Transition Prayer: Archangels Michael, Raphael, Azrael, and Raziel,
Fold your wings around my Earth Angel, (Animal's Name),
keeping her/him safe and protected.
Uplift and Release this beautiful Spirit from this earthly sojourn.
Infuse (Animal's Name) with Crystalline Rainbow Light Energy.
Illuminate this eternal journey enabling her/his Soul to fly freely home,
trusting the Rainbows of our Souls will intertwine throughout time,
meeting again at Rainbow Bridge, together once more.
And So It Shall Be.

August Chapter Sponsor – Rev. Vicki Snyder

AUGUST 5
Stay in Tune with ALL

By Lisa Clayton

Listen, and stay in tune with love melodies in your heart each day.
Be happy and joyous in listening to your heart with complete gratitude.
There are no mountains high enough that you cannot climb
as your faith in our love gives you strong wings to soar.

Your connection with and belief in Angels changes your life daily …
physically, mentally, emotionally, and spiritually …
as you open your heart to receive Divine Love and guidance.

Rejoice!!
Love from our Angel hearts is coming to you, like a swollen river,
overflowing its banks to water your heart seeds
and soul with faithful promise
to provide glorious passageways for your journey on earth.

Abundance flows in our river of love and creates a multitude of miracles.
Your Spirit Guides, Ascended Masters, Loved Ones in Light Form
collaborate and commune with us each day in pure love devotion;
sharing a common mission to reveal your soul's song and purpose.

Stay in tune with ALL of us.
Stay in your heart light. Stay in your Truth.
Stay in your Divine Feminine and Magnificent Masculine,
aligned by your Higher Self.

Miracles evolve naturally when you stay in tune to ALL
and give gratitude for our guidance, love and messages.

August Chapter Sponsor — Rev. Vicki Snyder

AUGUST 6
Focus

By Lisa K.

Time to take a break!

It's a good time to pause and think through how you spend your day.

What things are you filling your day with?

Many times you spend your time on useless things,
which don't allow you to reach your goals.

So focus on your path, your passion and your dream.

Don't stray from your focus.

Then let us do the rest to help you get there!

– Your Angels

August Chapter Sponsor – Rev. Vicki Snyder

AUGUST 7
May Peace and Harmony Reign

By Bobbe Bramson

Beloved Angels Kaeylarae and Charmiene,
May peace and harmony reign …ascendant throughout my being.
Make my mind to be like the moon's reflection
on a still and azure sea, shining and serene.

Imbue my heart with tranquil bliss, sweet as the sacred bees' honey.
Harmonize me with angelic grace and intertwine my heart and mind
as the dearest and most faithful of lovers.

From within this perfect union
let me shine with such radiant incandescence
that all who come in contact with me
may find themselves sighing in relief for no reason,
slowing down and seeing the beauty around them,
feeling a moment of inexplicable but welcome contentment.

And in *that* moment of magical reconnection
may seeds of Light be planted within them that grow and blossom
so that they, too, become beacons to all they meet,
and then through angelic miracles,
let the pattern repeat, irresistibly rippling outwards to countless others.

And so on and so forth,
touching every sentient being straight through to the heart of Gaia
until we are all joined together in a brilliant network
of Light, Love, Peace, and Harmony.
May my prayer be heard and its vision granted.
Thank you.

August Chapter Sponsor — Rev. Vicki Snyder

AUGUST 8
My Daughter, My Angel

By Dianna Vagianos Armentrout

My angel grew inside me until my womb swelled and my body opened.
Then she surrounded me with wings and love.
My daughter, Mary Rose, lived one sacred hour.
I held her in my arms and had to let her go.

Why am I still here a month later
when my body is heavy with grief and milk?
How do I answer the question "How many children do you have?"
Dead babies and miscarriages are taboo in our society
where positive thinking cures all.

But this angel…
Her energy is with me. I carry my daughter in my heart.

Mary Rose's portrait was painted months ago.
In the painting I hold my pregnant belly
and the angel holds me from behind.
Her wings are my sanctuary.
Prints of *Healing Companion* comfort mothers with infant losses.

Now I write to heal myself and others.
We women need each other to survive and bless this planet-in-transition.
We are standing on stepping stones to higher consciousness.
My heart is shattered and open.
I will not hide my third-eye sight and intuition any more.

Mary Rose, bless us.
Thank you for sending roses and feathers as you illuminate our path.

August Chapter Sponsor – Rev. Vicki Snyder

AUGUST 9
Archangel Gabriel, Prayer for Writing

By Shelly Orr

Archangel Gabriel,

I thank you for giving me the courage
to be vulnerable in speaking my truth.

Thank you for helping me to open my heart and share my words
so that they may be of service to others who resonate with my journey.

Please continue to grant me the courage and willingness to be a truth teller.
Please help me to stay motivated and focused as I write.

Help me to stay in my heart so that I may clearly sense
which writing opportunities are for my highest and best good.

And so it is!

August Chapter Sponsor – Rev. Vicki Snyder

AUGUST 10
Angel Prayer for Tranquility

By Suzanne Gochenouer

Dear Angels,

Help me find tranquility in my life
and to bring it into the lives of everyone I meet.

Inspire in me a deep relaxation
and a permanent peace that molds my life.

Show me ways to make my path smoother,
easing into each day with joy,
and ending each day
with the satisfaction of soul fulfillment.

Guide me to find the time and resources
to care for my physical, mental, and emotional bodies
so I am renewed each day in peace and joy.

Help me see the tiny moments within the busy rush of life
in which I can find solace.

Share with me a deep tranquility and relaxation,
especially in times of stress and need,
until these blessings become a part of every moment of my life.

Amen, Amen, Amen.

Thank you, thank you, thank you.

August Chapter Sponsor – Rev. Vicki Snyder

AUGUST 11
Prayer to Support Creativity

By Elizabeth Harper

Dearest Angel of Creative Expression,

Help my creative ideas and thoughts to flow easily and effortlessly.
Give me the confidence to express my creativity
both willingly and fearlessly.
Guide me to move beyond old limitations,
to lovingly accept my creative work as an expression of the Divine,
to love and approve of myself for who I am now,
and to know that it is safe to share my heart with others
now and forever.

When I accept myself as a creative being, I allow others
to appreciate and respect what I have to offer.
No person, place, or thing has any power over me.
I am free to be the creative genius I came to be.

Every day I create a joyful, peaceful world to live in,
one where I am free to express my creativity in a myriad of ways.
I am the creative power in my world

Thank you for providing me with everything I need
to live my life creatively.
And so it is.

AUGUST 12
A Prayer for Strength and Courage

By Tracy Quadro

Michael, you are the ultimate Warrior Angel!
Your righteousness is boundless,
your protection all-encompassing,
your strength unyielding, your presence eternal.
When my strength fails, when my Spirit flags,
when my isolation is profound,
please come to my aid.

Remind me that turning to you will bring
an instant unseen army of warriors to my doorstep.
Your sword is at my command,
your swift might my shield and fortress.
Open my heart and steel my soul.
Make me an earthly Warrior Angel in your company,
to conquer my fears and erase my hesitation.
Induct me into your legion of strength.

Michael, my Captain,
please empower me and make me feel invincible!

To whom do we turn when the whole world seems against us? When silence envelops us and leaves us feeling as though we are completely and utterly alone? When we feel as though our friends and family have problems and struggles of their own, and we are left to fend for ourselves? To the Angels, of course! And the mightiest of Angels, the Universe's personal "muscle" is always within calling distance when we need the extra shot of strength and courage during our darkest and loneliest of times.

August Chapter Sponsor – Rev. Vicki Snyder

AUGUST 13
A Prayer for I Am Enough

By Julie Geigle

Angels, Angels, Angels Everywhere

Enfold me in your wings of love,
lift me up and cut off this despair of pain and torment.
Surround me with lightness and ease,
Allow my burdens to be shed, one by one.
Reveal to me the divine truth of love,
so that I may be transformed and resurrected into my most High Self.

Empower me with courage and confidence
to make permanent, lasting changes in my life.
As I align with love, I fully embrace and step into my truth…
That I am not small, or weak, or not good enough,
But that I am bold and strong and more than I ever imagined I could be.

I am powerful beyond measure.
I am greatness personified.
I am good enough.
I am blessed
I AM

Thank you, Archangel Metatron,
for helping me to remember who I am and why I came here.
By the grace of God it is so.
Thank you. Thank you. Thank you.

August Chapter Sponsor – Rev. Vicki Snyder

AUGUST 14
Guardian Angel Prayer for Guidance

By Michelle Mullady

Angel of God, guardian dear,
I call upon your presence here.
Encompass me in your circle of perfect light.
Envelop me in your protective wings.
Drive me from every temptation and danger
as you surround me with your loving care.

Be a bright flame before me,
a glittering whirl of starlight above me,
a smooth path below me,
and a kindly escort behind me.
Today, tonight, and forever
lead me towards the Great Bright Spirit of eternity,
filling my awareness with our oneness.

May everything I think, say, feel and do begin with you,
continue with your help, and be done under your guidance.
May I grow in love and service.
May the goodness and miracles of heaven
pursue me along my journey all the days of my life.

* As you say this prayer, focus on your heart center and concentrate on breathing through the heart. Through rhythmic breathing, find the point of peace within, where all is calm and tranquil. Your guardian angel's sacred mission is to watch over, guide, and nurture you throughout the various stages of your life. They're always available to assist you; all you need to do is ask through the heart.

August Chapter Sponsor – Rev. Vicki Snyder

AUGUST 15
Mary, Queen of the Angels

By Trish Grain

Dear Mother Mary,
Enfold me in your soft cloak of pale blue light
and help heal and nurture my inner child
to feel safe and loved.

I know you will help me
to know that my situation will be guided to a fair outcome.

I trust and believe in goodness.

You are the divine, feminine energy
of balance, compassion, empathy and grace.

Please send your loving energy
to all places that are in conflict,
so that there can be peace.

AUGUST 16

Prayer for the Embodiment of Divine Love

By Marci Cagen

Oh, Great Spirit of many names, light a candle inside my heart
Use me. Be me. Free me.
That I may see you and the world in a new and purified way
Use me. Be me. Free me.
Please reveal yourself to me in ways that I will easily understand and trust.
Use me. Be me. Free me.
Clear away the debris of judgment
and fear that blocks me from receiving your light.
Use me. Be me. Free me.
Guide me as I spread your sacred light to others.
Use me. Be me. Free me.
May I be an instrument of peace,
so that I might bring love, light, serenity and awareness to all.
Use me. Be me. Free me.
May I be hollow like the flute,
and You, the life-giving breath that brings sweet melodies
to all those that seek to hear your loving tune,
and, especially those that don't.
Use me. Be me. Free me.
May I dance upon angels' wings
and always remember from whence I have come.
Use me. Be me. Free me.
So that I may be a reminder to all those around me
of your everlasting divine love

Use me. Be me. Free me.

August Chapter Sponsor — Rev. Vicki Snyder

AUGUST 17
Prayer for Healthy Eating

By Rev. Jennifer Shackford

Archangel Raphael,

please heal any unhealthy emotional relationships I have with food
and replace it with love.
Love for myself and love for my body.

Help me to fuel my body with healthy food for energy
and nourishment of my body.
Help me to cherish the vessel of my body.

Thank you, Archangel Raphael, for your love and support!

AUGUST 18

Healing Prayer –
'Re-connect to the Flow of Life'

By Gina Barbara

There is a river flowing to the sun;
although, with my struggles,
my life feels numb.

I pray to the Angels from above:
connect me again to the river of love
where the sun will glow upon my heart
and my spirit will show
that it isn't the END. . .
it's just the START.

I ask your blessing and protection, knowing that
as you guide me through the river flow,
with your love,
peace again my Life will know!

August Chapter Sponsor – Rev. Vicki Snyder

AUGUST 19

Healing from Archangel Raphael:
5th Ray Attunement

By Lisa Nicole Davis

Please, use this awareness tool as you see fit.
It is my gift to those who find themselves in this book, at this time.

The Emerald Green Ray of healing for your planet
runs through me, we are one.
My offering is to run this ray of healing through you,
only if you choose to accept.
If you are ready to move forward in your own healing,
I am here to support.

When you are ready: Sit quietly; breathe and relax
There you are, waiting ever so patiently. I see you.
Continue breathing. I am here, above you.

I begin to float down dropping in like a skydiver,
face-to-face, nose-to-nose,
gazing in your sparkling gemstone eyes.
With a smile, I admire your beauty and shine.
I adore you.

I ever so gently take your hands
and place them palms up, ready to receive.
Then, with my hands, beaming of brilliant green energy,
I infuse the Divine emerald rays into you,
through your hands, and so it is.
You are now able to call upon the 5th Ray for service to others,
and most importantly, service to self.
With a grin, wink and kiss on the check, our date is complete.

AUGUST 20
Mother's Angels

By Ann Phillis

I stare into the blue,
The deep, deep blue.
Into Mother's ocean
Of love and truth.

I fill my being,
Immersed in the new.
My courage uplifted,
I step forth, renewed.

I open my eyes
And see the love.
I listen to the whispers
Of everlasting grace.

I awaken my heart
To this love supernal.
And Mother's angels
Hold me, eternal.

August Chapter Sponsor – Rev. Vicki Snyder

AUGUST 21
Archangel Prayer for Animal Protection

By Tracy Una Wagner

Dear Archangel Ariel,

Please keep all
the woodland creatures,
the friends of the forest,
the animals of the wild
in the wild, the forest, the woods,
the grass, the brush, the trees,
the fields, and the streams.

Please help them understand that they have
shelter, food, and water,
friends, and family,
and that they
are safe and secure in those locations.

Thank you.

Amen, and So It Is.

AUGUST 22
Prayer for Healing, Protection, and Love

By Amber Lee Scott

Supreme Power, Divine Creator, ONE we call God.
Send your angels to surround me,
my home, my family, my friends.

We require your love; We require your light
Burn out the darkness with your flame of life.

Engulf us in feathery soft wings.
Calm our hearts. Strengthen our wills.
Let us see the TRUTH.
Let us live the TRUTH.
Let us BE the TRUTH.

Heal us, so we may see Wholeness,
Holyness, and LOVE from within.
I ask for your healing, protection, and
love for the Highest Good of ALL.

Amen.
And so it is!
Thank you!

I wrote this prayer while supporting my husband through his chemo, surgery, and healing from a rare form of abdominal cancer. I continue to pray for his recovery and the healing, protection, and love of my family and friends. May you also be surrounded by the love and light of the Divine. And may you always remember to call on your angels. Blessings - Amber.

August Chapter Sponsor – Rev. Vicki Snyder

AUGUST 23
Angels, Surround Me

By Noelle Goggin

Angels, can I hear your voices?
Guide me when I'm making choices
Gently whisper what is next so I know I'll do my best

Angels, can I see you here?
When I make my intention clear
Give me messages and signs each day
Synchronicities that are the soul's play

Angels, can you hold my hand?
When I'm down and feeling sad
Help me trust and give me courage
Keep me connected to my purpose

Angels, I know that you're there
lovingly supporting through the years
I thank you for the miracles you bring
and everything that makes my soul sing

Angels, whom I know by name
Helping me in this funny 'ol life game
Gone before me, why?
We don't know; Surviving and some more - we grow

Angels, who's helping me with my desire?
To live my life purpose and just fly higher?
Help me use my inner wisdom as I play in God's glorious kingdom

August Chapter Sponsor – Rev. Vicki Snyder

AUGUST 24

Reconnecting Through Archangel Metatron

By Michelle McDonald Vlastnik

I call out to you, Archangel Metatron,
Holder of the Keys, Flower of Life,
and Overseer of the energy grids of the Universe.
I ask that you work with me, reset and realign me to my True frequency.
Please raise my vibration so I may become my True Light Self.

I see your energy flowing in a never-ending figure 8.
May it flow through me, entering my heart center,
infuse in me focus and surround me on this journey.

I am ready to access my ancient wisdom
that has been seeded into me at SOUL level.
I embrace my expansion.
I Believe. I Trust. I Surrender. I Reconnect with ALL.

I breathe in the Light of Love;
come into me and use me as a Light onto my fellowman.
May my Light shine brightly, for I am a part of the Conscious Shift,
helping Mother Earth and all of her children.

I proclaim:
I now breathe with the Universal Oneness Breath.
I See with Love. I Hear with Love. I Do with Love.

Please keep my heart pure and may I always come from a place of Love.
So it is. Thank you. Amen.

August Chapter Sponsor – Rev. Vicki Snyder

AUGUST 25
A Special Angel

By Maria Gillard

Thank you for my childhood, for my laughing heart and soul
for all your magic, and for being bold
Thank you for being my mom's best friend
and loving me no matter what state I was in

Thanks for chives and roses, popcorn and TV
Thanks for always letting me be me
Thanks for rides to swim meets and yummy chocolate cake
Thanks for being strong and true when my heart was aching

Thank you for the blankets and pillow for my head
Thank you for the back hill and the Westside River bed
Thank you for the smell of melting butter on the stove
Thank you for the nickels you gave me for the store

You were a special angel sent to all of us
with your disguise of freckles, kisses, hugs and guts
We know you're out there somewhere and you'll stay inside our dreams
We know wherever you are there's a brilliant golden beam

Watch over us, dear angel, as you go on your way
and we will laugh and sing and dance again someday

Amen

August Chapter Sponsor – Rev. Vicki Snyder

AUGUST 26
Angelic Attunement Prayer

By Sandy Turkington

Oh, divine spirit,
through your grace,
I call upon Michael, Raphael, Gabriel, Uriel and Metatron.
Please bring their heavenly love and light to me now.

Bless, guide, and protect me from the North, South, East and West.
Strengthen my body, mind, and spirit, clearing all my chakras and energy.

Fill me with love, strength, and a deeper connection to the Divine.
Fill your light with my being with thee Holy Spirit.

Oh most beautiful angels, I thank you for sharing all your love and joy with me,
for your protection, guidance and love,
for connecting me closer to spirit,
and for keeping me and my loved ones safe.

Please continue to guide, guard, protect
and bless us, as we continue our journey.

And so it is!

AUGUST 27
Daily Prayer to the Angels in the Four Directions

By Virginia Pasternak

Dear Angels of the South, West, North, and East,
I welcome you into my day.
Protect me with your magnificent wings and songs of healing.

Angels of the South, home of warm soft breezes,
I hear your tinkling song and your laughing voices.
Thank you for warmth and joy in my heart.
I honor you with laughter today.

Angels of the West, where waters flow wide and deep,
I hear your gurgling song, your whispering voice.
Thank you for the gift of flow through my body,
the wisdom of my emotions, and the honoring of mystery.
I honor you with movement today.

Angels of the North, where my ancestors live,
I hear your murmuring voices in rocks, earth, and trees.
Thank you for solidity and self-knowledge, the gift of life on this earth.
I honor you with cleanliness today.

Angels of the East, place of light and miracles,
I hear your sonorous voices, your joyful song!
Thank you for clarity and insight,
for the piercing of illusion, and illumination of truth!
I honor you with my words and voice today.
With thanks and in beauty.
Amen. Amen. Amen!

August Chapter Sponsor – Rev. Vicki Snyder

AUGUST 28
Angel Prayer to Connect with Nature

By Amber Reifsteck

Nature Angels gather near
Fill my heart with joy and cheer
Dread and fear transmute away
Negativity send gone, to stay

Nature Angels help me feel
The power nature has to heal
The magic of a running brook
To replenish energy that was took

Nature Angels let me hear
Nature's power loud and clear
The calming wind to cleanse my soul
The singing of birds to make me whole

Nature Angels sit with me
Show me the magic in a tree
Fill my body with sunshine's love
And feel the warmth of the one above

Nature Angels show me the way
To gather strength in the everyday
Teach me to feel nature's force
Reconnect me with the source

August Chapter Sponsor — Rev. Vicki Snyder

AUGUST 29
To Surround Myself with Greatness
The Divine Armor

By Kimeiko Rae Vision ATP®, The Angel Warrior™

Dear Archangels, Please surround me.
Stand *all around me.*
Please stand beneath me *to lift me up!*
Please stand above me *to help me stay grounded.*
Angels, please help me to know that my true connection to God
is firmly planted within me and that this connection
is my infallible resource to stay *centered and determined.*

Angels, I count on you to stand by my side always.
Angels, please stand on my right side,
whispering encouragements of my greatness,
so that I may confidently make decisions,
take action and *go where I need to go!*
Angels, please stand to my left side and encourage me to whisper back!
Remind me of my innate ability to gracefully receive with joy
and *stand my ground like the Royal Figure that I am.*

With all of God's divine love and your angelic presence surrounding me,
I feel I am dressed in the divine armor of love and light,
and I am willing to walk in faith with my Angelic Royal Procession.
Thank you for helping me to commune with my Highest Self and with God.
Thank you for illuminating my True North.
I am grateful. I am energized. I am in great company.
Amen.

August Chapter Sponsor – Rev. Vicki Snyder

AUGUST 30
Truth Serum Prayer

By Tamika Schilbe

Dear Angels,
I trust in the light of my personal truth.
I honor my emotions,
listen to their messages,
and acknowledge them as guideposts to truth.

I am gentle with myself.
I listen deeply and honor the truth of others.
I speak with confidence,
not over or under exaggerating my truth.

When I veer off my true path,
I am guided back swiftly, gently and safely.
When truth's fire burns away what no longer serves me,
I call on my courage to guide me.

I share my truth where it is needed,
in the most loving way possible,
for the good of all Beings.
My truth is like the mountain, solid and strong.
It is also like the river, flowing and free.

I speak the truth, hear the truth,
and entrust in its wisdom now.
And so it is.

Thank you Angels for listening.

August Chapter Sponsor – Rev. Vicki Snyder

AUGUST 31
We Call on the Divine

By Sunny Dawn Johnston

We call on the Divine, the Angels and Archangel Azrael
to surround and comfort us in the everlasting white light
as we know that our loved one is now home.
We ask that you help us to heal… our hearts, minds and souls.
We ask that you lift our hearts above this heaviness
and help us to see and feel our loved ones bright light surrounding us.
Please help us to release our emotional pain so that
we may be released from the heartache and be open to the blessings
that can come through these changes in our lives.

We ask that you infuse our spiritual connection with healing loving energy
so that we may communicate with our loved one clearly.
So that we may feel their gentle spirit, see their beautiful face,
hear their voice and dream about them in our sleepless nights.
We know that they are nearby, watching over us,
and guiding us with patience and unconditional love.

As we move through our own pain, in our own way, let us be reminded
of how precious life really is…to appreciate each moment,
and to give thanks for our yesterdays and tomorrows,
but most importantly, our PRESENT moment.
Please help us to remember that our loved one is now home, free,
and dancing in the light! We thank you for lifting our thoughts
of pain and anguish to those of faith and trust.

In gratitude and appreciation, Amen

August Chapter Sponsor — Rev. Vicki Snyder

SEPTEMBER
Beyond Imagination:
The Signs of Light
Gina Barbara

Amongst the beautiful roses in the garden where I grew up, wafted the aroma of fresh produce cooking in the kitchen. A bright child blessed the butterflies with song. All the comforts of home promised me an idyllic childhood. It was not to be that simple.

I was to be both buoyed and bullied by an exceptional ability to feel when people were in silent emotional states. I felt compelled to take their hurts away. I found myself devoutly praying in the church pews. My family only went there for token visits as they struggled to survive in the corporeal world of their market garden.

When I was 6, I felt an immense need to pray to Angelo Di Dio (Angels of God) despite not knowing what the words even meant. Something about the *tune* of these words made me feel safe beyond measure. In this safety, the walls and ceiling of the church expanded into the skies. I remember my eyes suddenly turning toward an angel in the lead light window and warmth filled me.

This was the first moment of consciously meeting the angel - i*n my innocence and desperation, in came the spirit.*

That night when I went to bed, I called upon Angelo Di Dio to help everyone in their suffering. This practice became a normal part of my early life. As I grew older circumstances affected this connection. My safety became sourced from the shadow, no longer the light. Like many children I too found myself without someone to offer meaning, guidance and emotional support for these unusual experiences. Dread started to build as the sensitivity to these non-acknowledged feelings grew.

One day in church when my year-6 teacher was with us, I remember getting that dread feeling. I knew she was ill with a disease. The fear was unbearable. A month later, we were told that Mrs Duffy had cancer. We were asked to pray for her in our morning prayers, and to my knowledge she was a survivor. I grew very scared of these feelings and the accompanying dreams. I began to resist my connection to Angelo Di Dio. Looking back I can make sense of why this was the time I began excessively eating. I became an overweight child, diminishing my childhood joy and confidence greatly

My dad suffered a stroke when I was 15 years old. Around the same time I started to receive visits from imaginary figures. One I remember in particular was a massive man bandaged and mummified from head to toe. He was always silent. In later years I have come to understand that this was a figure reflecting my voicelessness. In this place of confusion and fear a growing sense of "shameful-weirdness" developed.

Even though I had stopped myself thinking about Angelo Di Dio, and would eat over my feelings, an increasing number of imaginary friends accompanied me in my dark places. As much as I resisted, they were still there. I tried to keep the fear at bay with bouts of bingeing and dieting. Other than my sister, I didn't dare tell anyone about my dream warnings. Two days before my dad would have a fit, my grandmother would visit in my dreams. My sister and I shared this trauma.

I made a decision to stop the pain and halved my size in a matter of weeks. This set in motion a vicious cycle of ill health that was to endure. Though I largely rejected the part of me that was connected to spirit, relentlessly it knocked on my door for self-realization. I gradually began to realize the signs of my light.

The courage to know that what I was feeling was real came after many years of research. I journeyed through self-help, experience, and study. With the love and support of a special guide Nicola, the reconnection to spirit has grown strong and has rarely left me since.

My prayers, dreams, and "the young girl's experiences in the church" came to have extraordinary meanings for me. My visitations from imaginary friends, premonitions, and my spiritual figures such as Angelo Di Dio became my evolutionary guides. My growing 'acceptance to self' transformed my appreciation of this communion with angels. I now love and nurture that little lost scared girl and I no longer fear the connection to Angelo Di Dio. Spirit and the angels are here constantly supporting each and every one of us on this sacred beautiful journey of life.

Gina Barbara is a passionate soul adventurer, an artist of the word and symbol, a lover of wisdom and student of life. Over the years, her commitment to growth and understanding has prompted her to participate in many evolutionary modalities involving the mind, body, and spirit, including Transpersonal Coaching, Holistic Counseling, Color Therapy, Crystal Healing, and EFT.

Gina is committed to embodying, sharing, and inspiring others to live their Brilliance Beyond Measure.

Gina offers a unique coaching and energetic healing style to motivated clients wishing to flourish in authentic lives; and to nurture and nourish themselves, others and the planet.

"I continue at the age of 48 to discover many more parts of myself that were left buried underneath my fear. Today I practice self-care in a special loving way, which allows me to support others when they feel a sense of pain and separation. Today, I help others discover the parts of themselves that they have lost connection to, and also bring messages from their own connection to the angelic realm."

Counseling Cert; Dip Transformational Life Coaching; Color Therapy LV III; Crystal Healing Cert, EFT Cert. and many other modalities. www.innerselfcare. com

SEPTEMBER 1
Brilliant Beyond Measure

By Gina Barbara

I pray to you Angels of Love,
call forth this 'Little Lost Girl' so deeply loved.
I measure a hip. I measure a thigh.
I measure my stomach; wish it were blind to the eye!

A soft whisper spoken so gentle and true,
"You are Brilliant Beyond Measure;"
Yet! You cannot see through, "Reflecting in the mirror of you."
I ask your love and protection, as I begin to shine through;
my hip and my thigh, my stomach too.
In comes the 'Presence' and the love of you

A Bright Light I feel emerging in me,
a heart and a beat; In me - assure me.
"You are Brilliant Beyond Measure,"
and so 'Let it be' at one with your heart,
no matter how skinny or how big you may be.

I ask you dear Angels to support me,
so that a hip and a thigh and a stomach too,
become the beat of pure Presence through and through.

The Whisper returns and now I see
it was this message that was meant for me
"You are Brilliant Beyond Measure," Is 'What is to Be,'
so I call on the Angels of Love and the support of Thee

SEPTEMBER 2

Archangel Uriel's
Guidance with Life Challenges

By Kimberly Marooney

Beloved Archangel Uriel,
When I cry for help, you come packing the power of divine Love.
When I feel lonely, you soothe my heart with companionship.
And when I stand in the Presence of the Divine,
you guide me to be your Earth Angel responding to the needs of others.

You are with me always.
You guide, nurture, and love me through all of my life experiences.
You help me to know that I AM a Child of Light.

Feeling your presence and guidance allows me to feel worthy
of working as an Earth Angel blessing others.
Help me to use the potent energy of Spring Cleaning to clear out my home
of the clutter that makes me feel helpless.
Guide me to let go of stuff that keeps me stuck in the past,
opening space for peace, joy and love to fill my home instead.

Strengthen me as I face the challenges of life.
I need a miracle.
Support me as I find the willingness to let go of long-time issues
and open my heart to new ways of seeing myself and others.

Uriel, I gratefully accept your guidance and am your willing Earth Angel.

So it is.

September Chapter Sponsor – Gina Barbara

SEPTEMBER 3
Archangel Zadkiel

By Trish Grain

Dear Archangel Zadkiel,
who holds the violet light of transmutation,

I ask you to shower me
with the gold and silver violet flame
to cleanse and transmute any and all negativity.

Thank you for guiding me into transformation
and helping me to release any ancestral patterns
and beliefs into a positive.

Clearing the way
so that I can experience
an alignment of my body, mind, emotions and spirit
and to accept a more beautiful higher frequency of light.

Thank you, Archangel Zadkiel.

SEPTEMBER 4
Prayer for a Safe Journey

By Rev. Vicki Snyder

Angels, I call on you to protect me on my journey.
Direct me to my destination unharmed.
I will show gratitude for arriving in the most magnificent fashion,
either by foot, car, motorcycle, train or plane.

Allow me to feel your wings envelope me
in pure love and protection, as I set out today.
Fill my heart with hope and excitement as I make this trip.
When I board the grand machine let the wind strike my face
and help me feel your angelic presence with every breeze.

Permit my senses to explode with the sights,
smells and sounds of this trip.
Let me thoroughly enjoy all the natural wonders
of God's brilliant work in action.

Permit me to sense you flying next to me
as I speed off to my destination.
Let me fully enjoy the ride with all its fantastic thrills.
Please keep me out of harm's way
and keep me alert to any circumstances that require a quick reaction,
ensuring my safety and the safety of others.

I am open, I am free, and I am expanding my consciousness
on this spiritual journey of life.

This journey is about my newfound love of a motorcycle - Vicki

September Chapter Sponsor – Gina Barbara

SEPTEMBER 5
Radiant Grace

By Ann Phillis

Radiant grace, amazing light!
In every color, brilliant and bright.

Flowing down on wings of angels,
Nourishing the earth, all life enabled.

Archangels, angels, sylphs and fairies,
Aligned in one purpose, your brilliance is present!

I open my heart to your loving downpour,
I welcome your hope, your infusion of splendor.

I become a brilliant sparkle of light,
A glittering soul in your wings so bright.

I stretch my arms wide, I reach out to bless,
I share with the Earth and all life you embrace.
I celebrate with joy, humble and free,
I honor your love, so happy, in your peace!

September Chapter Sponsor – Gina Barbara

SEPTEMBER 6
A Gift of Compassionate Connection

By Andrea Porter

I, Kuan Yin, the Angel of Compassion, invite you sweet one.
Come dance and play in the soul passion of you.

Come breathe with me.
I hold a safe space to consciously connect
with your soul in a special new way.
Breathe deep into you.
Invite your soul essence to come and join you now.
Let each conscious breath take you gently, deeper into the core of you.
Allow you to ride the breath of soul
into this space of authentic, passionate you.
Notice with each breath, you experience a new dance between you and soul.

Open to the gentle compassion of your soul's breath.
Let it wrap you in the soft, comfy love of divine you.
Breathe and notice; a new stillness surrounds you.
Your soul offers a gift of loving inspiration.

Breathe, receive this gift now.
Breathe and bring it with you, as you step into this day.
Watch, notice as this new breath of connection with soul
gently unfolds in your life. Know you can come back
to this sacred space any time throughout your day.

Just breathe; invite in your soul essence.
Soul truly desires to love, guide, and support you each moment.
Blessings Sweet One.

September Chapter Sponsor — Gina Barbara

SEPTEMBER 7
Prayer for Parents with Children Going Back to School

By Karen Paolino Correia

Dearest angels,
please watch over my children as they begin a new school year.
Please protect them as they travel to and from school.

Surround them in your love and support
as they meet new and old friends
and help them to choose wisely for their highest and greatest good.

Help them to believe in themselves, stay true to themselves
and to be confident in who they are.

Remind them to ask for help from their teachers and parents when needed.
I know you will watch over them and support them
to receive and experience their highest and best.

Thank you.
I am so grateful.

SEPTEMBER 8
A Prayer to Heal Worry & Fear

By Julie Geigle

Archangel Metatron,
Lately I have been consumed with worry and fear.
Nothing seems to be going right in my life.
I try and try, but nothing ever changes.
I feel defeated and hopeless.

I know the only way out of this pain
is to surrender my will to God.
I ask that you, Archangel Metatron, step in and act as a bridge
helping me to step out of this prison
created by my fear and worry.

As I step onto this bridge,
I remember there is another path filled with love and hope.
A path full of support and guidance from my spiritual team
of Angels, guides and loved ones who have passed.
I only need ask and the way will be shown.

I awake with serenity and love.
I remember I always have a choice.
When my mind begins to lead me down that rabbit hole,
I allow my breath to remind me of the bridge,
the bridge that leads me back to the truth.

As I align with the light of my Soul, magic and miracles
happen in my life and worry and fear disintegrate.
And so it is.

September Chapter Sponsor – Gina Barbara

SEPTEMBER 9
A Healer's Prayer to the Angels

By Michelle Barr

Surround us,
protect us,
guide us, and
direct us.

Heal what needs to be healed.
Reveal what needs to be revealed.
Lead me where you need me, and
speak to me in ways I always clearly understand.

Amen.

Say this prayer before doing healing and clearing work.

SEPTEMBER 10
A Prayer to Find Lost Hope

By Tracy Quadro

Dearest Angel Chamuel,
you help those who call upon you
to find things that have been lost.
I've lost my heart, my courage, and my faith
that things will turn around.
I have lost hope.

You are a being that soothes, comforts
and encourages us when we lose our way.
Please remind me that I'm not alone,
have not been abandoned or forgotten
and have not stepped off the path.
Remind me that there is a grand plan of the Universe,
with its profound and infinite Truth,
that knows much better than I how things will turn out.
Always for the highest good of all.
Guide me through the wilderness of my despair
help me to find my true direction.

Please take my hand and guide me
to the other side of this feeling of lack,
so that I might live my way into the knowledge that hope is eternal,
and the Universe is as it should be.
Always.

September Chapter Sponsor – Gina Barbara

SEPTEMBER 11
A Prayer for World Peace

By Cathleen O'Connor

Beloved Angels,
Guide our hearts in remembrance of who we really are –
beings of love and light – made from the same source.

Let our spiritual DNA spring forth
with acceptance for all paths as all paths are one path;
and remind us that what we hold as the only way
interweaves with the mystical path of truth.

Flood our world with love and light
so that each soul awakens in remembrance
of one human family; one spiritual ancestry.
Send us the grace of the open heart
so we may heal from loss and find again the way to love.

Shower us with blessings.
Enfold us in wings of starlight;
be beside us as we walk upon the earth
and remind us to tread lightly
with honor and gratitude for all that we have been given.

Awaken us to the dawn of a completely new day,
one filled with all the potential the universe holds.
Guide us to live this day as if it were the first day,
the only day – for that is what it is.
Give us today the gift of peace.
And so it is.

September Chapter Sponsor – Gina Barbara

SEPTEMBER 12
Angel Prayer for Divine Surprises

By Michelle Mullady

Angels of Joy,
please fill my life with divine surprises,
both big and small.
Open my mind and heart to miracles and rewards.
May you grant my precious spirit the willingness
to receive life's wonder and unforeseen treasures.

As I become receptive, help me release any expectations
about how and when they will manifest.
Grant me the faith that the Universe is in charge
of this unfolding abundance.

May I accept all blessings with a grateful heart.
Fill me with appreciation for every reminder
of the joy and happiness Spirit created me to experience.
As I accept each gift, may I know I am accepting Spirit's love.

* As you say this prayer, take a moment to relax and BREATHE Breathing in through your nose and breathing out through your mouth. Giggle. Give yourself a HUGE hug. Say: "I welcome a wonderful life." Smile. Breathing in, say: "I know that I deserve a wonderful life." Breathe. Say: "I willingly accept the highest and the best in my life now."

SEPTEMBER 13
To Surround Myself with Greatness
The Royal Procession

By Kimeiko Rae Vision ATP®, The Angel Warrior™

Dear Archangel Michael,
I know that I can trust you to lead me towards God's heavenly light.
As I embody my regal presence, please give me a Royal Procession,
send additional angels to walk ahead of me, clearing away cobwebs,
so that I needn't dread walking head first into sticky situations
that leave me feeling as though I was lured into a trap
and totally disgusted. ***Yuck!***

Instead, I will journey forward feeling protected and celebrated!
Thank you for helping me to communicate
with my Highest Self and with God.
Thank you for illuminating my True North.

Dear Archangel Raphael,
please stand behind me, beaming your healing light into my past.
I needn't worry that I have missed any important details,
that my past mistakes are irreversible, or that any missed detail
or mistake may come back to hurt me or to haunt me.
Please send a few powerful angels to walk behind me.

And now I can allow myself to be flexible, to grow, REACH,
and stretch into brand new milestones of my success.
I am grateful. I am energized. I am in great company.
Amen.

SEPTEMBER 14
My Precious Child

By Inger Marie Moeller

Stay with me, my precious child.
Heal in me, my precious child. For am I not your Mother?
of your Heart – of your Soul – of your Life?
- Your Mother

Hold my hand, my precious child.
Walk with me, my precious child. For am I not Your Mother?
of your Heart – of your Soul – of your Life?
- Your Mother

Cry with me my precious child.
Laugh with me my precious child. For am I not your Mother?
of your Heart – of your Soul – of your Life?
- Your Mother

Dance with me, my precious child.
Live in me, my precious child. For am I not your Mother?
of your Heart – of your Soul – of your Life?
- Your Mother

For you are loved, oh precious child.
Child of God, you have come home. For am I not your Mother?
of your Heart – of your Soul – of your Life?
- Your Mother

September Chapter Sponsor – Gina Barbara

SEPTEMBER 15
Angel Prayer for Clear Purpose

By Suzanne Gochenouer

Dear Angels,

Help me know and understand my purpose in this life.

When I am unclear about my next step,
guide me to the decision that moves me always closer to the Light.

Help me live my highest purpose in every action I take,
in every word I use,
in every thought that crosses my mind.

Encourage me when I grow weary of striving,
and remind me that I am part of a glorious plan
that I do not yet know.

Guide me to remain completely open
to a deeper connection to Spirit,
allowing me to fill my heart with the grace of loving purpose.

Share with me what I need to know
in order that I may share my Light with this world.

Amen, Amen, Amen.

Thank you, thank you, thank you.

September Chapter Sponsor – Gina Barbara

SEPTEMBER 16
We Are Always Here

By Lisa Clayton

Fear not, Beloved Child of love and light.
We are here with you always.

Archangel Michael loves you very much.
He is leading all Angels with so much passion, intent and power
of his sword to open doors
and let abundance and love flow to you with ease and grace.

Angels of the Golden Realm and your Guardian Angels are here.
The trees, flowers, deserts, ocean's waters
and mountains on Mother Earth vibrate with our love.
As you open your heart to receive our love,
new opportunities will rise up each day,
filling you with confidence and determination
in the name of unconditional love.

We are always here. Can you feel us?
We are the warm, gentle breeze that comes on a still day.
We are the feathers you find.
There is so much grandeur and grace living inside your heart
that we desire for you to experience.

ALL is Divinely well as we guide you to discover your love greatness.
Sing "Glory Be" each day. Sink into the AWE-someness of your juicy heart.
Speak of your love often. Know we are always with you;
lifting you higher and higher
through the power and glory of your heart's love.

September Chapter Sponsor – Gina Barbara

SEPTEMBER 17
For My Highest Good

By Lisa K.

How often do you come to us with your prayers?

We hear every one and respond quickly.

You may not know it yet,
but our answers are in the process
of bringing you the best that is for you,
whether you see it now, or see it later.

We always work for your highest good,
for your soul's purpose, and for your greater being.

Trust that you will receive answers in action
or in signs that your prayers are heard
and the Universe is acting upon it.

– Your Angels

SEPTEMBER 18
Conversing with an Angel

By Andrea Mathieson

Let listening be my prayer…..Angel, show yourself to me,
not in the wings and robes of my childhood fantasies,
but in your true light-guises.

I am not above you, distant, watching from afar.
I am near to you as breath. I touch you with a soft electric spark.
You see me in the purple hue of morning glory.
You hear my whispers in your heart. My blessing lives in all creation.
Your life, your breath is part of me; our gentle greeting quickens everything.

How can I come to know you?

You cannot search and not see me if your heart is soft and open.
You cannot find me when you try too hard if I am right there with you.
You cannot take a breath and not feel me if you sincerely let me in.
You cannot hide from me and say I do not care if one small bone is honest.
You cannot deny my presence shining everywhere if you say you are alive
You cannot say my miracles have been withheld if your hand is truly open.

I understand! There is no separation…
Your song — my joy expressed;
Your wings — my loving freed; *Your robes* — my radiance;
Your wisdom — my knowing; *Your blessing* — my compassion

Yes, you understand…
Now, take up your wings and robe and sing your song of joy.
Let me shine through you as together we restore the world's beauty.

September Chapter Sponsor – Gina Barbara

SEPTEMBER 19

Archangel Zadkiel ~ Violet Flame Heart Prayer

By Carolyn McGee

Archangel Zadkiel, Archangel of the Seventh Ray
and energetic guardian of the Violet Flame of love,
I ask you to help me open my heart, mind, body, soul and energetic field
to the healing and divine nature of the Violet Flame
to purify any negative energy that I carry from this or previous lifetimes.

Please use the Violet Flame to burn away any anger,
regret or sadness I carry within my heart.
Oh, Violet Flame burst open my Heart
so that I may forgive myself and those who have injured me.
Take any negativity and burn it clean
with the purifying love of the Violet Flame.

Archangel Zadkiel,
please use the Violet Flame and my loving intention
to open the hearts and minds of my family and friends
to the grace of love and forgiveness
and to bring healing and peace to my neighbors,
countrymen and all people of the world.

Oh, Violet Flame and Archangel Zadkiel bring peace,
healing and balance to our Mother Earth.
I am and we are the Violet Flame
and, with your guidance,
I am a living and breathing example of a life of Love.
And so it is!

September Chapter Sponsor – Gina Barbara

SEPTEMBER 20
Being Open to Angelic Guidance

By Rev. Jennifer Shackford

Angels, I ask that you raise vibration,
working through all energetic blocks in my body.

Fill the blocks with love and trust,
tapping into my intuition so I receive Divine Guidance.

Help me trust and know that it is YOUR voice I am being guided by.
I ask that you push aside my ego to allow me
to fully hear, see, know and feel your "voice".

I am open to your guidance!

Thank you Angels!

SEPTEMBER 21
Angel Phanuel and Intimacy: Loving Message for Relationships

By Bobbe Bramson

Dear Ones,
When you feel troubled within your relationships
by patterns that seem not to change for the better,
remember that there is hope,
for you are all intimately connected through One Love;

It binds you to those it is easy to love and those hard to love;
A Love so deep, so infinite, and so all encompassing
that it is difficult for you to believe deserving of it.
So you stay entrenched in your point of view
as if you only know the words to one song.

Let us remind you that there are many ways to see a situation,
many ways in which a heart that seems closed can open.
Allow others their ways, their roads, their desires –
just as you would wish them to see and support you in yours.

Release your small version of what is possible between you and another
and make room for something bigger and more splendid to occur.
Make room for a higher good and surrender your fears.
Tune into the sweetness of your innermost sacred heart
and know that just as your heart beats with love,
so does the heart within the other.

Listen closely: They beat as One with Love.

SEPTEMBER 22
The Seven Angel Rays Prayer

By Elizabeth Harper

Archangel Michael,
Fill my energy field with your blue ray of protection.
Shield me from harm. Give me courage to stay true to my values.

Archangel Jophiel,
Permit me to bathe in your yellow ray of wisdom and illumination.
Open me to ways to expand my knowledge and appreciation of all life.

Archangel Chamuel,
Let your pink ray of love saturate my heart and soul.
Help me to be truthful and honest, compassionate, kind, and forgiving.

Archangel Gabriel,
Flood my being with your white ray of purity; cleanse me of
negative emotions and beliefs so I may follow my divine mission.

Archangel Raphael.
Heal my spirit with your emerald green ray of balance.
Help me to expand my vision and open my heart to your abundance.

Archangel Uriel,
I am ready to accept your purple and gold ray of serenity and peace.
I am willing to be free of all fears and implore you to support my liberation.

Archangel Zadkiel,
Your violet ray of transmutation now burns away obstacles to my success
and leads me toward the fulfillment of my heart's desires.

September Chapter Sponsor — Gina Barbara

SEPTEMBER 23
Equinox Prayer

By Cathelijne Filippo

This Prayer is for the Autumnal Equinox in the Northern Hemisphere;
If you live in the Southern Hemisphere, read the Equinox Prayer on March 20.

Beloved Archangel Michael,
Please bless me on this Autumn Equinox,
when day and night are in complete balance,
signalling the need to balance the darkness and light within,
as I learn to navigate the Law of Polarity.

May I learn that after a time of activity,
I may now take time for rest and reflection.
And may I learn how, in the silence of darkness,
a period of gestation will help my soul to grow.

Dear Michael,
Please help me to go within,
making time to harmonize the feminine and masculine energies within,
as well as balance giving and receiving,
speaking and listening, being active and restful.

I now celebrate all the work I have done for the year.
I thank Mother Earth for her continued support and abundance,
wishing her a time of rest, as I take time for a repose in my own life.

So be it.

September Chapter Sponsor — Gina Barbara

SEPTEMBER 24
Affirmative Prayer

By Emily Rivera

Dear God, source, creator,
I invite the love, light, joy, wisdom, and peace
within, and all around me,
to expand with grace and ease.

I welcome and accept the support of the Angels
that guide my spirit with love.
May their wings carry me into a state of clarity, abundance, and harmony
everywhere I go, in everything I do, and with everyone I greet.

May my light, presence, and reality
always reflect their Angelic truth and Divine Love.

Breathe in silence, to integrate prayer/intention.
Visualize your heart expanding as you claim the last part of this prayer/intention.

In this moment and in all my moments,
I say yes to the expansiveness of my soul.
In much gratitude, so it is.
Amen

Our souls are in a perpetual state of honoring affirmations that reflect the awareness of harmony, love, peace, and beauty. Each of us from this space, emanates a song of truth and light. It is ideal through our prayers and intentions for us to claim and celebrate what our soul already knows. In that way we further invite and welcome these attributes of our Divine spirit and our Angels' love to reflect more clearly in our reality. - Emily

September Chapter Sponsor – Gina Barbara

SEPTEMBER 25
Prayer to Hold the Day Sacred

By June and Treena Many Grey Horses

Morning:
I welcome the daylight with Love and Gratitude.
I invite Creator and the Angels to be with me throughout the day,
to guide and protect me.
Thank you for this new day filled with Divine Blessings
and Gifts of Mother Earth's bounty,
All my needs are met and I allow the flow of ease,
joy and glory in and around me.

Midday:
As the midday sun kisses my face, I graciously accept all that is into my life.
I am thankful for the beauty in each and everything that the sun kisses.
I see with love, kindness and compassion.
I hear with love, kindness and compassion.
I feel with love, kindness and compassion.
I am love, kindness and compassion.
Thank you Creator and the Angels.

Evening:
I give thanks to Creator for a Blessed day as I see the brilliant sun set.
I give thanks to the Angels for all the signs and messages
given to help me through this day.
I give thanks to myself for all that I have given and received.
Creator and the Angels keep me safe and protected through the night.
Thy will be done.

September Chapter Sponsor – Gina Barbara

SEPTEMBER 26

Archangel Raphael
Prayer for Health & Vitality

By Ramona Remesat

Archangel Raphael,
I call upon you now.
Please encircle me,
and fill me completely,
with the emerald green light
of your Divine healing energy.

I know that in spiritual truth,
I am healthy and whole.
Please help me to actualize this now
by remembering to ask you,
and all of the healing angels,
for exactly what I want.

Please give me comfort, well-being,
peace, serenity and hope.
Please bring me energy,
vitality, strength and vigor.
I open my heart and accept
your healing gifts and your guidance.
As I do this, I tune into my body
and listen to her deep inner wisdom.
I trust and know that all is well and I thank you.

I now affirm that I am in complete and perfect health.
And so it is.

September Chapter Sponsor – Gina Barbara

SEPTEMBER 27
Right Back Atcha'!

By Peggy Shafer

Dearest Angels,
On most days, I ask of you a favor for myself or a friend.
Today, I'm sending all my love and thanks back in your direction.

Thank you for being with me, for guiding and protecting me
…always. I could never stop feeling your presence.
Your peaceful whispers announce the abundance of the Divine,
and surround me…in All Ways, always.

Your gentle touch - the light breeze from nowhere –
brings the deepest knowing that…I am adored for being me,
and supported by your love and guidance…in All Ways, always.
In childhood, I was told a story which began
…every Angel's highest joy is being a human's biggest fan.
And for that blessing, …Thank You!

Dear Angels, forgive me, please. I sometimes forget that
…I must ask for your help or you simply can't…help.
…Free will and all.
It's your highest joy to soothe me, uplift me, protect me,
…and also kick me into action.
But first, I need to ask …in All Ways, always.

You're never more than just a thought away.
And of course, …no request is beyond your power,
when I remember to ask and to also say in advance,
…Thank You.

September Chapter Sponsor – Gina Barbara

SEPTEMBER 28
Cascade of Angels

By Ann Phillis

Gentle, cascading, loving flow
Deep from the heart, the grace of God.

On angels' wings, it sparkles and glows
The deepest love our universe knows.

Open your heart, your arms, your being
Spread your wings, your awakening greeting.

Let wings merge with body, human angel become
Here on Earth, with your heart in love!

Make your difference now, powerful and free
We will change this world, the angels, you and me!

SEPTEMBER 29
Angels of Justice

By Chandra Easton

"On behalf of the radiant Ones we protect earth.
We align with the Great Bear, Sirius the Blue Star and Mother Pleiades.
On behalf of the Cosmic Christ, we stand.
We neutralize evil on earth and beyond.

We work for Justice. We restore balance on earth.
We stand within the Blue Flame. Wings outstretched, we form a shield.
We protect, we defend through the Heart of Justice.
We serve the Law. We uphold the Law. We embody the Laws.
Call upon us for Justice Divine. Call upon us for Justice for all.
Call upon us for the strength to persist.

Redouble all efforts for peace.
Redouble all resistance to outright evil.
Redouble the vision of planetary balance.
Redouble all contact with soul and beyond.

Redouble all actions of courage.
Redouble all actions of love.
Redouble all vigilance against sloth.
Redouble all deeds of conviction and love.

Together we form circles of allegiances.
Circles of trust, bonds of the heart. Unite with us now in peace."

* Visualize Lord Jesus, the New Jerusalem, within a six pointed star, radiating Light to Earth. Christ stands like a golden pyramid of hope and protection. Light triumphs.

September Chapter Sponsor – Gina Barbara

SEPTEMBER 30
Sacred Space Invocation

By Sunny Dawn Johnston

Today, we celebrate a time of new beginnings.
We stand in anticipation,
asking our Angels, Archangels, Guides, and Ascended Masters
to bless each of us here and those who are yet to come,
to fill the rooms and hallways of this space with divine light and love.

This is a sacred place; a place of peace and joy,
a place of love and healing, a place of understanding and knowing,
a place of interconnectedness.

May those who come to this space seeking wisdom find it.
May those who come seeking healing, receive it.
May those who come feeling guilt and fear be freed of it.
May they be able to reconcile the past
and be released to walk into the future
celebrating the gift of each life experience.
May all who enter this space be balanced, centered and grounded;
have peace and happiness; be healed according to their needs;
and have their hearts filled with the unconditional love of the Angels.

May the outward beauty of this place
summon each of us to the inward beauty of our hearts'.
May this space give birth to new and deeper connections
with the Angels in our lives.
May the energy of this space always be pure, full of light and love.
May the experiences of all who enter be for their highest good.
And so it is.

September Chapter Sponsor – Gina Barbara

October-November-December
The Energy of Eternal Love

with **Roland Comtois**

"Within He Speaks"

By Roland Comtois

There standing deep within the corners of my thoughts was a translucent hue of light that sent chills throughout my body, yet comforted my soul. Tucked within my prayers, hidden underneath my stress and embedded in my light, was a divine messenger ready to serve, support and guide me. The angels have always been here. From the beginning of time they have been a resource for inspiration and hope. They bring forth an unbelievable peacefulness that encapsulates every aspect of the soul. But this one angel in this time of life was different.

Aren't we all walking through life seeking the truth? Truth is that profound synchronistic event that tells you that your life's path is blissfully equivalent to your soul's mission. Truth lies somewhere between the breath and the heartbeat waiting to be rediscovered.

Fortunately, for all who choose it, there is an angelic crew ready to stand with us as we forge towards the celebration of the season. This is the time of trusting your internal and insightful knowing. Calling upon the angels who live in God's creativity will move you towards the true prosperity of your purpose and place in this world.

There I was perched upon a beautiful grassy hill, overlooking the beauty of nature and contemplating the journey of life. I spent some time calling on the angels as we all do when the transformation is present. I thought of each and every one of them that I'd had daily conversations with over the last years of my life. Thankful they never abandoned me if I asked for support, I especially thought of my guardian angel who has stood beside me through all of my life. I've discovered throughout my spiritual travels that with simplicity and quietness one can summon the angelic light instantly and directly from the universal cosmos. This awareness creates an everlasting bond that can always be evoked by remembering the feelings of when the angels are nearby.

The leaves that adorned the trees in the previous season are nearly all gone. There's one tiny little leaf that remains attached to the branch that has held it there for many, many months. The wind gently beckons it to let go and to return to the soil, a place where it will begin anew.

This season offers a quiet retreat allowing you to go inward to a place where you meet your angel "soul-to-soul." In this sacred space, through meditation and contemplation, much will be revealed to you. It is your time to harvest a much deeper, more profound relationship with the mystical courier that had guided you from the beginning of your destiny.

I called upon my beloved angels. To call upon them is simply to realign with the energy that you feel when they are present. A comfort emerges within a reverent heart and the angelic communication begins. I have returned, just as the leaf did, to a place to begin anew. I feel the evolution of my soul as I enter the place from where my pilgrimage began. Knowing my evolution is well supported, I celebrate the connection to the angelic realm with much gratitude.

I stretched across the universe from the place where I sat intently aware of my inner and outer surroundings. I looked deep into the blue skies above me and felt the coolness from the blades of grass. The vibrant colors that proceeded have transitioned into shades of white and gray. How beautiful was such a discovery!

Do you know that feeling when the blessings are so powerful and so loving that gratitude becomes your only mantra? Instantaneously, my heart opened to receive all of the blessings of unconditional angelic love. I sat patiently and purposefully waiting to see what was to come next. I was in awe of the gentleness that overpowered my restlessness. And, there he stood, radiant, magnificent and mesmerizing. An angelic force with a light that pierced my trepidation with such intense healing that I knew an archangel had touched my soul.

Unlike any other force, his spirit, his essence is extremely tangible and viable during this very special time of year. From my deepest thoughts as he stood in his grandeur, I heard "only in your stillness will you find the true treasures of the soul. The treasure is not measured by waiting, it is measured by knowing."

The celebration and the connection to everything, including our angels, is part of the fabric of life. The transformation that occurs in the last season, prompts this magnificent angel to bless the promise of our lives. I closed my eyes. He stood with such strength and tenderness that I was captivated by his beauty. Archangel Gabriel has found his way to me.

He stands with you right now. He awakens your quiet slumber to reinvigorate your destiny. He stands with a light and a message, beautifully illuminated, reminding us that the connection is the cause of the celebration. This ardent spiritual and insightful messenger knew that I had beckoned him. His name brings strength, perseverance and wisdom.

Each time you resurrect his name from the sepulchers of heaven during this season, a special message will be offered to you. When you call his name you reconnect to holy and divine energies. To witness his light, you must go within your sacred chamber. Just as the leaves release from the branches of the tree to begin anew, so must we enter a time of inner exploration.

Archangel Gabriel exists because he does. He exists in the universe and speaks directly to your heart. You exist because you do. You are part of the universal splendor, never to be separate. As you approach this monumental season of celebration, begin with going within. Take time to discover all that is within your grasp. Quiet down your voice, ease your restlessness and go beyond asking. Step beyond believing and harness the energy of knowing. The season of connection and celebration, and all that it offers you, will bring you a brighter today and a gloriously brighter tomorrow.

Remember that every roadway taken leads to a single, most precious and auspicious moment in time. What truly exists for us is an entourage of heavenly angelic voices that encourage us to celebrate our lives at every juncture, in every corner of our destiny and in every season of our lives.

Roland Comtois is a nationally acclaimed inspirational speaker, spiritual medium, and radio host. He is the author of two books *And Then There Was Heaven*, a memoir chronicling the author's personal near death experience and the after-life insights that define his life today, and *16 Minutes*, a poignant personal journal about the last earthly moments between a mother and son and a guidebook through grief. Roland is a professional healer and spiritual medium with over 30 years' experience as a gerontology nurse, Reiki Master, metaphysical teacher and grief specialist. His expertise extends from the physical to the spiritual, as he shares healing modalities and messages that nurture and balance mind, body and soul. His mission is to help people find comfort in life in spite of loss, show them how to move beyond grief with love and hope and to pass on the message that heaven and eternal love are real and always close at hand. He is the founder of Talk Stream Spiritual Radio and the After Loss Expo, now in its 9th year. Join Roland's mailing list right now at www.blessingsbyroland.com and get a FREE GIFT!

OCTOBER

Found by Angels
Lisa K., PhD

Angels found me even though I wasn't really looking for them, at least not directly. One day, many years ago, I was in the bookstore looking for any book on inner guidance or intuition that attracted me. Walking casually along the aisles I glanced over the rows of books, when one small book stood out and attracted my attention. It was a book on how to communicate with your angels through writing by using a few simple steps. I didn't know much about angels, but I liked them and angels seemed positive and uplifting. I bought the book, went home and tried it. I was shocked! I thought I would get just random words, but the words that came out had profound meaning! It was amazing.

With this newly developed skill, I continued to communicate with my angels through what I now call Automatic Angel Writing™. With it, I'd have a question for my angels and they would give me the answer through writing. I never knew what they were going to write. Words came slowly forming sentences and many times I didn't even know how they were going to end. Sometimes the sentences were short, other times I was given long paragraphs that seemed to write themselves. I was merely taking dictation.

All this time I was on a quest to learn more about inner guidance and how to develop the small voice inside that seemed to give you divine messages. I learned later that the small voice was your intuition and it was how angels speak to you. One day, with my angel writing and my intuition, I asked my angels, "What books can I read?" They responded, "Angels come and go." I took that phrase and I put it into the Amazon search engine to look for a book. One book came up that was titled, *"Divine Guidance: How to Have a Dialogue with God and Your Guardian Angels. By Doreen Virtue."* I had no idea who Doreen

Virtue was, but when I read it, it was just what I was looking for! I learned about using your intuition to connect to angels and receive divine guidance.

I became very curious about this Doreen Virtue lady. Who was she? What did she do? I discovered that she taught a course called the Angel Therapy Practitioner certification class. I loved the description of the class and I was so drawn to it. I kept going back to that web page and read it over and over, each time feeling very compelled to take the class and from the looks of it, the classes filled up a year in advance.

But, wait a minute! This was a class for people who wanted to be angel readers, or Lightworkers. "I'm not a Lightworker," I thought, "I don't want to do angel readings for other people. How can I take a class in the middle of October? I have to take care of my young son. Who's going to watch after him?" But I really wanted to take the class, I asked my angels what should I do, but they were silent. I had to choose for myself. They can't take away your free will to choose. I decided to trust. I figured, if it were meant to be the angels would make it happen. I signed up for the class and months later everything, of course, fell into place.

The class was unlike anything I'd ever done before. My angels brought me to a new level by combining all I had learned, experienced and researched already. I began doing angel readings for the public and soon had read for hundreds of people where I was often sold out at events.

But, I never wanted to be an angel reader, and I still don't. I have always wanted to share my knowledge with others on how to connect to inner divine guidance that comes through our intuition from angels and divine sources. I want everyone to learn how to connect to their angels and receive their own inner divine messages so they can live a better more fulfilled life. Because I learned from scratch how to build my intuition to connect to my angels, I know others can too. Anyone can do it, you can do it. God has given everyone angels to guide them, there are no exceptions, and all you need to do is use your intuition to connect to them.

Lisa K. is an author, speaker and seminar leader specializing in connecting to angels through intuition. Lisa teaches others how to develop their natural intuitive abilities so they can receive their own inner divine guidance. Lisa is considered the intuition expert and has taught hundreds of people about angels and intuition development in workshops and seminars. Lisa K.'s public appearances reach people around the world through guest speaking, online media and her popular radio show, "Between Heaven and Earth" on every day spirituality.

Lisa is a certified Angel Therapy Practitioner® and has helped hundreds of people through her angel readings where she is often sold out at public events. Lisa holds degrees in Electrical Engineering from Columbia University, PsychoBiology from the State University of New York, and a PhD on Intuition and Metaphysical Sciences from the University of Metaphysical Sciences.

As an author, Lisa K.'s work is frequently published in a variety of online widely distributed digital magazines including OmTimes Magazine. Lisa has made numerous guest appearances on both radio and television. Her speaking engagements are entertaining and informative, garnering high praise.

For more information about Lisa and free eBook with 16 intuition exercises go to: http://www.LMK88.com

OCTOBER 1
Daily Morning Angel Prayer

By Lisa K.

My Dear Angels,
I pray that you will be with me at all times to protect and heal me,
to give me strength and wisdom.

I ask for your blessings to hold my heart in Divine love and peace.
Help me always feel your loving presence.

Please help me to see, feel and know that you are always with me.
Assist me in clearly receiving and understanding your messages.

Keep me safe, loved and provided for and help me
feel joy and happiness throughout my day.

Amen

This Daily Morning Angel Prayer can be said daily along with your other prayers to bring your angels closer to you and help you connect with them. You don't need to be in any special place when you say this prayer; all you need to do is open your heart and mind to them. Know that they will hear you whether you say this prayer aloud or in your mind. Your angels always respond. Look for ways that they reveal themselves to you, the signs or perhaps the inner knowing that comes from your intuition that brings you their message in reply.

OCTOBER 2

Prayer for Peace, Comfort and Protection

By Rachel Cooley ATP®

Dear God, angels, and archangels,

Thank you so much for always surrounding me
and for bringing me your peace, comfort and blessings.
I ask for you all to be especially strongly present with me right now.

Please envelope me in your beautiful angelic wings of light.
Bring me comfort and peace of mind.
Bring me back to my true self.

I am so grateful for your presence in my life!
Thank you God and to your angels
for watching over me and my family now and always.
And so it is!

Amen.

October Chapter Sponsor – Lisa K.

OCTOBER 3
Prayer for Time

By Rev. Jennifer Shackford

Angels, I pray you slow down time.
I want to record and enjoy every moment I can.

Please help me to find the beauty within every situation sent my way.
I know everything is not sunshine and roses.
Even through the most difficult of times,
let me see and know the light at the end of the tunnel!

This life goes by so fast.

This life is so precious!

October Chapter Sponsor – Lisa K.

OCTOBER 4
Prayer for the Freedom of Peace

By Daniel Hyman

I know the key is to be at peace with loving myself,
not trying to love myself to bring peace.

One takes effort, work and thought while the other
takes a simple choice and sweet surrender.

One keeps me a slave to the pressure of my thoughts
while the other allows the space for freedom to be who I already am
and feel the love that is within my heart!!!!!

The time is now to let go of my fear,
so I can awaken and follow my heart.

I pray for the freedom of peace
I pray to the angelic rays for the peace of self-love
I release my fears to the angels

I awaken and follow my heart.

October Chapter Sponsor — Lisa K.

OCTOBER 5
"Maybe Not"

By Starlight

I had a dream
maybe not
I traveled far away
maybe not
I went to a land I have never seen
maybe not
I walked down marble hallways
maybe not
I ran around crystal buildings of brilliant light
maybe not
I played with dolphins and walked on water
maybe not
I danced with angels
maybe not
I laughed with those from long ago
maybe not
I smiled with love
A bird sang his song
Warm sunlight on my face
I woke
maybe not

What is real? What is not?
Love from the stars and back!

October Chapter Sponsor – Lisa K.

OCTOBER 6
Protection from Family

By Rev. Vicki Snyder

I call on Archangel Michael to keep me protected
when I have to face family members who are challenging.

I ask you to help me find the strength within
that will allow me to get through these times with grace and love.
I know that it is ok for me to remove people, family included
that are not for my highest and best good.

Michael, please use your sword to cut and remove
the negative family ties that bind me to unhealthy ways.
Use your powers to remove those things that cause my faith to be swayed
and force me to behave in ways not true to my authentic self.

Show me how to rise above the lower energies of family
that force me to be someone I am not proud of.
Offer me the confidence I need to remove these family difficulties
that are so heart wrenching yet so needed to eliminate.

Please collaborate with Archangel Raphael to cleanse my body,
mind and spirit of any negativity resulting from poor family relationships
and to heal myself with the best outcome possible.

Guide me to better relationships, which are based on
mutual trust, love and respect.

October Chapter Sponsor – Lisa K.

OCTOBER 7

Prayer for Releasing
Ancestral Blocks to Money

By Julie Geigle

Archangel Metatron,
I call on you now and the plethora of angelic support
to release any ancestral blocks to money that may be interfering
with my divine flow of abundance and prosperity.

I am aware and acknowledge many generations past
that have lived in poverty and lack.
The following old belief systems now evaporate:

"Money is bad." "There is never enough."
"It goes out faster than it comes in."
The chains that bind me and my ancestors now vanish.

I draw from the wellspring of God,
who has an infinite supply of all that is.
As the winds of change blow, new belief systems emerge:
"There is always more than enough money."
"My supply of money is infinite and endless."
"Money comes through people not from people."
"Money is a blessing; the more I have, the more I have to give"

I sprinkle these belief systems throughout my home,
repeating them throughout the day.
I give thanks to my ancestors
for the opportunity to heal my money story
and to impact future generations to come.
And so it is.

October Chapter Sponsor – Lisa K.

OCTOBER 8
A Prayer to Be Heard

By Tracy Quadro

Sandalphon, your gladsome task
is to carry our prayers before the face of the divine,
wearing them around you like a garment
encasing your magnificent wings, and spreading them wide
with the resplendent joy of this glorious purpose.

Then you whisper our greatest fears, pleas,
thanks and desires into the ears of the Source
from which all blessings and assistance flows.

Please hear my prayer, even when it is silent,
invisible even to my own consciousness.
Look into my heart and touch within me
the place where silence becomes words.
Help me to form those words into the prayer that resonates
with what is best for the highest and greatest good
of myself and all those I love.

And please carry that prayer to the heavens,
where my voice will finally be heard and understood
and my needs fulfilled.
Thank you for being my voice.

Silence is not always golden. When we feel as though we cannot be heard, the silence is stifling and oppressive. Sometimes the silence within our hearts is so pervasive and profound that we may feel as though even our prayers aren't being heard. At those times our Angels may be of special help.

October Chapter Sponsor – Lisa K.

OCTOBER 9

Angel Prayer for Empowering Your Radiance

By April-Anjali

Inner Radiance……..
Is about owning your experience in this lifetime
and recognizing that mistakes made
allow you to see the glory in what you have learned
and how great it is that your life lessons can be turned into gold
Inner Radiance………
Is celebrating every day with passion, love
And empathy for all living things because
If tomorrow comes - it's a gift
Inner Radiance………
Is about embracing the "what if" in life and that
nothing happens by chance but rather by divine destiny
and that your greatest moments in life are never planned
Inner Radiance…….
Could be about speaking your truth no matter what your age
and no matter what anyone else thinks.
It could be about beginning life anew on a whim or
making new friends or discovering something magical
inside of you that for so long went overlooked
Inner Radiance……..
Is being willing to dance your way through life
even when you don't know the song and
how sexy the internal flame becomes when you do
Inner Radiance……..
Is whatever you decide for it to be, because it's never too late,
you're never too old and the dream never ends.
Be Radiant!

October Chapter Sponsor – Lisa K.

OCTOBER 10
Angels of Light

By Ann Phillis

Nourish me, heal me, angels of light,
Hold my hand, show me the way of the heart.
Infuse my mind with clarity and vision,
Soothe my feelings with your love's pure intention.

I wake to your touch,
I feel your embrace.
I surrender to your knowing,
I walk my path in your grace.

Come to me, angels, the living force!
Nourish my heart, my strength, my choice.
Open my path to my vision and gaze,
Awaken my knowing of the Ancient of Days.

Stoke up the fires of my inner heart's furnace,
The splendor! The grace! The everlasting joyfulness!
The pulse of my heart is living light,
Awakening my destiny, my soul is bright.

October Chapter Sponsor – Lisa K.

OCTOBER 11
Prayer of Trust

By Lisa Clayton

I call upon my Beloved Angels, Spirit Guides and my Soul Family
in light form to join me in this Divine communion prayer of trust.
I trust in the God-guided plan unfolding.
I create positive thoughts and activate my faith to create daily miracles.

I fly to higher dimensions with Angel's golden light as my fuel
and my Guardian Angels as my co-pilots,
to keep me connected, and to trust Divine Source.
Through trust, I am fearless, free of worry;
taking one step at a time to expand my gifts and services to the world.

I am here to serve the highest good, to heal myself,
to help and guide others with love, through love and in love.
I activate and trust in my whole heart happiness and growth
through love infusion, love reunions and beloved communions
of the Archangels, Spirit Guides and Golden Angels.

I trust the windfall of abundance and prosperity is here at my fingertips
and resides in the core of my heart.
Faith has secured it.
My courage has initiated the movement for it.
Love has embraced it with purpose and the highest good for ALL.

I ask my intuitive soul to commune in trust always with the Angels.

October Chapter Sponsor – Lisa K.

OCTOBER 12
Angel Prayer for
Release and Letting Go
By Michelle Mullady

Angels of God,
my dearly loved healers,
please help me clear out and liberate whatsoever stands in the way
of pure love coming to me.

I pray to be set free of all that weighs my spirit down
and holds me back from giving and receiving Love.

I have a deep yearning to welcome love into my life.
I ask to be completely released of the pain, suffering and,
particularly self-doubt,
that makes me feel undeserving of love.

I pray to know the delight of love again
and to express it wholly.

Do this prayer for 21 days and feel your heart lighten. As you consciously release and let go of hurt, pain, negativity, and suffering, you allow your heart to melt into the flow of Divine Love that is your birthright.

October Chapter Sponsor – Lisa K.

OCTOBER 13

Prayer for Inviting
Forgiveness in Relationships

By Rachel Cooley ATP® and Kimeiko Rae Vision ATP®

Dear God, Angels and Archangels,
Thank you so much for bringing peace,
forgiveness and comfort in my relationship with…
…*(fill in the name/s)*

Thank you, angels, for helping me to release any attachments
to people, places or situations that did not match my expectations
or left me feeling betrayed or unloved.
I realize we were both/all doing our very best at the time.
I know I am always loved by you dear God, and by my angels.

Please release us from any unforgiveness, upsetting
or unresolved feelings we have towards one another
and clear us of any unforgiveness
so that we may move forward with love and light.
Please help us both to fully forgive and release each other
so that we can reach our own highest potentials with love, ease and grace.

Thank you, Archangel Michael,
for cutting any cords that I may have with this person(s).
I know that only the cords of attachment will be cut,
because the cords of love can never be severed.
I am so grateful for us both to be fully free now!
Thank you so much.
And so it is, Amen

October Chapter Sponsor – Lisa K.

OCTOBER 14
Guardian Angel: Prayer of Gratitude

By Cathelijne Filippo

Beloved Guardian Angel,

Thank you so much for always being there with me,
From the very moment I was born.
Thank you for guiding me along my way,
Protecting me when needed,
Holding my hand through the tough times,
And cheering for me during my successes.

Dear Guardian Angel,
Please let me become more open to you and your guidance.
Help me to experience your presence more clearly each and every day.
I now give you full permission to help me with _____.
Please show me the truth in this situation.
If there are positive steps I can take, may I receive clarity,
as well as the courage to act upon them.

I love you very much and send you my deepest gratitude.

OCTOBER 15
My Wings of Love

By Ann Phillis

I spread my wings with the flick of my arms
I shower my blessings upon all in my heart.

Sparkles of light, God's true grace
Descend to my world, make change with haste!

Our world in need, so great the hour
I dedicate my love, my abilities, my power.

To stand in the light, to stand in the world
To be one with heaven and one with Earth.
To open my heart and let balance rule all
My body, my mind, my feelings, my temple.

Although I stretch my wings so wide
I am here, human, in humble harmony with life.

The world needs my fullness of spirit and wings
And my body, my vehicle of loving care.
I am whole in your grace, I am whole in my heart
I awaken true spirit, here on Earth.

OCTOBER 16
Archangel Metatron

By Trish Grain

Archangel Metatron,
the mightiest of the Archangels,
Angel of sacred geometry.

You radiate the qualities of wisdom, commitment and discipline,
and I ask for your help in following my spiritual path,
so I may radiate the same qualities.

I call upon you so that I may assist children in learning
of their special gifts, abilities and qualities,
as a positive role model in their lives,
as they try to understand the world that they live in.

I ask for your guidance as I follow my path in helping children.

OCTOBER 17
To My Guardian Angel

By Adriana C. Tomasino

Dear Heavenly Harbinger,
Guileless Guide to the Sacred Sanctuary of My Soul,
Ageless, Timeless, Ever-Near.
The One Who Holds the Prelude to Posterity.
Caretaker, Companion, Charioteer....
Sometimes Unseen, Unheard, and Often Unsung,
You Always Aid upon My Request.
Appareled in the Fineries of a Time Long Past,
You Stand by My Side for Each Challenge and Test.
When tears rain down on the vast terrain that we call Life,
You arise, appear, like a ray of light,
Or, perhaps, as a fleeting feather on a warm summer night.
Matchless, Peerless, Luminescent....
You permit me to see the legacy in the lesson.

For arising out of the depths of despair,
The façade of fecundity remains.
For, Lo and Behold! Now, It Is Truly There....
Thanks to Thee! Uplifting, Inspiring, Ever Admiring....
The Mystical Memory of Evocation and Transmutation has been rekindled
As I am serenely swathed in Eternity's Embrace.
No longer confined by the Limitations of the Physical Realm,
My Search for the Illumined Path continues
in the Antechamber of Heaven's Gate,
As I Yearn to Break Free of the Soul-less Quest.
With Gratitude for the Grand Guardian of My Soul's Signature,
Who meets me with Magic, Wonder and Delight.

October Chapter Sponsor – Lisa K.

OCTOBER 18
Angel Prayer for Guidance

By Suzanne Gochenouer

Dear Angels,

Help me hear heavenly guidance as I travel through this life.

Guide me to be open
and willing to receive the messages Spirit sends.

When I am uncertain or lost,
empower me to understand the guidance I receive
in signs and messages.

Help me think clearly and rationally
when I need to make a decision.

Please make your messages clear
and easy to understand,
as you know my earthly energy vibrates
at a lower level than your angelic energy.

Help me quickly and easily connect with you,
so I may always be blessed with your guidance and love.

Amen, amen, amen.

Thank you, thank you, thank you.

October Chapter Sponsor – Lisa K.

OCTOBER 19

Prayer for Healing with the Emerald Green Ray

By Cathelijne Filippo

Beloved Archangel Raphael,
Please send your emerald green ray of healing to my side.
May it surround me and move through me.
Bringing healing to my physical, emotional, mental and spiritual bodies,
In all directions of time and space, and through all dimensions.
May your emerald healing energy fill every atom and molecule of my body.
May it heal every cell, organ and tissue,
Bringing restorative energy, filing me with true balance.
Energize me with vibrant vitality.
For as I heal myself I also heal the world.

May I be a healing channel for Angelic Vibration.
May I share your healing energy with others,
Through loving words and gentle touch,
Through compassionate eyes and accepting silence,
Through wise inner knowing and a loving heart.
For our hearts are the vessels of love,
And love heals all wounds, be they inner or outer injuries.
Love sees the perfection within us all,
Making us realize that we are already healed and whole,
In the eyes of Father/Mother/God.
And so, may I be healed and whole now,
In the perfect image of my Divine Blueprint.
So be it.

October Chapter Sponsor – Lisa K.

OCTOBER 20
Prayer to the Angels for Nurturance

By Shannon Navina Crow

Today, may I find time to nurture myself as easily
as I care for the creations, children and beings in my life.
May I see my basic needs as priority,
water, nutrition, breath and sleep, and know that I am worthy.

When I open to receive love, energy and time,
those that I care for and the life work that I serve will benefit.

I am doing my best in this moment.
It is enough. I am wonderful exactly as I am.
May I be gentle with myself and see my "mistakes"
as a way to learn and grow.
Mother Earth supports me with each breath.

Inhale, visualize the unconditional love
of mothers of present, past and future,
and fill up with the love and support needed
for challenging moments.
Exhale, release doubt, criticism and fears,
and ground into the present.

Allow me to feel that I have the answers I need,
filtering other's advice through my heart.
May I stay connected to whom I am.
May I ask for help and nurture the mothers around me.

OCTOBER 21
Archangel Michael, Guide My Day

By Lisa Wolfson

As I wake in the morning,
I ask you, Archangel Michael, to guide my day.
Help me to rise and greet the day with gratitude and a warm heart
that I may handle all that this day holds
with an even temper and integrity and not be easily swayed.

Protect me and those I love from harm and
guide me to be mindful in my thoughts and actions
so others are protected from hurt as well.

May I draw strength from you to meet the challenges of the day,
always knowing how lucky I am to walk with you beside me
and that in your presence and light, only good can prevail.

And when evening comes and I reflect on the day,
may I be content with all that I have said and done,
knowing I followed your example of strength, protection and love;
And that all who encountered me today have experienced the same.

As I lay down to sleep, may I be grateful for the day I had
and hopeful for the one to follow.

Forever guided by you, Archangel Michael.
Forever grateful to you!

October Chapter Sponsor – Lisa K.

OCTOBER 22

In Praise of Ariel, Archangel of Nature

By Bobbe Bramson

I sing a song of praise to you, beautiful Ariel,
resplendent Queen Angel of Nature.
Praise to you who orders with such gracious, loving rule
all of the Devas - the Shining ones -
each one of them a unique and precious expression of the Divine.

Such myriad wonders:
the colors, the infinite variety of design, the feeling sense of every place,
the mathematical miracle echoed over and over again within each and all.
Oh, praise to you, Ariel, who paints God's boundless creativity with
artful, yet wild abandon, imprinting all you touch with radiant perfection.

I sing praise to the Devas:
Of copse and grove, field and meadow,
valley and plain, jungle and swamp - of ocean, sea, marsh, and shore;
lakes, streams, rivers and glaciers -
of each creature…winged one, swimming one, crawling one,
two-legged and four-legged -
of each blossoming one…tree, flower, cactus,
grain, fruit, vegetable, scrub and brush -
of cave and hidden place, mesa, desert, stone, and crystal -
of cloud, sky, sun, moon, wind and weather -

I sing your praises, blessed Ariel, for the glorious rapture that is Gaia
and for my sense of place, oneness, and belonging within it.
Thank you for the bounteous life-sustaining treasure you bestow.
Amen.

October Chapter Sponsor – Lisa K.

OCTOBER 23
Angel Invocation Prayer

By Elizabeth Harper

Angels, Angels, Angels
Give me the strength to share my heart
with those who need love.
Give me the courage to share my truth
with those who seek guidance.
Give me the faith to share my wisdom
with those who need support.

Give me the power to share my healing gifts
with those who need relief.
Give me the permission to share my vision
with those who need direction.
Give me the confidence to share my knowledge
with those who seek to learn.

Give me the energy to share my passion
with those who need uplifting.
Give me the discernment to share my wealth
with those who need abundance.
Give me your love dear angels,
so that we may share our combined energy with those
who need to trust that we are there for them, always.

Angels, Angels, Angels
I thank you for your support.
And so it is.

October Chapter Sponsor – Lisa K.

OCTOBER 24
Gratitude Prayer to God and Angels

By Katerina Naumenko

I bless the day that I first felt your touch.
I bless the day you caught me in my fall.
My heart beat with your wings…
and, Oh! So much
my life has changed for richer
since answering your call.

I thank the God that sent you to my side.
I thank you for your care, your love, and gentleness in leading me.
The hand that holds mine now has been my gentle guide,
that led me to a life of wondrous miracles I see.

My heart dost overflow with Gratitude and Love,
the Light I see around me is shimmering and pure,
the land I knew before has changed as if overnight,
and blesses me with beauty, bounty,
and visions of delight.

I pray both friend and foe find peace and joy tonight.
I pray that those who hunger satisfy their need.
May hand that holds mine find yours as well tonight,
and blessings fill your day
and Godly love you feel.

October Chapter Sponsor – Lisa K.

OCTOBER 25
A Prayer for New Beginnings

By Julie Geigle

A new day dawns
fresh, clear, crisp.
I set aside my unease
and align with the sanctity of my Soul.

The promise of a miraculous experience
is ignited with each breath I take.
I see my life in terms of opportunities
all judgments of good and bad evaporate.

As I open up to all that I am,
I trust that in this moment of time,
I am exactly where I need to be.

My obsession with what people are doing or not doing
renders me powerless, this I know.
And in that knowing I reach for a new thought;
I choose to stay in my own business of loving, caring and honoring myself.
This choice renders me powerful, this I know.

It is in this knowing that I remember who I am and why I came here.
I allow God, the Angels and Spiritual Beings of Light
to wash away that which no longer serves me.

New beginnings flood into my life.
I release the past and begin again.

October Chapter Sponsor – Lisa K.

OCTOBER 26

Daily Guidance Prayer to Archangel Jophiel

By Susan Huntz Ramos

Dear Archangel Jophiel,
with all its twists and turns,
please guide me on my path through this life.

Show me how to release my ego
and to connect with my Higher self,
the Christ Consciousness within myself.

Help me to carry the scent of a rose,
the beauty of a sunset,
and the warmth of the sun
in my heart
so that my thoughts, words, and actions
attract harmony, beauty, and joy
in my life
and the lives of others.

With deep gratitude.
thank You for your loving guidance.

OCTOBER 27
A Prayer for Living Lost Souls

By Rev. Vicki Snyder

To all angels, please shine your light brightly
for the lost living souls to see; so they may find their way.

Some on earth are lost and do not see the path ahead of them.
It has become dark and void of love for self and others.
They have lost hope and their direction is twisted.

Show them signs of how they can get back on their path.
Guide them to the proper people and places
that can best help them to do this.

Offer your wings to transport them as needed
to the place of joy and happiness they so long for.
Lift them with your wings and help them
to come out of the darkness they have created.

Offer them forgiveness.
They do not know what they do
and lack spiritual insight into how their actions affect us all.
Show them that with your love and light
they can see the forest through the trees.
This will help to better the universe for all living souls.

This is the time to undo the negativity these lost souls have spilled
and replace it with the light and positivity of your higher love.

OCTOBER 28
Daily Prayer for Love and Light

By Cathleen O'Connor

Dear Angels,

Please hold my heart in your hearts today.
Guide me in my thoughts, feelings and actions.
Keep me present and self-responsible.
Open me to forgiveness of self and others.

Direct my energy to where it is most needed
and remind me that I am never alone.
No matter what comes my way, easy or difficult,
help me stay in gratitude for the gift of this day.

Show me the sacred nature of my work
and infuse my spirit with love and light
today and all days to come.

And so it is.

OCTOBER 29

Praise Song to Raziel:
A Prayer for Diviners

By Rachel Pollack

We sing our angel Raziel, giver of secrets,
giver of letters. He who gave the Book,
blessed among the seven wonders that lived before creation.

The Book of Secrets—
All that is hidden, all that will come,
known and seen long ago, revealed in paradise,
Sung to Adam, to Eve, soft among the leaves and pomegranates.

The Book—not pages—a sapphire,
radiant with letters of flame.
Praise Raziel, who gave it to Adam, to Eve,
hidden from the angels, hidden even from Gabriel of the Horn,
Raphael the Healer, star-eyed Michael of the Sword, even Uriel,
the Light of God—known only to Eve, only to Adam,

The Book of Secrets, passed to Noah to light the Ark,
to Abraham and Sarah concealed in their cave,
to Joseph, our beloved, our brother, our ancestor,
Joseph the Diviner, Joseph the Dreamer,
who saw all that was hidden, all future, all beauty.

We sing and praise you, Raziel!
Giver of Secrets, Giver of Letters, Giver of Truth
Kayn y'hi ratzon
So mote it be.

October Chapter Sponsor – Lisa K.

OCTOBER 30
Samhain Prayer

By Cathelijne Filippo

Beloved Archangel Uriel,
Bless me during All Hallows Eve,
when the veils between the worlds are at their thinnest.
May I be connected to the Saints and Ascended Masters,
and may the appropriate Ascended Master step forward,
as I open myself to my spiritual guides of light,
to guide me on my journey.

Dear Archangel Azrael,
Please help me to connect to loved ones that have passed away,
as I shine my deep love to their souls.
May I be visited by loved ones or guides
from the Light Worlds as I sleep tonight.

Help me to use this time to let go of anyone
I am still holding on to emotionally.
Let me reflect on the beautiful memories,
as I see their light shine from their spirit.
Help me to let go of pain and sorrow,
in the knowledge that we will meet again,
rejoicing in all the love once shared.
I know I am ever supported and never alone.

So be it!

OCTOBER 31
A Blessing for Your Journey

By Roland Comtois

Dear Angels,

Bless us as we embark on a journey of divine purpose.
Help us to become more who we are and give us the inspiration
to fulfill our destined path.

Dear Angels,

Bless humanity with the strength
to overcome the stillness of fear,
and lead us collectively towards the global heart.

And Finally,

May the angels, guides and guardians be ever so present,
in every moment, in every day,
in every obstacle, in every wish,
in every lesson learned and in every breath.

Love peacefully, compassionately and joyfully
with all that is divine and holy.

October Chapter Sponsor – Lisa K.

NOVEMBER

My Badass Warrior Angel
Tracy Quadro

Angels are beings of light and infinite love. They are kind, unfailingly loving, unconditionally generous and exclusively benevolent. But, they are also Badass Warriors! They are courage. They are strength. They are protectors, bodyguards, and bouncers. They keep us safe. Sometimes even from ourselves and our choices. And they take their job very seriously.

The first time I saw my Angel I was in pain. The faithless and fearful way I was living my life was taking a terrible toll on my body. Every movement was painful – I was having trouble sitting for too long, standing for too long, sleeping – I was pretty much in constant discomfort. My toxic thoughts were painful too. I had been wallowing in a state of hopeless despair, feeling that nothing would ever get better and I was doomed to a life of misery. It was a deep, dark and lonely place.

I tried everything at that time to get "better," looking for an external fix of an internally-caused dis-ease. I had exhausted the allopathic healing route. I tried osteopathic, chiropractic, homeopathic, and "experimental" modalities. I turned to bodywork, massage, Reiki, Cranio-sacral - you name it I tried it! Then one day, I was having some polarity therapy done and something unusual happened. The therapist literally took a few steps back, and I saw her, the Angel I have come to know as Annie. She has shared some of her other names with me since, but Annie is how I knew her then and my nickname for her now.

If I had to use only one word to describe her, though it would be terribly insufficient to describe all she was and is, it would be... *Intense.* Intense power and energy! She didn't speak to me in words, but intuitively, in feelings and her attitude. With my limited perception, her attitude seemed to be: "kick ass." She was driven, no-nonsense, take-charge, "get out of my way, I'm working here." She wasn't smiling. She came at me like a whirlwind, swirling with white and shining with purpose, furrowed brow, her long dark hair pulled back so her vision would be unobscured. And she placed her hands upon me, not gently, not roughly, but deliberately and efficiently, like an EMT at the scene of an accident, expert, serious and determined.

As her being coursed through me like painless electricity, her message was unmistakable - "Knock it off." She was telling me to stop hurting myself with my thoughts, stop anticipating the worst, stop feeling helpless, to get off my duff and feel my power. She showed me *my own* intensity, *my own* strength, *my own* determination. She wanted me to set loose the Warrior Angel inside of me and live my life with deliberate purpose. She wanted me to get out of my own way and let my higher self take charge. She wanted me to let her shine through me and heal myself. She is the epitome of "Tough Love," but Love nonetheless.

It took many years, with Annie occasionally trying again to get through to me, though never as intently as that first time, for me to finally understand what she was saying and start living my life differently... mindfully... purposefully. Now that I "get it," I connect with her frequently for strength, for guidance, for a renewed sense of purpose. She gives me pep talks when I need them, and a boot in the butt when I need that. She doesn't listen to pessimism or self-pity. She wants action and helps guide me to solutions. No whining allowed.

Although my outlook is sunny as summer weather most days, occasionally I still feel myself slipping into the dank dreariness, bitter winds and fading light of the autumn days of my heart. I turn to my spirit companion, my Badass Warrior, when I feel tapped out and my energy and optimism store begins to feel depleted.

Annie tells me to meditate and reach her when my tank is empty. "Just ask," she says.

"Guardian, today I feel the coldness of despair beginning to creep into the warmth of my peace. Please remind me, that I am protected by a fearless Warrior, and that her strength lives inside me. Please remind me that challenging change exists to wrest me from my complacency and point me toward my new direction to warmer days. Thank you for accompanying me on this journey and showing me, always, how brave and strong I really am."

Tracy Quadro is one of those rarities - a right brain and expansive Spirit embodied in a mostly left-brain profession. Attorney and mediator by day, Tarot card reader, artist, writer and jewelry maker (in addition to playtime outdoors) on evenings and weekends. Balance is the key! She has been an empath for many lifetimes, an intuitive, and a person whose senses can perceive what many others' cannot. Tracy has always known that other beings share our space with us, and has been reading to learn and understand more about them for as long as she could read, and, most recently, writing what she's learned.

She has had the un/fortunate experience of having had some very close earthly companions pass along into their new form as infinite beings, who send her messages and guide her on her journey. They have joined her Badass Warrior Angel Legion. Tracy has been blessed in many ways, most significantly in having been given stewardship of four wonderful young people and a beautiful piece of our earth on a lake in the heavenly state of Maine. Life is truly good.

Connect with Tracy at www.tracyquadro.com, on FB at www.facebook.com/TarotByTracy. Visit her e-shop at www.etsy.com/shop/TarotbyTracy.

NOVEMBER 1
Prayer to Your Guardian Angel

By Tracy Quadro

Dearest Spiritual friend, protector, guide,
please be with me through the most challenging moments of my life.
Remind me to turn my face and heart to you often,
and speak with you daily to begin to understand the unique essence of you,
who have been matched to the unique essence of me.

When I'm wounded, grant me your healing hand.
When I'm striving, lead the cheers.
When I'm in despair, lend me your soothing shoulder.
When I'm complacent, light the fire.

Take me from who I am now to who I am meant to be, one breath at a time.
Whisper your sweet words of love, of encouragement, of strength, of comfort,
into the places of my heart and mind and body that most need to hear them.

Protect me from harm, whether from
my own internal demons or those outside myself.
Make clear to me the distinctions between
the light and dark energies around me.
Engage me in accepting my successes and joys with gratitude,
with eyes open to the abundance that constantly surrounds me.

And don't hesitate to tickle my ribs, stroke my hair or nudge me forward,
granting me the humor, grace and fortitude
to triumph through every day of my life.
With thanks and a trusting heart, so mote it be.

November Chapter Sponsor – Tracy Quadro

NOVEMBER 2
A Note from Heaven

By Lindsay Marino

Dear Sweetheart,
Please know that I'm always with you.
I know you may not see me, but take the time to feel my presence.
I'll reach out to you in ways that must not go unnoticed.
My message may come to you in a song or dream.
Pay attention to the signs around you
because I'll find ways to communicate with you.

Remember that I did not die.
My soul is still alive and I want you to know that I am here for you.
I'll be the first one to greet you when it's your time to come back home.
There's a reason why you aren't able to be here with me now.
Know there's more work to be done.

In the meantime, live fully.
You aren't alone in your journey.
I'll be walking with you every step of the way.
Don't worry about me.
There is an infinite amount of love and peace here.
I've been receiving your prayers.
Thank you for all of your beautiful love.
Since I'm on the other side, I can take care of you even more.
Be open to receiving my gifts.

I'm sending you all of my love from heaven.
I Love You Always

November Chapter Sponsor – Tracy Quadro

NOVEMBER 3
Angelic Prayer for Addiction

By Rev. Jennifer Shackford

I send you Angels.

I send you strength and courage!

I send you Archangel Raphael to clear your auric field,
remove any low energy attachments to you.

And I send you Archangel Michael to send them to the light!

I pray you once again are restored to the love you had for yourself
when you were a child.
That you can take one minute, one day, at a time.
That you utilize all the tools that await your use
to help you along your healing journey.

I pray you see what the world has to offer you.

I pray you find peace within yourself.

You can and will overcome!

And So It Is!

November Chapter Sponsor – Tracy Quadro

NOVEMBER 4
Forgiving Love

By Ann Phillis

Oh the joy!
The love of forgiving
Released from the past.
My heart is singing.

The threads that bind
Are freed from my being.
Angels of hope,
Resurrect my living.

I stand in the grace
Of my heart, renewed.
My soul, like fire,
Energizing my path forward.

My surrender complete,
My wings stretch wide.
I am of the light,
Fully here, on Earth.

NOVEMBER 5
Beloved Angels, I Pray

By Lisa Clayton

Beloved Angels, I ask you to bless my heart and soul
in this offering of prayer today.

I pray for love and forgiveness to be the banner I fly.
I pray for the highest vibration to emulate from my heart,
to attract those I am to be of service.
I pray my services rise up from my passionate heart
so I may sing my soul's song.

I pray "Now" envelops my deep consciousness
so I can be in tune with the present
and joyfully invite all opportunities to fill my heart's desires.
I pray the beautiful dreams that live inside of my heart manifest
into good deeds for every living being and spirit I am in touch with daily.

I pray that those who honor, respect, support and encourage me
are ever present in my life.
I pray for the greatest truth and wisdom to be reflected
in every word spoken and action taken while I'm here on earth.

I pray to no longer remain asleep in my heart
so I may see the wonder of each day's dawning
through eyes that penetrate beyond the obvious.

I pray to my Beloved Angels to help me live this day through love.

NOVEMBER 6
Prayer from Archangel Metatron

By Dona Ho Lightsey

Glorious is this life of mine,
to have to hold, to create divine.
We welcome the cup of God's holy word,
received in grace and truly heard.
We awaken the mind to what is bright,
illuminated by Holy sight.

Grace come to me, to reveal the truth,
to quickly shift what is the root
of all that is not light or love,
we now release this, like the peaceful dove,
who will carry me home on Angels' wings,
to the divine perfection of all sacred things.

We invite in now, God's holy light
to bless and heal what is not right,
inside the heart and body and mind,
we ask for truth, to seek and find...

The Chalice, the Cup inside the heart
frees ONESELF, no longer apart,
but ONE NOW, in Holy Trinity,
revealed, reclaimed in divinity.

Amen

NOVEMBER 7

Surround Me
with Your Loving Embrace

By Sue Broome

Dear Angels, Angels Everywhere,

I ask you to surround me with your loving energy and your sense of peace.
I feel my heart expand when I know you are with me.
Every cell in my body overflows with your loving embrace.
I see each color of the rainbow and beyond,
and feel your calm, reassuring presence.

You inspire me, you encourage me, you help me to see
what's right about the world and I am grateful.
When things feel off, you wrap me in your love and
encourage me to see things in a positive and clear light.

Come into my life every moment of each day.
Fill me with your energy, your light, your protection,
your guidance and your unconditional love.

I invite you into my life and into my heart, more today than yesterday.
I am open to receiving your love and your guidance,
listening with my whole being.

I know you are with me, Angels, when I call upon you.
You are always just a breath away.
Thank you, dear Angels, for your loving embrace.
I love you.

November Chapter Sponsor — Tracy Quadro

NOVEMBER 8
Angel Prayer for Expansion

By Suzanne Gochenouer

Dear Angels,

Help me see life's infinite possibilities
in every part of my life.

Guide me to expand my consciousness
and Love to the limits of each possibility,
and then give me the courage to move beyond those limits.

Help me learn to recognize opportunity and blessings
that come to me in ways I don't expect.

Remind me to ask for new ways to explore the depths of Light and Love.

Guide me to be open to new truths and revelations.

Excite my soul with the limitless Universe of which I am a part.

Share with me a love for endless learning
and for moving forward in Faith and Love.

Amen, amen, amen.

Thank you, thank you, thank you.

NOVEMBER 9
NOVEMBER 9 ~ LAUVIAH (Victory)

(from the tradition of the 72 Angels of the Tree of Life)
By Terah Cox

Dear Lauviah,

May your light remind me that it is the nature of life that I, and each,
should "win" at being who we truly are, and that in the "fight for existence,"
the battles worth winning cannot be fought.

When either success or seeming defeat
makes me forget the treasure of my inner light,
may you take me unto the altar of my heart to remember that true success
belongs to the soul and defeat belongs only to the world.
Thus may I strive toward my soul-purposes with dignity and integrity,
surrendering only to co-creation with the flow of life.

Help me to say the *yes* of acceptance to each circumstance that comes
so that I might receive its gifts, and yes to who I am right now
even as I am still bringing forth the more of me.

With your light may I see that I will always
come to where I need to be – and that there is no place
like now-here for finding my way to where I truly belong.

And above all, let me always know that I will triumph in my endeavors
one way or another, sooner or later, when I triumph in love today.
Amen

NOVEMBER 10
Prayer for Being Your True Self

By Linda Goodings

Almighty god, higher self and Archangel Jophiel,
Thank you for allowing me to be a reflection of your magnificence
in my personal life and in my life's work.

Thank you for allowing me to remember whom I really am.

Archangel Jophiel, thank you for guarding and guiding my thoughts
so that they are always based on peace, health, joy and love.
No matter where I go.

Allow me to hear, speak, see and know only love, like you do.
I'm willing to forgive everyone who has ever hurt me
or told me something other than the truth, including myself.

Please purify my emotions, intentions and anything that is blocking me
in this or any other lifetime, in any way.

I know I AM your greatness.
We are one, now and forever more.
Blessed be it.

Thank you and Amen!

November Chapter Sponsor – Tracy Quadro

NOVEMBER 11
Angel Jewels

By Ann Phillis

Ruby red, the depth of love
Violet fire, transforming heart
Green of nature, healing to soothe
Golden sunlight, nature's cocoon.

Orange spark, vitality's presence
Rose pink of love, Mother Christ's essence
Deep blue of cosmos, encompassing heaven
Pure white of grace, nourishing pearlescent.

Here we are, the angels of blessing!
Here we live, in harmony with the present.
A gift in every color, for life's every effort
We sparkle every nation and every heart to be radiant!

November Chapter Sponsor – Tracy Quadro

NOVEMBER 12
Prayer of Love for Mother Earth

By Inger Marie Moeller

"I place you Earth as a living pearl, in the chamber of my heart"
We step on you, don't feel your pain
Your cry turns into sand
into the sky You call in vain
across the desert land

"I place you Earth as a living pearl, in the chamber of my heart"
When will we hear, when will we see
what we have done to you?
When will we understand the tree
the birds, the lion, flowers too?

"I place you Earth as a living pearl, in the chamber of my heart"
The rivers flow, the oceans grow
the snowcap disappears
the waste of ignorance we throw
ignoring all your tears

"I place you Earth as a living pearl, in the chamber of my heart"
But listen now, the sun breaks through
Your children are awake
and hand in hand we stand by You
Your heart to us we take

"We place you Earth as a living pearl, in the chamber of our hearts"

November Chapter Sponsor – Tracy Quadro

NOVEMBER 13
Angel and Elemental Shamanic Blessings

By Karen Cote

Blessings to the Angels and Spirits
of the Upper, Middle and Lower Worlds.

Blessings to the Spirits of the East, where the sun rises.
May my metaphoric branches go as high as my roots do deep.
Thus may I feel the power of Your wind
yet stay anchored in the Earth.

Blessings to the Spirits of the South, direction of the healer.
May the power of Your fire burn away my ego and false pride
so I can be a "hollow bone" to channel Your light.

Blessings to the Spirits of the West,
the direction we go when we die.
Give me the strength of metal so that I may cultivate
truth, justice and integrity as I prepare for
my final journey home to You.

Blessings to the Spirits of the North.
May I forever anchor myself and be as grounded as the Earth.
Since I am autumn wood that burns hot with too much fire,
may the power of Your water come to cool my fires
so I do not burn myself out.

I ask that Your light may always come into my body,
purify my soul and guide my way all the days of my life.

November Chapter Sponsor – Tracy Quadro

NOVEMBER 14
Healing Blessings from Archangel Metatron

By Joyce Willson

As I close my eyes to connect to heavenly energy
I invite in the loving Archangel Metatron.
I begin to feel his presence in a split second.
His gentleness, love and support arrive
as I feel the tingling sensations trickle over my entire body.

I see the sparkling, glistening light pour into my crown chakra
and travel like the swiftness and gentleness
of a waterfall as it pours into my entire being.

I am grateful for this loving connection to Archangel Metatron.
I open to receive what message and healing he brings forth to me this day.
I remain quiet and still to feel and experience his presence.
I am grateful.

I feel the love and strength he sends forth so that I may be the person I AM.

I AM love, I AM kind; I AM a child of God.
I AM peace, I AM compassion, I AM whole.
I AM gentle, I AM power, I AM joy.
I AM free, I AM ease, I AM safe.
I AM light, I AM truth, I AM whom I AM.

I pray to you, dear Archangel Metatron, to shine your light upon me this day.
Amen.

NOVEMBER 15
Angel Prayer for Healing

By Michelle Mullady

Angels of the realm of holy love and vibrant light,
I call upon your presence to aid me in my healing now.
I ask that a powerful surge of emerald green healing energy
fill my being at this moment; cleansing and purifying
every organ, muscle, joint, tissue and cell of my body,
restoring me to full well-being.

With my heart open to God's rejuvenating love, I accept my healing.
Give me the faith to know, in my core, that the power of God
sustains and blesses me with perfect health.

Darling angels, in prayer each day,
guide me to contemplate the life of Spirit within.
Help me to affirm that I am a creation of Spirit,
an ever-renewing expression of divine life.
I am health and wholeness,
and my body continues to respond with life and vitality.

Please assist me to use the power of my mind to visualize myself
as a vibrant, walking, talking phenomenon of God's Light.
Thank you for supporting my ability to heal
and for leading me to peace of mind,
a transformed sense of calm, and a strengthened spirit.
And so it is.

Amen

NOVEMBER 16
Invoking the Angels

By Trish Grain

I invoke all Angels to join hands
and to let their rainbow energy flow into my being
and to open my heart,
creating a magical bridge
between heaven and earth
so that I may be empowered and inspired
to be of service in helping others to reach for the stars.

I open my arms and heart to receive your blessings
bringing hope, love, joy, abundance and spiritual enlightenment.

The angels are sending you sprinkles of magic and miracles now.

Thank you, Angels

November Chapter Sponsor — Tracy Quadro

NOVEMBER 17
Prayer to Zagzagel-Angel of Wisdom

By Bobbe Bramson

Zagzagel, oh, Zagzagel
Blessed Inner Angel of Wisdom-
Bring me into healing alignment
with the Light and warmth of your presence.
Return me to the innocence of my pure
and glowing Self fully embodied as Love.
Zagzagel, oh, Zagzagel
Make me wise and help me to treasure the stillness
of my Higher Self's company.
Give me inner sight to look within, to seek and find
each pearl of wisdom that awaits me there.
Give me inner hearing within the subtle silence
to intuit the still, small voice of God.
Give me inner knowing and take me to the innermost sanctuary
of my heart where quiet repose resides.
Zagzagel, oh, Zagzagel
Still the chatter of my ego mind, the endless drone of static
that feeds self-doubt and negativity,
And instead tune me into the clear channel,
resonant with the harmonic of My Truth and My Inner Knowing.
Zagzagel, oh, Zagzagel
Teach me your art of Wisdom and make me expert in it,
that I may cultivate a rock-solid trust in myself
that cannot be swayed by any outside influence.
Surround and infill me with your halo of Divine Truth
and guide me to shine my soul's radiance upon my path.
Thank you, beloved Zagzagel.

November Chapter Sponsor – Tracy Quadro

NOVEMBER 18
Prayer for the Release of Suffering

By Juancarlos Soto

God,
Though I may feel alone, I know I am not.
Though my ego tells me that I am unworthy,
I know I am Worthy.
I am willing to release those beliefs that limit me
so that they may be transmuted into strengths
that will help me to succeed.

I know that in your eyes I am perfect.
I, at this moment, choose to accept this perfection within me.
Help me, loving Creator, in this time of need, in this time of suffering.
I know that I no longer have to suffer in silence
that I no longer have to suffer at all.
I no longer carry these burdens alone.
You and the Angels help carry them now
and transmute them into learning experiences that will only serve
to make me better, to make my life better.

I affirm that your Love, Grace and Harmony flow into my life.
I affirm that your Love, Grace and Harmony, nurture me and renew me.
I proclaim that it is so.

Amen.

NOVEMBER 19
Ariel, Bring the Rains of Remembrance

By Kimberly Marooney

Beloved Ariel, How I miss you.
The illusion pulled me away with the needs of the world.
Too much to do! Not enough money.
Worry, anxiety doing it all myself.
That rut is deeply worn and I was stuck in it.

Thank you for sending your rains of remembrance
to soften the soil and liberate me.
You have provided an influx of energy that has set me free.
Thank you. I feel so blessed and loved.

With your help, I can feel an immense shift in my consciousness.
I see this shift happening all around me in the world.
I witness millions of others in prayer, co-creation and endeavor
calling your Presence to dwell on this Earth.
The age of darkness is passing and your Golden Light is dawning.

I am deeply grateful that you are opening the collective consciousness
to make life easier. I feel supported!
Perhaps this support has been there all along
and I'm just opening to experience it.
Could this be the state of enlightenment?
Becoming aware of how much loving support is Present already?

I feel peace, joy, love, freedom. My heart is singing with solutions.
Hold me in this state of loving Oneness today.

November Chapter Sponsor – Tracy Quadro

NOVEMBER 20
My Forever Friend

By Marian Cerdeira

I hold out my hand to you,
my beloved Guardian Friend.
Please be here.
Let me feel your loving presence with me now
and close to me throughout this day.

You hear my prayer.
I feel it in my soul.
You deeply know me
and my heart is safe with you, always.

I reach for your loving hand, my Guardian Friend,
to join with mine as I walk through the unknown of this day.
My mind is open to all that I am guided to see and to do.
I'm thankful you are here and I am under your loving watch.
Blessed that you are forever close keeping me out of harm's way.

As I lift my thoughts to God and this inner light,
I think of you holding my hand.
My heart is deeply grateful to you,
my beloved Guardian Friend.

I love you.

NOVEMBER 21
Daily Invocation for Healthy Eating

By Gina Barbara

I pray to you Angels of pure light,
that these foods I eat
my Soul ignite.

As the rays of the sun,
touch the morning dew,
my desire for unhealthy foods
I hand over to you.

May the nourishment and gifts you bring,
heal my mind, body and spirit too;
as I grow In Gratitude,
for all I say, Eat and Do!

NOVEMBER 22
Archangel Uriel: Prayer for Peace

By Cathelijne Filippo

Beloved Archangel Uriel, Angel of Peace,

I ask you to shower me with your peace today.
Please help me be at peace with myself and with the world.
When I experience inner turmoil,
please bring me tranquillity and renewal of hope.
When I experience fear, help me to return to a state of love and trust.
When I experience anger, show me forgiveness and understanding.
When there is misunderstanding, please give me insight.
For as I forgive another, so do I forgive myself.
And as I strive to understand another, I find a new sense of peace.
Please harmonize all my relationships and my environment,
so that I can live peacefully.

Dear Archangel Uriel, Flame of God,

Please bring your Light to places of darkness on this earth.
Let it permeate fear and anger, hate and violence.
Please replace chaos and war with peace and understanding.
I especially ask you to send your Light and peace to _____.
May _____be resolved perfectly for the Highest Good of all.
Help mankind live from the heart, opening up to a sense of
unity and brotherhood.
May Divine Justice always prevail.

So be it.

NOVEMBER 23

Archangel Uriel's
Prayer for Emotional Healing

By Stacey Wall

Archangel Uriel,
You know my heart and the challenges I've faced.
You know where I've been and how events have made me whom I am.
I know that every happening served as a learning opportunity.
With gratitude for these lessons, I ask you to help me move forward
and leave these events in the past.

Help me heal any emotional wounds
that hold me back from living my life fully.
Bring healing to any relationships that may be strained or damaged.
Help me move beyond old hurts.
Fill me with forgiveness for myself and others.
Remove any fear of allowing myself to heal.
Fill my body, mind and spirit with the light of pure love.
Transform my brokenness and restore me to perfect balance and health.

Give me strength to let go of old beliefs.
Give me courage to heal.
Give me the freedom to shed the pain of the past
so that I may live as the fullest expression of my authentic self.

Archangel Uriel, I thank you for your quiet strength and unfailing love.
And so it is.

NOVEMBER 24
Angel Prayer for Self-Connection

By Simona Hadjigeorgalis

If these words resonate with you, read them out-loud. Gift them to yourself.

I am a beautiful and vibrant being.
I am in harmony with my authentic self.
I connect with my inner power and light.
I honor the light within me by being the best me I can be.

I believe in my inner wisdom.
I gain clarity of who I am and my unique gifts
by staying curious, observant, and radically honest with myself.
I fully embrace all the hues of my human-ness.

I trust in the greater picture.
I embrace my loving and playful heart.
I am radiant and flowing.

I am fulfilling my soul's purpose, and along the way
I am enjoying positive and loving relationships,
flowers, smiles, warmth & sunshine, happiness,
laughter, joy, vitality, positivity, passion,
wonderful interactions and experiences,
and the radiating white light of love.

I live a vibrant and well life.
I shine from the inside, out.

November Chapter Sponsor – Tracy Quadro

NOVEMBER 25
Angel Prayer of Protection and Direction

By Brenda Dowell

Angels, Guides, Ascended Masters, Teachers
and all who walk with me in love & light,
please come into my life now.

Guide, guard, protect and keep me safe from harm.

Please allow me to be a pure and open channel
for your love and healing to work through me.

Please give me clarity of purpose,
courage to follow my dreams and compassion to be of service.

Not my will, but thine be done,
for the highest good of all concerned.

And so it is.

November Chapter Sponsor – Tracy Quadro

NOVEMBER 26
Being Thankful

By Lisa K.

Being thankful is a tricky thing,
but you have much to have gratitude for.

Within the realm of this or that,
your life has brought you many good things.

You just need to take a moment to realize how much you have!

With your gratitude you will generate an aura of positive energy
that will surround you with a magnetic attraction to all that you desire.

When this happens, we can easily bring you all the people, places and things
that you need to manifest what you want.

– Your Angels

NOVEMBER 27

Archangel Raguel:
Prayer for Friendship and Harmony

By Cathelijne Filippo

Beloved Archangel Raguel,

please shower me with the energy of true friendship today.
Let me be my own best friend, enjoying my own company
as I treat myself with loving-kindness.
Let me extend that loving kindness to those I meet,
in order to become the friend for others that I would wish for myself.
Please send me like-minded friends for mutual support.

May I truly connect from heart to heart and from Soul to Soul,
as I see the Light within myself and within the other.
Please help me to communicate openly and honestly
as well as truly listen to another.
Help me to stay centered within my own heart,
whilst reaching out to others.
In that way, all my friendships will hold the quality of the heart.

Dear Archangel Raguel,
please mediate in any situation between me, and my loved ones
where there is disharmony. Please help us resolve the cause of this,
be it misunderstanding, irritation, frustration, anger, jealousy or resentment.
Help me to always see the lesson in any situation
as I step back and let my Higher Self lead the way.
Thank you for your friendship, Archangel Raguel.

NOVEMBER 28

Angel Guidance:
Yesterday, Tomorrow and Today

By KipAnne Huntz

My dear Angels I ask you please;
balance my empathy and compassion with my courage and strength.
Should I begin to sway from this path we journey on
I ask you please, gently guide me back around.
Though my dear Angels you already see the paths that have
yet to unfold before me
you know it is I who must choose ~
I ask you now and always my Angels far and near please guide me true.
As this day unfolds before me it is my heart's desire,
my passion too that in addition to whatever it is I create with you
we also bring beauty, love and strength to those whose paths we cross today.

As was yesterday and will be again tomorrow,
I begin today with a heartfelt thank you.
Thank you for surrounding me as I awaken
to all of the new possibilities this day holds.
Yesterday's challenges and triumphs will always be a part of who I am.
Tomorrow's blessings have yet to unfold.
Today is a blank canvas ~ full of infinite possibilities
on which to build and create.

My Angels ~ I ask you once again,
guide me true for this day belongs to me and you.

NOVEMBER 29
In Divine Service Prayer

By Elizabeth Harper

Great Spirit, Angels, Guides, and Elementals.
Surround me with your love, light, peace and power.
Protect me, help me to be at one with you.
I ask that you bring light into my mind, body, spirit and emotions,
cleanse me of anything that does not belong to me
and no longer serves me.

Bring light into my space, above me, below me, and around me.
Spread your light and love into every area of my being,
past, present and future, in this lifetime and all future lifetimes.

I ask that you ground my energy and help me
to reach the highest vibration possible
that is in alignment with my current level of awareness.

I call upon my Angels and Guides to work with and through me today
for my highest and greatest good
and for the highest and greatest good
of all those I come into contact with.

Angels, protect me as I share my gifts with those in need.
Help me to serve from a place of integrity, love and compassion.
Help me to hear your messages, to see your divine light,
to receive clear and accurate guidance.

With the power of your love, I thank you
Amen.

November Chapter Sponsor – Tracy Quadro

NOVEMBER 30
Behold, Behold

By Roland Comtois

Hear me, I am your guardian angel.
For the mighty light shines upon you.
As you ascend towards your enlightened self
know that I will always be with you.
You have come opened to expand your vibration.
Open your heart now and release pain.

Be Love.
A soul that suffers cannot ascend, grow, expand or become.
Behold, Behold for the light will give you strength.
Your true strength already exists deep within the soul, deep within you.
For today, as you ascend towards your truth,
place your hands upon your heart and know
that I am with you.

Be Love.
Behold, Behold for now we are one,
in union with the Source,
in union with the Divine,
in union with Self.

Be Love.
I call upon your soul
To REMEMBER
To REAWAKEN
To RENERGIZE
Your Divine purpose.

November Chapter Sponsor – Tracy Quadro

DECEMBER

Angelic Encounters
of the Loving Kind
Bobbe Bramson

The Angels' presence in my life has always been a bit of a mystery to me—the exact when, where, and how of it. Up until middle elementary school I was completely unaware that Angels existed at all, yet even before that I felt a soft and sweet protection surrounding me, a magic cloak woven of music, beauty, and nature; a cloak of much-needed comfort in a big and scary world. Common knowledge would have it that to invoke Angels we must ask them to come, but that isn't how it happened for me. Instead it was as if *they* led me to *them* sending out quietly persistent Angel sonar that patiently awaited my heart's response.

The Angels came to me as I was wrenched from the warm amniotic sea, whispering assurances that brought me through a difficult birth. They came to me, the lonely little Jewish girl, in the sparkly winter light of Christmas, as I played carols that beckoned with harps of gold and joyous strains, all of it so magically wondrous. They escorted me safely at 3AM in Manhattan to my car on the fifth floor of the deserted municipal parking garage. Angels sat next to me in darkened concert halls, my heart fair to bursting at music so achingly beautiful my soul would sing. And when I crossed the Tappan Zee Bridge in New York, and the car to my left began spinning cartwheels at 60mph across all four lanes, they delivered me to the other side unscathed.

My seminal Angel moment came in 1994, a few months before my mother died. I'd never had a direct angelic encounter, but I was about to be initiated. During a past life regression to 1850s England, on my deathbed and struggling to breathe, there appeared before me on my right side a huge and resplendent Angel whose outstretched wings glowed with luminous hues of amber, russet, brown and gold. The otherworldly glory of its presence was awe inspiring and yet I felt waves of transcendent calm flow through me, infilling me with a deep peace. In that moment I knew that all would be well, even in death.

As comforting as this angelic vision was in terms of my mom's impending death, it was so vivid and real that I knew on some core level that I had been changed irrevocably and there was no turning back. The invitation had been sent: the Angels were calling me to seek them actively, to engage with them as healing change agents. This wasn't always easy. I was forced to suspend my disbelief. I was challenged to step away from my father's atheism and the stultifying rigidity of an abstract and vengeful God. I was asked to surrender all constructs of what might or might not be possible, and I was gently but firmly encouraged to journey into the density and darkness within me that I might heal unto wholeness and overcome decades of false limitations, suffocating fears, and outmoded ways of being. I could never have braved this inner terrain without the constant guidance, love, and protective support of the Angels. They brought me through it and I have gotten so much stronger, braver, wiser and compassionate for having made the effort.

Over the years my relationship with the Angels has flourished through millions of delicious synchronicities and transformative miracles of angelic alchemy. I cannot begin to describe in mere words the sheer joy and Divine Magic of our co-creative partnership of healing and evolution. They continue to urge me to go deep that I may ascend higher. They embrace me when I falter and feel afraid. Through them my vessel expands daily to hold more Light and express more of my Highest Essence thereby enabling me to help others to do the same.

My communion with the Angels is a gift that keeps on giving, and I am exceedingly grateful for its reciprocal nature. The more I seek to deepen my connection with them, the stronger my connectivity becomes. The more I devote myself in gratitude to walk with them, the more radiantly they shine their grace upon my Spirit path. I feel honored and blessed to be one of many channeling the Angels' Love and Light into the world at this time. What a blessing it is to share my love of the Angels, transmitting their healing frequencies and uplifting messages of hope, so that each of us may awaken to the powerful truth and transcendent glory of who we really are.

Bobbe Bramson is a licensed, ordained interfaith minister through the Angel Ministry of Gateway University, and is of the lineage of the Order of the Seraphim. In her work as an angel medicine woman, energy healer, intuitive, and teacher she helps people uncover and reconnect to the beautiful and radiant Soul Treasure that they are. Using her 35 plus years of experience in the creative and metaphysical/spiritual arts she synthesizes a perfect blend of healing techniques and transformational tools ***custom-designed*** for each individual to help them awaken to, explore, and express their unique gifts.

She is known for her attuned and insightful wisdom, her genuine caring and warmth, and her ability to be an innovative and inspirational catalyst for positive change. Bobbe enjoys creating beautiful sacred environments where she facilitates Reiki Wisdom Salons, Angel Alchemy Circles and Soul-Awakening play-shops to nourish the heart, mind, and soul. Certified as a Usui and Karuna RMT, IET Master Instructor, and VortexHealing® practitioner, she is also a lifelong musician, songwriter and environmental and animal rights activist. The guiding intention in all of her work is to empower people to shine their most authentic Light into the world. Connect with Bobbe at bramsongs@verizon.net, on Facebook at https://www.facebook.com/AngelHearttoHeart or via her website www.AngelHeartToHeart.com.

DECEMBER 1

Archangel Chamuel
Prayer for Self-Love and Acceptance

By Bobbe Bramson

Most beloved Archangel Chamuel,
teach me to love and accept myself
from the inside out, to see myself as you do.
You, of the purest, highest octave of love and adoration,
please infuse every layer of my being
with your golden pink ray of unconditional love and acceptance.

Shine it into every cell of my body so that I might learn
how to treat this temple with respect and tenderness.
Purify my mind and emotions of patterns of neglect,
self-judgment, and harsh expectations,
and surrender me into the peace of a trusting, open heart.
Enfold me and the hurting disowned parts of myself
in the warmth of your compassionate embrace
that a healing re-union may occur.

Reveal within me the truth of my perfection right now, as I am,
and deliver me from the need to look outside myself
for validation of my worth.
Empower me with such a strong and unwavering love
that I honor my own authenticity, cherishing it as a rare and precious jewel.
Glorious Chamuel, I give thanks for your radiant Presence in my life
and for the joyful assurance it brings to my heart and soul.
May you be blessed a thousand-fold.
Amen

December Chapter Sponsor – Bobbe Bramson

DECEMBER 2
Communicating With Spirit

By Lisa K.

Never before has there been a best time to renew
your interest and strength in spirit.

You will find that it is easier and faster than ever before
to connect to your higher realms of consciousness
and to, what you call, Spirit.

The land of Universal Consciousness
awaits your reaching in and connecting.

So, be still, wait for your answers,
as they will come to you in symbols, words, thoughts, images and sound.

We will always try many ways of communication to reach you!

– Your Angels

December Chapter Sponsor — Bobbe Bramson

DECEMBER 3
A Prayer for Harmonious Communication

By Tracy Quadro

Angel Gabriel,
you have been the harbinger
of so many pivotal spiritual moments.
You have shared the glad tidings of births, salvation,
the promise of a new life and other happy news.
But even when you foretell unhappy events,
there is hope in your message.

Please help me to find peace through understanding that
everything happens for a reason, and all news is good news.
Guide me to resonate with your strength,
so that I may see every piece of information that comes to me,
even the words that strike me at first as unwelcomed, as a gift.

Please guide me through my rough passages,
strewn with misunderstandings and strife, with grace.
Please remind me to be merciful and forgiving of myself
when my reaction to what others tell me falls short of graceful.
Give me the skills to help others to find common ground
and to break down the communication barriers that lead to conflict.

Empower my voice so that my words are a welcomed comfort to others.
And please help me to find the skills to communicate so that
all I impart will sound like good news,
and that all I hear will sound joyful.

December Chapter Sponsor – Bobbe Bramson

DECEMBER 4
You Are Not Alone

By Linda Wheeler Williams

An Angel intervened on my behalf in 1990.
I was driving to work, thinking about my day.
I'm not sure how long I had been on autopilot,
but when I came back to reality, I was too close to a semi.
I felt a sense of calmness, while thinking, "It's my time."
You are not alone.
A heavy force pushed my foot,
like someone placing their foot on top of mine
and pressed down on the accelerator.
My car speeded up and I heard, "Turn, Turn, Turn,"
as the force took control of the wheel,
steering my car around the truck and passing it.
Ask your Angels for guidance.
My car was then guided across the grassy medium,
onto the freeway, headed in the opposite direction.
I heard "Brake, Brake, Brake." I slowed down and pulled over.
My body was shaking fiercely. What had just happened?
They are here to assist.
That incident was the theme of my thoughts that day.
Over the years I've had other experiences.
I used free will, which was typically
the opposite of what I was guided to do.
When I listened, I enjoyed a peaceful life.

I am not alone. I now ask my Angels for guidance.
Thank you Angels for your grace and assistance.
Amen.

December Chapter Sponsor — Bobbe Bramson

DECEMBER 5
Archangel Michael's
Divine Love and Light

By Lisa Clayton

Beloved Archangel Michael,
I trust in your courage and protection to infuse my heart each day.
Miracles occur when I remain focused upon believing in the power of love,
through connecting with your Divine Love.
Anything is possible, through opening my heart to Divine Light,
from the Golden Realm of Angels, led by You.

My heart beats in perfect rhythm with Divine presence of your Love,
which activates my inner compass for freedom,
happiness, joy and abundance.
The Golden Realm of Angels offers me Divine Light
laced with harmony and grace to raise the vibrations of my heart.
I feel their golden essence flowing through my veins with each breath I take,
replacing the pulse of fearful situations that appear impossible to overcome.

These are false illusions.
The essence of Divine Love and Light shines upon dark times,
dissolving fear as unpredictable life situations unfold.
Archangel Michael reminds me
Divine Love and Light always trumps fear.
The Golden Realm of Angels' wise guidance I receive
through faithful prayer is the angelic communiqué
that opens my eyes, ears and heart's voice for reception each day.

I am forever grateful for these blessings
activated by Archangel Michael's Divine Love and Light.

December Chapter Sponsor – Bobbe Bramson

DECEMBER 6
Prayer for Abundance

By Rev. Vicki Snyder

I pray to Archangel Ariel to create abundance in my life.
I ask that we partner together on this task of creation.
My thoughts attract all that is positive and good for me.
I only ask for what I need,
that my wants are in line with my actual needs
and that my wants and needs all always in sync.

I show gratitude for all I have and I ask for prosperity in all areas of my life:
family, friends, love, good health, opportunities and money.
With your help and the law of attraction
I witness a cornucopia of prosperity
and I share these blessings with all I love.

I also ask Ariel to shower others with blessings of abundance.
With this mutual abundance there comes a shift in the world.
Let us not have to work so hard to provide for our families,
so we may enjoy more quality time together.
Allow this abundance to let people and families fall back on old family values.

Help me and others not to come from a place of lack
but from a place of wonderful gratitude for each day we have.

December Chapter Sponsor – Bobbe Bramson

DECEMBER 7
Prayer from the Glen

By Trude A. Xanders

Come Angels, Lovely Larks Celestial,
make your nest in the deep wildwoods of my heart.

A cavern in quiet, a twined canyon,
where branches and brambles roam,
urging rebirth throughout this secret cave.

I seek sure solace beneath your Wings.
Softly, swiftly, wind your feathered passage
in loving answer to my Spirit's Quest.

Inspire the peeking violet towards the far sun,
free the gleaming streams along their emerald paths;
Caress the currents with opalescent beams of Rainbow,
pour Iris Light through every crevice, curve and hollow.

You, tranquil Treasure unseen, bless this dappled forest.
Your Medicine, Grace,
My prayers, Answered.

December Chapter Sponsor – Bobbe Bramson

DECEMBER 8
Angel Prayer for Inner Peace

By Michelle Mullady

Angels of Serenity,
in the silence of this moment,
I thank you for connecting me to the place within
that is untouched by any form of turmoil or distress.

Guide me to tune in to this inner reservoir of divine peace
and allow serenity to soothe my soul
as I rest in the fulfillment of God's love.

May I listen to the quiet and feel the peaceful presence of God inside me.
In these sacred moments of conscious communion with the Divine,
lead me to understand that I can reconnect with this inner peace
at any time throughout the day.

*As you say this prayer, sit quietly and settle down. Take several deep breaths. Let go of whatever worries you have and be in this moment where there is only peace. There is loveliness around you, paradise within you and you feel tranquil and calm. Nothing can overthrow this feeling. You are safe and secure in your peacefulness and choose this place, this space whenever you want stillness and relaxation.

DECEMBER 9
Prayer to Your Angel Guides

By Virginia Giordano

Dear Precious Gifts from God,
Thank you for surrounding me with
Love and light every moment of every day
Asleep or awake
You guard and protect me
Because of you
I am never alone
You are my true spiritual soul-mates
No one knows me better
No one loves me more --
Unconditionally
No one judges me less--
Including myself
I know that with you by my side
ALL IS WELL, ALL IS WELL, ALL IS WELL

So Be It

December Chapter Sponsor – Bobbe Bramson

DECEMBER 10
Mother Mary: Prayer for Gentle Self-Care

By Cathelijne Filippo

Beloved mother Mary, Queen of Angels,

Please surround me in your peaceful,
caring energy of soft, aquamarine, blue Light.
May it surround me like the warm embrace of a mother,
healing me on all levels.
May it bring gentleness and security to my inner child.
Please heal my inner child and help me connect to it.
May it awaken within me the ability to play and enjoy life to the fullest,
As I care deeply for this child in me.

Dear Mother Mary,
Please help me to be gentler towards myself.
Let me accept myself fully. Let me acknowledge my true self.
Let me love myself completely,
And let me take time to rest, replenish and recharge my inner batteries.
Please teach me gentle self-care.

Now let me extend that gentleness and kindness to others.
For only after I take proper self-care, can I truly be there for others.
I acknowledge this fact and vow to be there for myself
and to not only honor others' needs but also my own.
By doing so I become more whole and complete,
adding these energies of healing and care to the Earth.
So be it.

December Chapter Sponsor – Bobbe Bramson

DECEMBER 11
Prayer for Stress-Free Holidays

Whatever your holiday ceremonies, let this inspire you to smile away the holiday stress

By Cathleen O'Connor

Beloved Angels, the Holidays have arrived once more
with menus and planning and shopping in store.
The social whirlwind begins; my calendar fills
and I can't find a minute just to sit still.

There are cards to write and presents to buy;
phone calls to make and giftwrap bows to tie.
There are lists from the kids of 'must-haves' galore
and no elves in sight to lessen the chores.

The weight of expectations begins to take its toll;
Will the roast be flavorful? Will I have enough rolls?
Should I sit cousin Bill next to Ted's new wife
or will old family tensions erupt in strife?

It's just too much; I feel I can't cope
so you have to help me or there is no hope.
I feel overwhelmed and less than enthused;
even the batteries have been over-used!

Please step in and take me in hand
and remind me this whirlwind was never the plan.
Help me to see that what matters most
are the hugs and the love and keeping us close.

Send us your light, your grace and your love,
with soft, gentle whispers of calm from above.
And remove all our stress as the holidays near
and replace it with only angelic good cheer!

December Chapter Sponsor – Bobbe Bramson

DECEMBER 12
Angels of Creation

By Ann Phillis

Flowing light, angels bright,
Creating change in our world tonight.
Touching all hearts, all consciousness waking,
Steeped in the knowing, our planet is waiting.

Waiting for love, for light, for hope,
To overcome hatred, the fear and the dark.

Choose, dear souls, choose the awaking,
Join with the angels, the Masters evolving.
Choose and be free in the light of our making,
Us all, together, in the new world we're creating!

December Chapter Sponsor – Bobbe Bramson

DECEMBER 13

Healing Prayer for –
'Inner & Outer Conflict'

By Gina Barbara

I call upon the Angels of peace to comfort me
at times of inner and outer conflict in my life.

I ask that I be clearly understood
and able to express myself easily and freely
without doubt, fear or judgment,
in what I do or what I say.

I ask to grow towards a much deeper understanding of myself and others,
allowing the beauty of grace to unfold and to move beyond
the illusion of doubt, fear or judgment, in my everyday challenges.

By so doing I ask you to help me bring peace and love to myself,
others and the world, through the clarity of your light.

I am now at one with all that is!

DECEMBER 14
Wear a New Heart Wardrobe

By Lisa Clayton

Significant shifts are occurring on planet earth, Beloved:
less mind, more heart.
Practice emptying your mind, connect with your heart
and learn to listen to your heart messages
as you open up to Divine Guidance.
First thing each morning, focus on your soul.
Stop thinking so much.

Your experiences are the result of your thoughts and intentions.
Let your intentions be created from your heart
by letting go of what your mind thinks you should do.
Learn to listen to the voice of your heart.
This is easy when you connect to our Divine Love and Light
and allow it to enter your heart.
Bring in this energy through your crown chakra.
Honor your brain and cleanse it of thoughts that no longer serve you;
thoughts that hold on to anger, resentment, jealousy, and greed.
Cleanse your mind with love energy.

Wash your brain daily.
Dress your heart with a new wardrobe,
one that makes you sing, dance, laugh, love ALL
and soothes the soul with peaceful colors.
What's in your new heart wardrobe to wear each day?
It's time to go heart shopping! Commit to follow your heart's voice
and listen to what it desires to wear each day.

DECEMBER 15
A Prayer to Heal Overwhelm

By Julie Geigle

Archangel Metatron,
There is always so much to do.
The days never seem to hold enough time to get everything done.
I seem to be missing my life, always busy,
running from this thing to that.
I am in constant anxiety that I will never get it all done.

Please help me to awaken to these truths….
I did not come here to get it done.
"How am I feeling?" measures my success.
If anxiety arises, I STOP what I am doing and breathe deeply three times.
My breath helps me shift out of ego consciousness and into Soul consciousness.
I radiate love, light and harmony from my Soul.
I am a Miracle Maker, a Divine Manifestor of my reality.
Time only exists within Ego Consciousness, the root of overwhelm.
Time dissolves within Soul Consciousness; where energy and motivation are endless.
The limitations of my ego vanish as I embrace timelessness.

I am not powerless,
I am POWERFUL!
I am a glorious, magnificent Soul
who has come forth to experience love.
And as I align with that truth
overwhelm dissolves.
And so it is.

December Chapter Sponsor – Bobbe Bramson

DECEMBER 16
A Prayer to Be Present

By Lee A. Baker

Rushing through a busy day,
I took a deep breath to center.
A Voice said, "Slow down to the speed of life."
Sighing, I replied, "That is easier said than done."
To which the Voice answered,
"We could have said,
slow down to the speed of light which is much faster!"
I laughed.

In that moment, a valuable lesson was learned.

How long does it take
a butterfly to rest, a bird to fly, a snowflake to form,
a new leaf to unfurl, a flower to bloom, a raindrop to fall,
a breeze to blow, a whisper to be heard, a prayer to be answered,
a heart to open, a tear to dry, a laugh to spread,
a wound to heal, a body to dance, a human to BE?

May I open my awareness to the present moment
and accept it with gratitude and grace.
May I listen to the stirrings of my soul and follow the wisdom within.
May I surrender to the Divine timing and growth of my highest potential.
May I allow my light to shine and merge with the radiance within All.

Thank you.

Amen.

December Chapter Sponsor – Bobbe Bramson

DECEMBER 17
Prayer for Committing to Your Divine Path

By Samantha Winstanley

I ask for the Highest Divine Light

To move through me

From this day forth

So I may serve as a vessel

For the Highest Good of All

Amen

This prayer is simple but very powerful when used every day. I believe that working with angels doesn't have to be complicated. Divine light is always present and accessible to everyone. To receive guidance and help all you have to do is ask with a sincere and loving heart. Your answer may not come immediately, but you can trust that it will arrive, when you are ready and the timing is right.

This prayer is for all those who wish to act as a bridge of light for humanity and work in service for the Divine. It will invoke angels to support and guide you on your Life's journey, clear a pathway forward and illuminate your heart. Remember that one step at a time is all it takes to reach your goals.

God loves you very much.

-Samantha

DECEMBER 18
Bless us All Angels

By Inger Marie Moeller

Angel of Truth, your color is blue.
You show us all that we need to dissolve all the darkness
the past has brought and turn our doubts into Faith.

Angel of Love, your color is rose.
You guide us to follow the heart to love and to hold,
the grace that will flow to cherish the life on this Earth.

Angel of Peace, your color is white.
You glide like the wings of the dove
You tell us: Stop fighting. You help us forgive
and recognize God's Love in all eyes

Angel of Joy, your color is gold.
You help us to laugh and to smile.
You wipe all the tears from faces of pain
and heal every child of man.

Angel of Light, your colors shine through
like the rainbow across the sky.
We go through the changes the Earth will need
for the life to continue unfold.

Bless us all Angels. Give us Thy Light.
Lead us to let it stream forth from heart to heart,
from mind to mind-and the Earth will be whole again.

December Chapter Sponsor – Bobbe Bramson

DECEMBER 19
Prayer to Archangel Michael for Strength and Courage

By Susan Mavity

A New Earth

Ignite within your world the true Beauty and Grace of your Being.
Claim your divinity within the Blue Ray of our light.

Dear Ones,
stand bold and strong in the light of the new energies.
Visualize the sacred wisdom within your hearts.
Send forth a beam of light for all to see.

Dear Earth Angels,
hold this truth in your hearts.
You are all one, connected within the
Divine Blueprint of All That Is.

Dream within your hearts a vision of a new world.

December Chapter Sponsor — Bobbe Bramson

DECEMBER 20
The Reach for the Stars Prayer

By Mitzi and Brynn Patton

My angels so dear, I ask you to come near
to be with me throughout my day.
Wrap me up in white light,
keep my smiles super bright,
and keep me safe while I play.

I know you give me hints
in the sun rays that make me squint
or when I find feathers or dimes.
Encouragement you give to me,
I feel you, I don't have to see,
you are here with me all of the time.

Thanks for being my friend,
with you I know there's no end
to the possibilities that before me lie.
You'll help me get anything done
if I ask and even make it fun,
with you it's great finding my way.

Whatever I do, you help me get through,
and even raise the bar.
You expect the best for me,
higher and farther than I can see.
With angels, I can reach the stars!

December Chapter Sponsor – Bobbe Bramson

DECEMBER 21
Solstice Prayer

By Cathelijne Filippo

This Prayer is for the Winter Solstice in the Northern Hemisphere;
If you live in the Southern Hemisphere, read the Solstice Prayer on June 25.

Beloved Farlas, Angel of Winter,
Bless me with your presence during this Winter Solstice,
and shower me in Yuletide blessings.
May I go deeply within during this shortest day
and longest night of the year.
May I use this time for quiet contemplation.

Let me look back on the past year,
being grateful for all blessings,
letting go of all that no longer serves me.
As I rest in the knowledge that this is the time to relax and rejuvenate,
awaiting the new light to be brought forth.

Please help me to celebrate the return of the light
on this turning point in time.
As I realize all darkness must come to an end,
I know it is now time to shine my inner light.
show me my heart's deepest wishes,
and the next steps on my soul's journey.
I am ready to embrace the light within
and radiate it out into the world.
And so it is.

December Chapter Sponsor – Bobbe Bramson

DECEMBER 22

Light Heart Space for Releasing the Past

By Carolyn Burke

Divine Angels of Light,
Surround me in your loving embrace as I let go of the old.

Thank you for helping me to have the courage to face my fears
and the wisdom to move forward on my path,
for the highest good of all.

As I effortlessly let go of negative thoughts
and patterns that tie me to the past,
I thank you for helping me discover new ways to live my life.

As the weight of relationships that no longer serve me
begin to lift, I feel light and free.
Thank you for helping me to create space
for new energy to flow in.

I am grateful for the light that radiates from the center of my being,
penetrating any darkness as I shift my perceptions
about myself, and my world.

I feel healed on all levels by the power and presence of love in my life.
My heart space is light, open and always expanding.

Thank you Angels for helping me shine my light in the world.
And so it is.

December Chapter Sponsor – Bobbe Bramson

DECEMBER 23
In the Hands of an Angel

By Leela Williams

Dear Guardian Angel,
Hold out your hands so that I may rest within them.
Hold me gently and securely in this healing haven.

Thank you for this loving and soothing space,
where I feel safe enough to remember,
I am all I need to be.
Wise, honest, strong, resilient,
patient, compassionate, determined, resourceful,
vulnerable, powerful, kind, courageous.

Through struggle and in laughter,
I am at peace and complete.
All that I am, is all that I need
to serve the world as it serves me, in love.

All that I have, is all that I need
To share this grace as it is shared with me.

Thank you.

December Chapter Sponsor – Bobbe Bramson

DECEMBER 24

Archangel Sandalphon
Prayer of Gratitude for Music

By Lori Kilgour Martin

Archangel Sandalphon,
I would like to share with you my deep appreciation for music.
Filling my soul with its vibrant colors and rich tapestry, I am blessed.
Beauty, Grace and Divine expression hold the glory
into which I feel whole again.
The soft melodies breathe contentment into my heart.
They give me permission for the vulnerabilities to be revealed.

Sacred harmonies shimmer;
ancient tones wash through like a soothing balm.
How mighty, how gentle, those soothing sounds welcome the Christ light.
Distant, quiet drumming echoes. They clear a path for blessings to come.
Thank you for the harp, the Angels' beautiful instrument.
It evokes feelings of warmth and the pure love from heaven.
Ever flowing, this wondrous weaving of music brings peace.
We are connected to the eternal presence, to God.
The orchestra is in place, the artists are ready to join in.

The sun lies down, they begin.
The moon shines bright, the stars sparkle with delight.
The Earth and planets are smiling too.
Oh, how lovely, when the new, bright, magnificent dawn rises,
we will rejoice and sing again.

Archangel Sandalphon,
thank you for your love, your presence and for the music.

December Chapter Sponsor — Bobbe Bramson

DECEMBER 25
Calling the Archangels for a Beautiful Christmas

By Samantha Honey-Pollock

Archangel Jophiel,
All these beautiful things I see!
Please allow what is best for me.

Archangel Michael,
with wings so strong,
please show in my family
where I may have "seen" wrong.

Archangel Raphael,
tall and sweet,
allow us all healthy choices to eat.

and

dear Archangel Metatron (you know so much!),
make the technical knowledge I have,
for the young ones . . .
Enough.

December Chapter Sponsor – Bobbe Bramson

DECEMBER 26
ANGELS

By Debbie Lyn Toomey

Angels be by my side

Never let me stray

Guide me to my greatness

Enlighten me with wisdom

Lead me to my dreams

Surround me in your light.

December Chapter Sponsor — Bobbe Bramson

DECEMBER 27
Beloved Angel Guardian

By Gabrielle Zale

Beloved Friend, silent and unseen, I ask you -
Accompany me as I journey into the sacred canyons,
and cradle me as I lay upon Mother Earth's skin.
Bear witness, as I wrestle with my fears and sorrows,
and protect me in the dark unknown of the night.

Cherished Friend, I pray —
Open my eyes, so I may see what is real,
clear my ears, so I may hear the truth you speak.
Quiet my mind, so I may discern the guidance you offer,
open my heart, so I may feel the warmth of your love,
and know whom I AM.

Bathed in the light of the sharp-eyed moon
I surrender.
In stillness you speak …
through rustling pines' whispers and night owl's cry.

And come the dawn, may I remember,
that the dark yields to the light,
and that I am never alone.

December Chapter Sponsor — Bobbe Bramson

DECEMBER 28

Archangel Michael
Energy Clearing Prayer

By Alicia Isaacs Howes

Dear Archangel Michael
Help me to clear my heart, mind, body and energy field
of anything and everything that no longer serves me,
my highest good or that simply isn't mine
as I now realign with my soul's wisdom, healing power
and highest frequencies of love and light.

Breathe in and feel, imagine or visualize blue light coming in with each inhale.
With each exhale release anything and everything
that no longer aligns with you or your highest good.
Repeat 1-3 times or until you feel complete.

I ask that the results of this clearing
are greater than anything I could hope for, dream of or even imagine.

And so it is.

Amen. Amen. Amen.

Use this prayer if you're feeling **STRESSED, CONFUSED, OVER-WHELMED** or **OUT OF SORTS** even if you don't have a particular reason for feeling that way. Wonderful if you're a **HEALER, THERAPIST, COUNSELOR** or **EMPATH** who tends to take on energy from others or your surroundings near or far that is not yours and can overload your energy system.

December Chapter Sponsor – Bobbe Bramson

DECEMBER 29
The Path

By Lisa K.

As this year draws to a close,
know that you are well on your path to your life's purpose;
that the road that you chose to follow was not an easy one
because you wished to attain some great gifts and lessons.

You are doing well, you are okay
and you have not strayed from your purpose.
All is happening the way it should
and we are here to make it all happen with you.

Plan your new year with gusto and gratitude,
for you are doing well!

– Your Angels.

December Chapter Sponsor – Bobbe Bramson

DECEMBER 30
Angel Prayer for the Future

By Suzanne Gochenouer

Dear Angels,

Help me find empowerment for my bright future.

Remind me each day that life deserves
my enthusiastic presence and participation.

Bring me clear thinking and planning
as I look forward to what I can be
and what I can share with others in the future.

Inspire me to think not only of what I would like to be and do,
but also of what this world and Heaven require of me.

Help me feel strong and safe
even when I cannot clearly see what my future holds.

Help me find excitement and promise in every possibility.

Give me a deep desire to see what may unfold,
and give me a clear understanding
of how my future work will help me grow into my higher purpose.

Amen, Amen, Amen.

Thank you, thank you, thank you.

December Chapter Sponsor – Bobbe Bramson

DECEMBER 31
The Angels Experience of God

By Roland Comtois

I love my God for He never forsakes me.
He gives me light to see.
He gives me wisdom to teach.
He gives me love to share.

My God is a radiant beam of warm light that fills my heart.
My God speaks to all the people of the world…
None are left hungry.
He fills all of us with the freedom to experience His love.

By His virtue He gives love unconditionally.
He embraces you when silence needs to be filtered through.
He lifts you when the walk seems so tiring.
He loves you when you feel alone.
My God is your God,
and your God…and your God.

My God is in you…building a temple that will house His love.
My God lays the foundation so His strength
will permeate your temple.
My God gives you light to see the true palace.

My blessings are your blessings because
My God is your God, and your God …and your God.

December Chapter Sponsor – Bobbe Bramson

Author Biographies

We encourage you to meet the wonderful co-authors of the book. The co-authors are listed in alphabetical order by first name. Please visit their websites or send them an email letting them know how much their original prayers have touched your heart. Each co-author brought an energy of love and light to the project creating a circle of blessings and joy.

Adriana C. Tomasino is an Angel Communication Master, a doctoral candidate in medieval literature, pursuing research on Hildegard von Bingen, a student of Dr. Jean Houston, and President of Heaven Seas: Wings and Harps, a business dedicated to providing individuals with various tools for empowerment. Please visit www.wingsandharps.com or e-mail dreemstar1@yahoo.com

Alicia Isaacs Howes, founder of www.yoursoulstory.com and Soul Connection expert, is here to help those struggling with a health, relationship or money story. A former management consultant, her health crisis led to becoming a healer, teacher and intuitive coach. She channels whatever is needed to guide others in practical and graceful ways.

Allison Hayes, The Rock Girl® is a Professional Psychic, Medium, Past Life Channeler, Healer and High Priestess of Stones. She is a popular Radio/Television Personality, International Speaker and founder of The Rock Girl Sacred Stone School® where she offers classes and workshops in Reiki, Psychic Development and her own Master Stone Program®. www.TheRockGirl.com

Steward of eARTh and Heart-Perceptive Leader, **Amber Lee Scott**, is on a mission to Ensoul Language with creativity, passion, truth and LOVE. She combines her knowledge of project management, marketing, social media and writing experience to facilitate her client's vision and values into their very own True U Voice. www.trueUvoice.com

Amber Reifsteck is an organic flower farmer and artist. She spends a lot of time working with the nature angels and fairies that make their home on her farm. She also has a line of recycled paper greeting cards bearing images of her nature photography. www.TheWoodlandElf.com

Passionate about listening to Nature, **Andrea Mathieson** created the Raven Essences. Trained as a classical musician, she is now a Mid-life Mid-wife focused on tending soul gardens through intuitive sessions and private retreats. Her books include *A Love Affair with Nature, Gaia's Invitation,* and *Earth-Light,* currently in progress. www.ravenessences.com

Andrea Porter is an Intuitive Spiritual Counselor, Life Coach, author, and artist. She is a teacher of soul-led, compassionate transformation and life design from the heart. Her work inspires individuals to release their past while discovering a new way of living consciously and passionately from their true self. Visit Andrea at www.passionately-you.com

Ann Phillis is an author, soul seer, angel clairvoyant and Earth lover. Ann's own personal journey has been deeply influenced by her connection with the angels. Ann shares her love, hope and vision through www.NourishingSoul. me, where she offers meaningful insights, soul wisdom and practical how-to's that empower you to walk your heart path.

Known as 'The Angels' Voice', **Anna Taylor** is a singer-songwriter, certified Angel Therapist® and Theta Healing Practitioner® offering private sessions and workshops to clients worldwide. She hosts her own radio show, "Anna and the Angels," and her debut album, Already Here was featured on BBC and Hay House Radio. To receive your free weekly inspiration visit: www.anna-taylor.co.uk

April-Anjali is an inspirational, high vibrational healer, speaker, teacher, entre-preneur and voice of the goddess. Through illness and disease, she transformed her world. By embracing her power within, what once appeared as a dark journey, became an amazing story of a return to love and the discovery of a dream healer within. Connect with April-Anjali at www.AprilAnjali.com.

Asher Quinn (Asha) is an English singer-songwriter, multi-instrumentalist, intuitive mystic and mystical balladeer. He channels his inspirations about Divine levels of being and about all the beautiful, extravagant bridges there are between Divine creation and human existence into song. Read more about Asher and his work at www.asherquinn.co.uk and listen to him sing 'I Wish' on his You-Tube channel at: http://youtu.be/jV_6RlNtcgc

Asia Voight is an internationally known Animal Communicator, Intuitive Counselor, Teacher, Inspirational Speaker, and Radio Host. Asia is also a published author featured with Dr. Brian Weiss and Jack Canfield. Her work has been shown on ABC, NBC, CBS and Fox TV as well as Coast-to-Coast, and Hay House. www.AsiaVoight.com.

Audrey Simmonite, has followed many paths to seek knowledge and to find her 'own truth'. She is a Reiki Master/Teacher and Medium, she uses Tarot and Angel cards to bring messages of comfort to any in need. She also takes an active part in helping to run Angel Radiance (www.angel-radiance.com).

Avianna is an international intuitive, psychic medium, awareness mentor and meditation teacher. Her passion is educating souls to live awake and authentic, creating a reality that is spiritual, deliberate and meaningful! Join Avianna as she spreads metta and travels abroad hosting spiritual development and meditation retreats. www.aviannacastro.com

Belle Salisbury is a Psychic Medium and Spiritual Counselor. She is the owner and creator of Bellesprit Magazine, a free online magazine. Belle hosts her own online radio show, Live with Belle Salisbury which airs each Friday at 8:00 pm ET. Visit her web site at www.bellesalisbury.com.

Beth Lynch is a Spiritual Medium, Intutive Consultant and founder of Inner Light Teachings. She is the author of *Journey To Light*, "Meditation for the Soul" and *Discovering the Divine IN You* books, audio and ebooks. Her children's Meditation CD/Book is *Donald's Journey To the Tree*. www.innerlightteaching.com.

Betty Sue Hanson works with the Angels in her practice as an IET® Master Teacher and Karma Release Practitioner in Westchester, Orange and Passaic counties. Her belief is that ultimately YOU are the healer – she facilitates this process through the angelic realm. Betty Sue can be reached at email: angelwork444@gmail.com.

Bob Kenney is a professional psychic medium and stage IV cancer survivor guided by spirit to help others. Bob's readings may focus on life challenges, messages from departed loved ones and how to advance spiritually. Bob also has been teaching many how to contact loved ones in spirit directly. www.bobkenney.wordpress.com.

Bobbe Bramson is a licensed, ordained interfaith minister through the Angel Ministry of Gateway University. Certified as a Usui and Karuna RMT, IET Master Instructor, and VortexHealing® practitioner, she is also a lifelong musician, songwriter and environmental and animal rights activist. Connect with Bobbe at bramsongs@verizon.net, on Facebook at: https://www.facebook.com/AngelHearttoHeart or via her website www.AngelHeartToHeart.com

Brenda Dowell, E-RYT 1000, is an advanced level Registered Yoga Teacher, Yoga Therapist, Anatomy Instructor and Energy & Body Worker who teaches in Ontario, Canada, and worldwide. Through her passion for life and deep desire to support others, she inspires, empowers and guides people home to their hearts. www.brendadowell.com.

Caitlyn Palmer is a young woman who grew up moving throughout Western Australia, and at the age of 15 discovered the world of angels, crystals and Reiki. Since then she has pursued a life of healing and spirituality. She is currently a Reiki Master and hopes to heal and teach others. Contct Caitlyn at caitlyn_palmer@hotmail.com

Carolyn Burke, MSW, E-RYT, is co-founder of DevaTree School of Yoga in Canada. She is an international yoga educator, family therapist and parent of two earth angels. She shares her passion for working with the subtle realms through her teaching, helping others nurture the sacred in their everyday lives. www.devatree.com.

Carolyn McGee is a master intuitive combining angel communication, color therapy and energy work into her coaching to help you uncover your passion, inner radiance and live joyfully. She co-authored the International Best-Seller *"Embracing Your Authentic Self"* and is BTR host of "Angels on Air" and "The Spiritual Book Club". www.GatewayToYou.com

Cathelijne Filippo is a psychologist, Angelic coach, healer, artist, spiritual teacher and author, bringing together the spiritual and creative in her business, Angel Light Heart. She creates angel sculptures and drawings, oracle decks, essences, gives workshops, consultations, readings and healings. Read more about her work on her website: **www.angellightheart.com.**

Cathleen O'Connor, PhD is a metaphysician, writer, speaker and life/business coach. Cathleen is co-founder with Elizabeth Harper, of www.spiritualliving.com, an online metaphysical community. Cathleen, known as "The Balance Whisperer," believes in the power of the mind and heart to co-create miracles in all areas of life. Find Cathleen at www.cathleenoconnor.com.

Chandra Easton strives to Live In Light, bringing Heaven to earth. She loves the starry realms, angels, sacred sites and humanity. As an esoteric astrologer, healer and visionary, she empowers others and shares joy. Blessed to meet and train with Lady Ananda Tara Shan, she works for the Earth. www.starastrologyhealing.com

Cher Slater-Barlevi, MA, is the author of *Dog of God* the *novel*, a wild romp through magical worlds. She holds a Master's in Spiritual Psychology and is an artist, writer, Spiritual Counselor, Speaker and Illustrator with 40 years experience as a medium offering readings and 'SOUL' paintings for people and pets. Learn more at www.dogofgod.com.

Christina Scalise is an Author, Certified Reiki Master, Professional Organizer, wife and mother of three, always paying attention to the signs, laughing like crazy and never taking life too seriously. Her newest books are: *Are We Normal? Funny, True Stories from an Everyday Family* and *Organize Your Life and More.* www.authorchristinascalise.com.

Cindy deJong DSW, ATP® is an Angel Guide, Reiki Master, Shamanic Practitioner and Coordinator at Awakenings: Center for Psychic Sciences and Healing Arts in beautiful Goderich Ontario, Canada. She has assisted many during her years of study and practice with her down to earth approach to spirituality. Email: cindy.dejong@yahoo.ca

Cindy Nolte is a TV personality and author of Finding Peace in an Out of Control World. She runs a private practice where she offers workshops and 1-on-1 sessions. Cindy is an internationally known Certified Hypnotist/Instructor, Reiki Master/Teacher-for people and animals, medium, intuitive, coach, keynote speaker and more. www.freshlookonlife.com cindy@freshlooknolife.com

Connie Gorrell is a certified Mind, Body, & Spirit Practitioner and founder of the **DreamSTRONG™** movement which provides resources for empowerment, enrichment, and education of women. She is passionate about helping women of all walks of life overcome adversity and identify and establish their personal and professional goals. www.conniegorrell.com; www.dreamstrong.us

Coryelle Kramer is a naturally gifted seer & communicator who has been connecting and speaking with animals, Divinity & spirits since childhood. Her life's purpose is "Divination" to foresee, connect and be inspired by the Universe. She communicates with spirits, guides, and animals to interpret their messages for you. www.coryellekramer.com

Cynthia Helbig is an Angelsteach Angelic Life Coach and a member of the Living with the Angels community. She is also a Meditation coach, Bowen Therapist, Attunement Teacher/ Practitioner and Reiki Master. Meditation is her passion and she loves to share angelic wisdom, guidance and joy through her meditations. www.empoweredheart.com.au

Daniel Hyman: I am love; I am a humble, empowered and awakened soul on earth serving as a vessel of an example, bringing light to darkness from what was forgotten from long ago. I am all that I am of whom I am in this exact present moment. Connect with Daniel at www.earthstar18.com.

Debbie Lyn Toomey RN, Health & Happiness Specialist™, is the founder of Ultimate Healing Journey, LLC. She combines over 25 years of nursing, Six Sensory™ Leadership, Master Energy Healing Coaching, and Positive Psychology coaching to deliver the most comprehensive services to all her clients. Visit www.ultimatehealingjourney.com to learn more about her proven and powerful services.

Debby Tamborella is a Reiki Practitioner, Angel Card Messenger and loves to make natural soaps, lotions and teas using herbs from her garden and bees-wax and honey from her beehives. www.facebook.com/lavenderangels

Debra Snyder, PhD is an inspirational speaker, spiritual teacher, and the award-winning author of *Intuitive Parenting* and *Ignite CALM*. She holds a Doctorate of Philosophy in Metaphysics and focuses on bringing her methods and techniques to the world to inspire, promote healing, and enhance loving communication between people. www.heartglowliving.com

Diana Blagdon, Psychic Life & Business Coach, assists clients in aligning with their Divine purpose. She is a radio show host, author, teacher and Reiki Master who utilizes energy work, past live regression and coaching techniques in her practice. She owns StarGazers Metaphysical Resource Center in Fish Creek, WI. Visit Diana at www.dianablagdon.com.

Diane Hiller is honored to be recognized as one of the Top 100 Psychics in America today. The founder of Elemental Empowerments, LLC, she is a tested and Certified Psychic Medium, Psychotherapist and Certified Feng Shui Master. Diane's prayer is about the loss of her twin soul and how their connection has evolved, even after death. Chiral refers to 'mirror image.' Connect with Diane at www.elementalempowerments.com.

Dianna Vagianos Armentrout is a writer, teacher, poetry therapist and workshop facilitator. Her workshops create the space for people to be still and access their own words, images and metaphors as they step into their healing. Her website is www.diannavagianos.com.

Dona Ho Lightsey, the Creator of Violet Alchemy® Multi-dimensional Healing for the evolution of Your Soul and Certified SoundHealer since 2005, channels songs, languages of light and love, and offers messages and dispensations from the Archangelic realm. As a Master Energy Healer and Divine voice channel, she supports Humanity's evolution to birth the New Earth.

Elizabeth Harper is an internationally acclaimed metaphysical artist, psychic medium, teacher, and award-winning author of *Wishing: How to Fulfill Your Heart's Desires*. Her intuitive knowledge of color sparked the creation of the ColorScope and AstroColorScope oracles featured online and in magazines. With Cathleen O'Connor she is co-founder of spiritualliving.com an online metaphysical community. www.SealedWithLove.com

Having encountered her first Angel at the age of 17, **Ellen McCrea** began an earnest inquiry of the Angelic realm. She writes "Angel Letters" for people seeking healing and love. She also does Angel card readings. She can be reached at ejmccrea@yahoo.com

Emily Berroa-Teixeira of Halo Angel Therapy and Healing is an Angel Intelligence Practitioner, Angel Medium, and skilled intuitive residing in Taunton, Massachusetts. Emily's soul purpose is to bring forth messages from the angelic realm promoting the confidence for others to ignite their own passions and purpose. Connect with Emily at: www.facebook.com/haloangelhealing and emilyberroa@yahoo.com.

Emily Gilghrist is a Reiki master, Integrated Energy Practitioner, retired massage therapist, Nurse, wife, mother and grandmother. Reiki Master and Teacher Wayne Lemmon, and Integrated Energy instructors Leon Pelletier and Phoenix Rising Star attuned her. She is actively involved in children's church guiding them with her energy and light.

Emily Rivera is a national speaker, spiritual counselor, and energy healer who lectures on the power of eternal consciousness and serves as a channel for Ascended Lights. Her popular events as well as her private readings explore these principles and offer insights, advice, and guidance to people all over the world. www.theangelcoach.com. Email: emily@theangelcoach.com

Eve Picquette is the author of *Open Your Heart for Happy Relationships – What Your Angels Have Been Trying to Tell You for Centuries* on amazon.com. She is certified in Angel Therapy, is a NLP life coach and has a MSN from Vanderbilt and JD from the University of California. Visit her website – AdvisorIsIn.com for a free angel card reading.

Gabrielle Zale is a nationally certified reflexologist and past-president of the New York State Reflexology Association. A student of shamanism and spirituality, Gabrielle is also an artist able to express in various media. Gabrielle's compassion and gentle presence are accompanied by her intuitive guidance offering a deep healing experience. www.holdingthesoul.com.

Gayle Kirk is a well-respected, compassionate International Psychic, Medium & Channel. Gayle is in the *Register of the United States and World's Best and Most Trusted Psychics, Mediums and Healers* as a Qualified Psychic & Medium, Psychic Life Coach, Messages from Heaven, and Trance Channeled Reader. She conducts online & in-person classes. Visit Gayle online at: www.GayleKirk.com.

Gina Barbara offers a unique coaching and energetic healing style to motivated clients wishing to flourish in authentic lives; and to nurture and nourish themselves, others and the planet. Counseling Cert; Dip Transformational Life Coaching; Color Therapy LV III; Crystal Healing Cert, EFT Cert. and many other modalities. www.innerselfcare.com

Giuliana Melo is a new contributor. She is 50 years old and prides herself on being able to always use love and kindness as her guide. Her friends call her the love and angel lady.

Guy Isabel (Gisabel) is a spiritual medium who receives communications through a kind of automatic writing. He communicates regularly with his guardian angel, spiritual guides, and souls that are part of his family of souls in order to receive guidance in life and messages of love. His website is: www.gisabelspiritualmedium.com.

Helen White Wolf is a spiritual healer and intuitive who has worked consciously with healing angels since her teens. She offers workshops and training programs in Soul Centered Healing internationally and offers sessions by Skype and phone from her home in New Zealand. She can be contacted at polarisandhelen@gmail.com and via her website www.living-presence.org.

Helene Kelly is a retired RN, cabaret "manager/performer/director", and flight attendant. An agnostic who totally believes in Angels and their enormous power to assist and teach us every day, Ms. Kelly is honored that her work "Angels Are Everywhere" is included in this lovely book.

Inger Marie Moeller, from Denmark, works closely with the Divine Mother and the Angelic Kingdom for inner transformation of Earth and Humanity through Heart Flow Worldwide: www.heartflow.org, and through her work as a healing minister at Earth Healing Services Center in Copenhagen: www.heartflow.eu. Since 1984 she has taught meditation, healing and Theosophy and joined the Global Peace Initiative of Women 2008: www.GPIW.org

Ingrid Auer is one of Europe's leading mediums, channeling messages and energized symbols and essences from both the Angels and the Masters. Her main emphasis is writing. She continually gets information and messages from the spiritual world, which she passes on in books, blogs, newsletters, and on internet platforms. Visit Ingrid at www.IngridAuer.com

Jan Harper is a Reiki Master, specializing in working with horses. She is a water color artist, painting botanicals from 1542 to 1900. Owning horses and competing in horse shows was when her soul slowly started to reveal itself. At age 62 she is still riding horses and is studying evolutionary astrology.

Jennelle Deanne is a Canadian psychic medium and life coach who tunes in and assists clients in areas such as; money and finance, careers, relocation, vacations, romance, family issues, life path, and finding peace in knowing their loved ones are safe beyond the "physical plane." www.jennelledeanne.com.

Jennie Degen is the owner of The Sacred Self in Canton, MA. She is a healer, Licensed Massage Therapist, Reiki practitioner, Intuitive, and Past Life Regressionist. She has always loved helping people and recognizes that the best way to help others is through physical, emotional, and spiritual assistance. Contact Jennie through her website www.sacredself.com or jensharples11@gmail.com.

Jennifer Parr facilitates group classes, virtual programs and individual sessions for women and children helping to awaken their truest hearts' desires, purpose and joy. She is an expert on self-love. Jennifer is a certified Reiki Master, laughter yoga teacher and is accredited with the American Association of Drugless Practitioners. Visit Jennifer at www.jennparr.com

Rev. Jennifer Shackford is an Angel Messenger and Advanced Angel Practitioner enrolled at the Divine Blessings Academy for her Bachelors in Spiritual Healing and Holistic Practitioner Certification. She is also a Certified Psychic Medium and member of the American Federation of Certified Psychics and Mediums. Connect with Jennifer at www.faithandangels.com.

Jennifer Shaffer is an Evidential Spiritual Psychic Medium and was voted 2014 Psychic of the Year by Shay Parker's Best American Psychics. She has appeared on CBS Television, HLN and FOX. Certified by World Renowned Master Psychic Lisa Williams as an Advanced Medium and Advanced Psychic, Jennifer Shaffer can be reached at www.jennifershaffer.com.

Jill M. Jackson is an award winning International Psychic Medium, Animal Communicator, Spiritual Teacher, Speaker, Radio Host, and Author. She is a member of Shay Parker's Best American Psychics and is tested through Certified Psychic Society. She can be reached at www.jillmjackson.com or by email at admin@jillmjackson.com.

Jillian Leigh is a teacher with a Master's Degree in Holistic Thinking from the Graduate Institute. She has a certification in Angel Communication from Rev. Elvia at AngelsTeach.com and is a certified Reiki 2 energy healer. Jillian enjoys sharing her love of the angels with others. Visit Jillian at www.angelicawakenings.net.

Jodi Chapman is the creator of the inspirational blog, Soul Speak, and the Soulful Life Sanctuary. She also co-wrote the bestselling Soulful Journals series with her husband, Dan Teck. She would love to help you reconnect with your soul! Receive a free soulful meditation and ebook here: www.jodichapman.com

Joe Randazzo is a retired police lieutenant. He worked for 25 years as a member of the NYPD in a variety of patrol and administrative assignments. Since leaving the force he has dedicated most of his time and efforts to the study and practice of shamanism and energy medicine.

Joy Elle is the owner of www.healingvisions.org, and works with organizations in the spiritual and metaphysical communities. She guides Indigo and Crystal children and has been giving intuitive medium readings all her life. She is an Ordained Minister, Cantor, Reiki Master, Chakra Balancer, Theta Healer, Spiritual Counselor, Crystal Healer, & Animal communicator.

Joyce M. Jackson, the *Sane Psychic,* is *Your Guide on the SANE Side* of the metaphysical world. She makes the chaos clear. She's a San Francisco based Psychic Medium, Shamanic Practitioner, Reiki Master and Healer. She brings a calming, reassuring message in easy language to clarify your life questions. www.thesanepsychic.com.

Joyce Willson is an RN, Energy Healer and founder of The Art of Reiki. She shines her inner light brightly as she follows her passion of energy work. Connecting with the angelic realm of light and love, inner peace and truth is rediscovered thus allowing one to move joyfully forward into the world. Visit Joyce at www.theartofreiki.com and jwillson@theartofreiki.com

Juancarlos Soto also known as "The Modern Oracle" is a natural born clairvoyant, oracle, author, life coach and spiritual teacher. Juancarlos' mission is to *Empower You, Transmute Any Situation in Your Life, Manifest Your Highest Good* and *Reveal the Possibilities.* www.modernoracle.weebly.com

Julie Geigle is an International Psychic Medium, & Certified Guide for The Casa, assisting people on a healing journey of transformation through the John of God experience. She is an awakened Spiritual Healer, Teacher and Archangel Metatron Channel and a member of **Shay Parker's Best American Psychic** directory. www.heavensenthealing.us.

June and Treena Many Grey Horses are dynamic Gemini sisters, and Kainai First Nations. They are gifted to the Spirit Realms, Angelic Psychic Mediums, Reiki Master Teachers, Angel and Spirit Facilitators, who own Angel Abundance 8, and are on Facebook. Their email is angelabundance8@gmail.com.

Karen D. Cote is a Shamanic Minister of The Circle of the Sacred Earth, hypnotherapist, Reiki Master/Teacher, Shr Jye of T'ai Chi Chuan / Qigong, and member of The International Chinese Boxing Association. She has written articles for The Door Opener Magazine, has been featured on WFSB-TV3's Better Connecticut and spotlighted in Hartford Magazine. www.thewellct.com

Karen Cowperthwaite is a gifted angel whisperer, healer and soul nurturer. In her private practice, Souly Sister Coaching & Energy Work, her gentle nature supports individuals of all ages to move forward and reconnect to their spirit. She is lovingly nudged by the angels to grow and share her experiences with her clients. Visit her at www.soulysister.com.

Karen Paolino Correia, is known as "The Miracle Messenger". She is recognized as a caring intuitive and teacher who has shared her talents with thousands across the globe. She is the author of four internationally acclaimed books and she can be reached for speaking engagements and readings at www. CreateHeaven.com

Kari Samuels is an Intuitive Counselor, Happiness Coach and Numerologist with a gift for making the mystical mainstream. It is her passion to help people reclaim their natural INTUITION so they can truly SHINE THEIR LIGHT and live their soul's purpose. Visit her at www.karisamuels.com.

Karri Ann Gromowski is a Spiritual Intuitive & Healer, Angel Therapy Practitioner ®, Medium/Spirit Communicator, and aspiring author. She shares her talents by illuminating, inspiring, and empowering others to "Let Their Soul Shine!" through facilitation of her services, workshops, and retreats, helping both people and animals. Visit Karri Ann at www.kaleidescapesofli-ght.com and www.KarriAnn.com.

Katerina Naumenko is an amateur artist and poet and is soon to publish *"Song of Raven"* through New Generation Publishing" She practices energy healing modalities of Integrative Energy Therapy (Master Instructor Level), Marconics No-touch, and KIA Reiki. Visit "Katerina-Naumenko - Dreamer's Dream" on Facebook and her sites at: **www.fineartamerica.com/profiles/ katerina-naumenko.html.**

Katherine Glass is an international psychic medium, energy healer, and spiritual intuitive counselor. She has enjoyed a private practice in Concord, MA. for the past 22 years. Katherine shares her gift through television and radio, as well as live appearances for groups. Readings are by phone, Skype and in person. www.katherineglass.com

Katrina L. Wright was born in Philadelphia, Pennsylvania and is currently living in Southern California. She is a consummate artist, energy worker/healer, and certified Massage/Spa Therapist with an M.A. in Spiritual Psychology. A yogi and life-long seeker of Truth, she loves living in the "ashram of the heart" and helping others. Email at: KatrinaLWright13@yahoo.com.

Keysha Sailsman/Alberga is a Licensed Angel Therapist or Angel Therapy Practitioner®, certified by Doreen Virtue, PhD. and a Licensed *Heal Your Life* ® Coach and Workshop Teacher. Keysha believes we are all Spiritual beings with unlimited potential. Her website is www.birthofangels.com; email: Keysha@birthofangels.com

Kia Abilay, a resident of Hawaii, is an interfaith minister, Akashic Records Teacher and Healing Touch Practitioner offering sessions for 13 seasons at the Wellness Center at Omega Institute in Rhinebeck, NY. She holds a BA in Humanities from the New College of San Francisco with an emphasis on ecology, culture and sustainable community. Visit Kia at www.rainbowheart. net.

Kimberly Marooney has helped hundreds of thousands of people worldwide have personal experiences of God's love that result in profound healing and greater self-awareness enhancing relationships and bringing priorities into sharper focus. Kimberly is a gifted mystic, teacher, radio-personality, internationally acclaimed author of Angel Blessings Cards, founder of TheAngelMinistry. www.KimberlyMarooney.com

Kimberly Thalken is a psychic-medium, energy healer-teacher, hypnotherapist and the Founder *of Love First. Where Life Transformations Happen.* She works with clients worldwide using a holistic and integrative approach to empower and support the individuals she works with and regularly facilitates workshops that help to promote self-healing: www.lovefirst.co

A master artist of Angelic Realm Communication, **Kimeiko Rae Vision** ATP®, The Angel Warrior™ loves introducing you to YOUR guardian angels so that you can always access your Divine Guidance and Support! Kimeiko is a Transformational Speaker, Entertainer and Angel Therapy Practitioner® certified by internationally renowned New York Times Bestselling Author Doreen Virtue. www.AngelWarriorVision.com

KipAnne Huntz: Artist ~ certified in level one Healing Touch. I've been drawing with Angels since 2001 and am a conduit for the Angels who wish to be seen. I incorporate healing energy into drawings and t-shirts that I create with the Angels. FB and Etsy: Angel Vision Creations. kipannehuntz@gmail.com

Lee A. Baker is a channel and intuitive healer. She is an IET Master/ Instructor and certified graduate of the two year School of Spiritual Healing and Prophecy offered by Fellowships of the Spirit in Lily Dale, NY. Lee resides in Indiana and can be contacted at lebake444@gmail.com

Leela Williams began psychic readings at age seventeen and her career includes editing, writing and publishing. Her career in metaphysics spans more than twenty-five years. She complements her role as production manager of the International Psychics Directory with editing and writing projects and is currently undertaking a degree in religious studies. Visit her at www. spiritguide.com.au

Lilly Wong, www.lilly-wong.com "I share my creative expression by guiding women and men in their spiritual development. I see myself as an LIFE ARCHITECT giving energetic support in designing and structuring life through private sessions, workshops, conferences and life channelings in Spanish, English and German."

Linda Goodings is a psychic angel medium, reverend and teacher. She is the Founder of The Earth Angel and The Earth Angel Fair, a columnist and she facilitates workshops and events helping people to find answers, guidance and help in getting in touch with their own angels and spiritual gifts. Her websites are www.earth-angel.nl and www.earthangelfair.com.

Linda Wheeler Williams is a spiritual teacher & writer who inspires others through spoken and written word guided by the Archangels. Her approach is heartfelt, powerful and touches the soul. Linda continues her journey of discovery by serving others. She currently resides in Phoenix, AZ and may be contacted at www.lindawheelerwilliams.com or lindawheelerwilliams@yahoo.com.

A 10th generation clairvoyant, **Ms. Linda Xochi** appears on internationally-syndicated Television Network, Telemundo, as a spirituality expert in the study and communication of angels. With 15+ years experience, Ms. Xochi's passion is helping women struggling with relationships to find clarity, guidance and direction, and to learn to trust themselves and each decision they make. www.lxavalos.com

Lindsay Marino is an International Medium, Energy Healer and Radio Host. After losing the love of her life in a tragic accident, her heartache turned into a spiritual awakening and her gift was uncovered. She started receiving messages from loved ones from the other side. Connect with Lindsay at www.LindsayMarino.com or email Lindsay@LindsayMarino.com.

Lisa Clayton is founder of *Source Potential,* serving as master teacher-facilitator, intuitive coach, inspirational speaker and spiritual leader helping individuals reclaim their passion, power and potential through inner-heart learning. Lisa is an ordained Angel Celebrant and provides intuitive services working with Archangels, Spirit Guides and Golden Realm Angels. Connect with Lisa at www.lisaaclayton.com.

Lisa K. is a speaker, author and teacher of intuition development. She is a contributing author to *OmTimes* Magazine and writes frequently about intuition. Lisa K. appears publicly through guest speaking, online media, as an

Angel Therapy Practitioner® and on her radio show, "Between Heaven and Earth." Connect with Lisa at www.lmk88.com.

Lisa Nicole Davis is a spiritual lightworker who embraces love and self-healing. Helping guide others through their journeys and trials of life is her passion. Freeing hearts of fear and grief so they can fly is her mission. For readings, sessions, private retreats, events and ceremonies, please visit www.lisanicole.net.

Lisa Wolfson is a breast cancer survivor who dedicates her time to spiritual and holistic growth of herself and others. She is a Reiki Master Teacher, Ordained Interfaith Minister, End of Life Doula and Crystal Healer who guides her students in Reiki training and advancement, works with clients on a regular basis and facilitates workshops for holistic, psychic and spiritual growth. Email Lisa at: **reikiwithlwolfson@gmail.com.**

Lori Kilgour Martin is an Earth Angel Mentor and Musical Theatre Artist from Canada. She received her Angelic Life Coach certification through Angels Teach. Grateful for the Angelic Realm; our guiding lights holding us in grace and love, Lori enjoys walking in Divine partnership with them in sacred service. Visit Lori at www.diamondheartangel.com.

Lori Siska is a spiritual medium and a certified angel card reader. She provides energy healing and Reiki for animals wherever needed in the world. Visit Lori at www.guidedbyspirit.ca.

Lorraine Appleyard is a psychic medium, Reiki Master and energy healer. Lorraine is committed to helping others through her abilities and with the help of her guides. Lorraine is able to help identify energy blockages in the aura and chakras that create illness and create blockages in life. Lorraine works to provide guidance and insight to those seeking. www.soulsolutions.com. Email: soulsolutions@hotmail.com

Lynn Waddington is a medium and medical secretary from South Yorkshire, England. Her ambition is "to be the best I can be."

Maddy Vertenten is an outspoken advocate for women living full-spectrum lives. A wellness and beauty coach for women who believe that cultivating their essential feminine sensuality profoundly impacts the harmony of their loved ones, their communities and the world. Maddy's programs, services and products teach women of all ages how to care for themselves inside and out. Find her at www.MaddyV.com and maddy@vibrantone.com

Maggie Chula is a Spiritual Teacher and Channel for the Archangels and Ascended Masters. She is also the Master Teacher and Earthly Channel for the Spiritual Healing and Mystic Certification course Open the Doorway to Your Soul: the Akashic Vibration Process. Learn more at www.MaggieChula.com.

Marci Cagen is a licensed nurse and massage therapist, herbalist and clinical aromatherapist. Her mission is to inspire others to live happy, healthy, and love-filled lives through various holistic healing modalities and community education. She has dedicated her life to teaching others about the wonderful world of natural healing. Visit Marci at www.marcicagen.com

Maria Gillard is a talented singer, songwriter, and educator from the Finger Lakes Region of New York State. Her compelling voice draws you into her lyrics which, when combined with memorable melodies, head straight for the heart. She tells stories through her music in ways that are soul stirring, evocative, contagious, lively and energizing. www.mariagillard.com

Marian Cerdeira is an intuitive channel and medium. In 2004, she began a beautiful connection with Spirit, initially with Angels and individuals who had transitioned from the physical worlds, and eventually to a beloved group of Beings known as The Brotherhood. Her messages from spirit and the Brotherhood are posted on her Facebook page - A Slice of Light: www.asliceoflight.com

Marla Steele, in 2001 became a professional pet psychic with the helpful nudging of her Arabian horse. Her approach to animal communication contains a blend of intuition and energy healing including Reiki, Matrix Energetics, Flower Essences, and Aromatherapy. She is the author of the Animal Chakra reference charts and the voice of Animal Communication Journeys, a guided meditation cd. Visit Marla at www.healingwithenergy.com.

Mary O'Maley is a holistic healer and psychic medium. She is a blogtalkradio personality, co-author of *Your Soaring Phoenix,* award winning Hypnotherapist, and professional instructor of Holistic modalities. Learn more about her psychic medium gifts at www.themerrymedium.com, and her unique and powerful approach to personal transformation and healing at www.R4wardmotion.com.

Melanie Barnum, CH, is a psychic, medium, intuitive counselor, hypnocoach, and hypnotist and hosts workshops & teaches. Melanie is the author of multiple books including *The Book of Psychic Symbols: Interpreting Intuitive Messages, The Steady Way to Greatness: Liberate Your Intuitive Potential and Manifest Your Heartfelt Desires,* and *Psychic Abilities for Beginners: Awaken Your Intuitive Senses.* Visit www.MelanieBarnum.com.

Michelle Barr is The Business Coach for Intuitive Women, training and supporting the helpers and healers of the world to turn their life's calling into a profitable, freedom-based business so they can create a vision of the life they want to live and create a business that supports and sustains them. Visit Michelle at www.michellebarr.com

Michelle Beltran is an expert, innovative spiritual guide whose work brings forth powerful changes on a personal level. Michelle's gift of intuition has served everyday people, entrepreneurs, therapists, professional athletes, CEOs, celebrities, housewives, teachers, and others who seek understanding and want to live life wholeheartedly and to the fullest. www.michellebeltran. com

Michelle McDonald Vlastnik, Mind Body Fitness and Wellness Specialist, is a NASM Certified Personal Trainer, Mystic Intuitive, Hypnotherapy and Intuitive Body Energy Practitioner who holds a Bachelor's of Science Degree from Grand Canyon University, majoring in Corporate Fitness and Wellness. She also studied at the Southwest Institute of Healing Arts. Visit Michelle on Facebook at www.facebook.com/HighEnergySixSensoryPersonalTraining.

Michelle Mullady is an internationally known Joyful Living Mentor, Master Energy Intuitive, Spiritual Guide and award-winning author of *The Joy of Loving Yourself: 101 Ways to a Happier You*. Through private consultations, workshops, radio appearances, and writing for 20 years, she helps others to heal their lives and discover authentic happiness. www.michellemullady.com

Mitzi Patton has carved her own beautiful path and wants to inspire others to do so. She lives with husband Robb and their son, muse and rhyming partner, Brynn. She is the creator of Littlebird photo jewelry, made to touch, move, and inspire others by capturing life's special moments. Visit Mitzi at www.littlebirdphotojewelry.com.

Nicolebeth is an Evidential Empathic Medium, Healer, Certified Spiritual Counselor and Kundalini Reiki Master. She attended a private mentorship program with Shirley Ryan PhD, CCHt, at Working Together Institute. Nicolebeth works exclusively in her field and can be reached by email, nicole@nicolebeth.net. Further information is available at www.nicolebeth.net.

Noelle Goggin is a qualified and highly intuitive coach. She works with clients to support them in getting more from their lives and helping them to manifest their hearts desires. Contact her at www.noellegoggin.com

Odalys Villanueva-Hernández, born in Puerto Rico, is a New York-based licensed massage therapist. Her work has an eclectic approach that fuses Nature-Science-Angelic healing and Energy work, applying her Eastern and Western therapeutic skills. Her studies have been developed through years of practice, research, self-healing, intuitive development, and angelical guidance. Email Odalys at: odalys.villanueva@gmail.com

Patty Nowell is a Certified Angel Messenger, Artist, and Certified Life Coach. She uses her skills in all three areas to help others rekindle their creativity, reinforce their own magnificence and reconnect with hope and dreams. www. Soaring-Heart.com

Peggy Shafer is an Intuitive Coach/Mentor, writer and an 'Inspirational Listener' who challenges and motivates her clients to dream bigger and boldly say, 'YES!' She coaches groups and individuals via phone, Skype and in person at her office in Granville, Ohio. Learn more about Peggy's work at www. BeYourOwnBestSelf.com

For over 15 years **Rachel Cooley** has helped her clients tap into the angelic realms for healing & guidance. As an Angel Therapy Practitioner® certified by Doreen Virtue, Rachel is dedicated to serving moms who want to stop the chaos and start enjoying the calm and confidence available when supported by the angels. www.rachelcooley.com

Rachel Pollack is the author of 36 books, including two prize-winning novels. Her book on *Tarot, 78 Degrees Of Wisdom*, is known as "the Bible of Tarot readers." Rachel created *The Shining Tribe Tarot* deck as well as *The Burning Serpent Oracle* together with artist Robert M. Place. Rachel's newest novel is *The Child Eater*. Visit Rachel at www.rachelpollack.com.

Ramona Remesat is a Spiritual Life Coach and Angel Therapy Practitioner, certified by Doreen Virtue. Women who feel unfulfilled and stuck in life hire Ramona to help them discover what makes their heart sing so they can start creating, and living, the life they truly deserve. Visit Ramona at: www. RamonaRemesat.com.

Robert Haig Coxon: Canadian Composer and worldwide Performer, he is best known for his meditative CDs of Sacred Music that include *The Silent Path*, *Prelude to Infinity* and *The Infinite...essence of life*. www.robertcoxon.com.

Robin "Raj" Munger is a psychic medium, a healer, animal communicator and karmic soul coach. She has been a massage therapist and healer practicing energy medicine for over twenty five years. She has studied with some amazing teachers including James Van Praagh and continues to enhance her psychic medium abilities. www.rajmunger.com.

Robyn Clark is a Ka Huna bodyworker and a Reconnective Healing Practioner. Robyn is passionate about helping people to find balance in their lives, to be the very best they can. Her favorite quote is, "be the change you want to see." Robyn can be contacted through Facebook at alohamassage, twitter @alohamassge10 or email alohamassage10@gmail.com.

Roland Comtois is a nationally acclaimed inspirational speaker, spiritual medium, radio host and author of *And Then There Was Heaven*, and *16 Minutes*. Roland is a professional healer with over 30 years experience as a gerontology nurse, Reiki Master, metaphysical teacher and grief specialist. He is the founder of Talk Stream Spiritual Radio and the After Loss Expo. www.blessingsbyroland.com

Rosemary Boyle Lasher, RM, IETP, was able to sense the body's subtle energies from childhood. As a practitioner of Reflexology, Reiki, IET, Chakra Balancing, and Aromatherapy, Rosemary guides her clients into a deeply relaxed state through which the body can re-balance and heal itself. Contact Rosemary through her website: www.rosehealingcenter.com.

Rosemary Hurwitz, MA.PS, spiritual teacher, author, presenter and coach, works with groups or individuals in the Chicago area and online. She is on the faculty at Common Ground, The Present Moment and Harper College. Her focus is the Enneagram and deepening the intuitive process. Her Enneagram book is expected in 2015. Find her at: www.spiritdrivenliving.com or www.facebook.com/rosemaryhurwitz.

"Blessed Angel Guide!" **Samantha Honey-Pollock** assists individuals across the globe reconnect with their heavenly knowledge via retreats, skype, and in person. She is also a Cosmopolitan and Women's health columnist. Visit Samantha at www.samanthahoney.com. *"Truly inspirational: I felt heard, and understood, and I'm so happy that the angels are right here with us."*

Samantha Winstanley is a soul-inspired, heart-based creative designer and artist. She creates websites and brands that assist leaders, healers and entrepreneurs in the spiritual professions to step up, shine and inspire greater numbers of people. She infuses all her work with the energy of pure love and spirit. www.ArtoftheAngels.com

Sandy Turkington has 35 years of experience as a teacher and demonstrator in disciplines of Angels, house blessings, mediumship and teaching. She is a minister and Ph.D. with the Universal Life Church with degrees in Divinity and Spirituality. She is certified in many other courses as well. Contact her at: sandyturk236@gmail.com.

Sarah De La Mer is IRELAND'S Famous Mystic, Seer, Life Coach, Writer, Radio Host, TV Personality & Consciousness Facilitator. Ashton Kutcher identified her on Jimmy Kimmel's Show as HIS psychic, and Simon Cowell was stunned when she predicted the FULL line up of Irish Popstars SIX before he had even decided himself. Find Sarah at www.sarahdelamer.com.

Sarah Dennison is a Spiritual Teacher, Angelic Life Coach, Animal Communicator, TV Personality, Author & Public Speaker. Her goal is to educate and share with people all of these modalities & awaken these intuitive gifts within each of you. Visit Sarah at www.beamerslight.com.

Shalini Breault began her journey in corporate America with a MBA in Finance. Life took a turn in 2006 and she is now a Reiki Master and Hypnofertility coach. Her passion for Vedic chanting, making jewelry, knitting ruffle scarves and designing bling apparel makes her a natural with artistic expression. Connect with Shalini at shalini_chandini@yahoo.com.

Shannon Navina Crow, E-RYT 500, RCYT, RPYT, CTYMP is co-director of the MamaNurture (100-hour Prenatal Yoga Certification) of DevaTree. Shannon helps students uncover and nurture their own yoga. She is known for creating a playful, vibrant, and supportive learning environment that is accessible to everyone. Visit Shannon at www.sacredawareness.ca www.mamanurture.ca

Sharina is one of Australia's most popular celebrity psychics. She hosts 2UE Radio's Psychic Encounters and appears regularly on Channel 9 Mornings with Sonia and David. Her best-selling book, "The Fortune Teller," is a RAW award winner and her star columns appear in eight newspapers across New South Wales and Queensland, including Take 5 Magazine. www.sharinastar.com

Sharon Pugh, known as the 'Southern-Style Medium," is considered one of the top 10 Evidential Mediums in the world. Sharon is a Certified Psychic through Shay Parker's Best American Psychics and is a highly sought after TV and Radio Personality. Connect with Sharon at www.sharonpugh.com.

Shelley Robinson, known as Mystic Shelley is a natural born Psychic Medium who reads your energy and brings light and insight to your situations-past, present and future. She is a member of Shay Parker's Best American Psychics, and a Reiki Master who also has expertise in Tarot, numerology and astrology. Connect with Shelley at www.mysticshelley.us.

Shelly Orr lives in Oklahoma with her husband and young daughter. She is currently working on writing projects which share her journey of self-discovery, self-acceptance and self-love.

Rev. Sheri is an internationally known psychic medium and spiritual teacher who is dedicated to helping others communicate with Heaven – without the need for an intermediary. She is the founder of Angel Messenger, a website that provides free online Angel card readings to hundreds of thousands of monthly visitors. www.AngelMessenger.net.

Simona Hadjigeorgalis is the co-creator of www.FueltheBodyWell.com, which is the go-to spot for home study courses in wellness. When she's not writing about fueling the body well, you can usually find Simona 'wellness adventuring' with her family. "May we each shine from the inside, out!" ~Simona

Stacey Wall is an ANGEL THERAPY PRACTITIONER®, Animal Intuitive and Spirit Medium. In addition to intuitive readings, she shares her passion for healing as a practitioner and teacher of Animal Reiki and Integrated Energy Therapy®. Stacey uses Communication with Love® to assist others on their self-healing journey. www.connectionsforhealing.com.

Starlight "I am love. I am a visitor from far, far away. A soul on her journey to complete her purpose and then go home." Visit Starlight at www.earthstar18. com

Sue Broome is an intuitive energy healer, Angel Card reader and teacher. She has published *Signs From Your Loved Ones*. Sue loves to spread the word of Angels in her workshops and talks. Embrace your spiritual journey through empowerment and self-healing. Connect with Sue at su.broome@gmail.com, www.SueBroome.com, and on Facebook at Empowerment4You.

Sunny Dawn Johnston is an internationally renowned author, dynamic and engaging inspirational speaker and gifted psychic medium. Sunny has performed thousands of readings and has spoken internationally on the subject of Angels, Mediumship and Intuition. Sunny's latest book, *The Love Never Ends: Messages from the Other Side* was released in October 2014. www.sunnydawnjohnston.com

Susan Huntz Ramos is a Certified Holistic Life/Wellness Coach and Reiki Practitioner. With the guidance from Spirit and the Angels, her passion is teaching people how to tap into their own inner wisdom, inspiring a healthy balance to their mind, body, and life. www.susanhuntzramos.com

Susan Mavity is an Intuitive Therapist. She has a Master's Degree in Metaphysics and Spiritual Counseling, and is the Author of *The Light Within the Gift of a Rose*. Susan is a guide, teacher and mentor. Her work brings the aspects of self to a place of peace and balance. Connect with Susan at www.guideyourspirit.com

Susie Robins lives in Wichita, Kansas, with her husband, Dave. She is a mother of four children and eight grandchildren. Susie is a Usui and Karuna Reiki Master and currently works with special needs students in the public school system. Susie loves sharing Reiki with family, friends and students. Contact Susie at srobins4444@gmail.com.

Suzanne Gochenouer is co-author of four books, author of published articles and stories, and editor/publisher of a poetry and art book. She posts weekly on www.TransformationalEditor.com about editing and writing. Certified as an LOA coach, and as a ghostwriter, Suzanne is passionate about helping writers define and reach their goals.

Tamika Schilbe, MSW, E-RYT is an author, award-winning counselor, consultant, yoga educator and truth-archaeologist. She is co-founder & Philosophy Instructor at DevaTree School of Yoga in Canada. An experienced speaker and trainer, Tamika guides people to share their authentic voice in the world to create clearer, more purposeful lives. www.tamikaschilbe.com

Tammy J. Carpenter, M.A., is an acclaimed N.A.T.H. hypnotherapist, teacher and psychic medium. Tammy has written several books, including *Channeling Ezekiel: A Daily Guide to Inner Beauty, Wisdom & Balance*. Tammy facilitates workshops on Meditation, Intuitive Writing and Intuitive Doodling and uses her psychic skills to volunteer with www.findme2.com. Visit Tammy at www.mindoverbodyhypnotherapy.com/About.html.

Terah Cox is the author of **The Story of Love & Truth,** the **Birth Angels Book of Days** series **You Can Write Song Lyrics,** and more. She is also a "truing-up" mentor, writing coach and lover of words as gates to meaning and connection. www.TerahCox.com

Tracy Quadro is an empath, intuitive and a person whose senses can perceive what many others' cannot. Attorney and mediator by day, she is a Tarot card reader, artist, writer and jewelry maker on evenings and weekends. Connect with Tracy at www.tracyquadro.com or via email at Novemberfire62@yahoo.com.

Tracy Una Wagner, CHT, is an Intuitive Transpersonal Life Coach who works with the Angelic Realm by using creatively fun approaches to guide people to reach their goals, dreams, and desires. Tracy empowers individuals to finally know true abundance by living their uniquely authentic Life Journey. Visit Tracy at www.versatileinspirations.com - 2Inspire4Gr8Ness or tracy@versatileinspirations.com.

Trina Noelle Snow, born in Wheeling, WV, enjoys creating unique pendulum art pieces for her site, Snow Angel Hemp Pendulums, and working with angel cards. At age seventeen she had a poem featured in a collaborative publication by *The World of Poetry*. She is author of, *Roadtripping the Dream*. Visit Trina at www.iamsoulbeautiful.com.

Trish Grain is an Angel teacher, a Reiki Master, Heal Your Life therapist and Relax Kids teacher who loves to help others nurture their own inner light. She is certified in counseling and has a diploma in Hypnotherapy/Psychotherapy. Connect with Trish at www.angel-radiance.com which reflects the heart and soul of her work.

Trude A. Xanders, Creative Dream Artist, flourishes in Angelic Alliance to bring Inspiration through a different lens. She explores, writes and plays in league with pleasure, Genius and joy. Her adventurous, individualistic spirit engages hearts across the world through a remarkable spectrum of Artistry. Visit Trude at Muse Mentor Headquarters: trude.xanders@gmail.com.

Rev. Vicki Snyder is certified as a Medium, Angel Card Reader, Realm Reader and Spiritual Healer. She teaches classes in healing, mediumship, and Angel Card Reading and facilitates monthly angel card reading practice groups.

Receive her free weekly angel messages on her facebook page, Divine Angel Messages. www.vickisnyder.webs.com.

Virginia Giordano is the chairperson of the Barbara E. Giordano Women's Health and Education Foundation whose mission is to empower women by providing them with opportunities that support and nurture their spiritual, emotional and physical health and growth. You can visit the Foundation at www.giordanofoundation.org.

Virginia Pasternak is a sought after shamanic practitioner, teacher, and healer in Santa Fe, New Mexico, and a student of shamanism and healing practices for over 15 years. It is her great joy to bring light and wholeness to all beings. www.virginiapasternak.com.

Be an Angel for Us!

We hope you have loved the messages of light, hope, healing and joy that so many wonderful angel messengers around the world have shared within the pages of this book.

Now you can be an angel for us if you liked the book by going to our amazon.com page or our goodreads.com page and posting a review.

The more reviews we have the more visible the book becomes and the more the light of the angels shines.

And make sure to join us on our facebook page:

www.facebook.com/365DaysofAngelPrayers to join in the monthly prayer circles and connect with others who love the angels as much as we do.

With gratitude for your support of this project,

Cathleen and Elizabeth